Victoria Woodhull

Victoria Woodhull's Sexual Revolution

Political Theater and the Popular Press in Nineteenth-Century America

Amanda Frisken

PENN

University of Pennsylvania Press
Philadelphia

10   9   8   7   6   5   4   3   2   1

Published by
University of Pennsylvania Press
Philadelphia, Pennsylvania 19104-4011

Library of Congress Cataloging-in-Publication Data

Frisken, Amanda.
    Victoria Woodhull's sexual revolution : political theater and the popular press in
nineteenth-century America / Amanda Frisken
        p.   cm.
    ISBN 978-0-8122-2188-6
    Includes bibliographical references and index.
    1. Woodhull, Victoria C. (Victoria Claflin), 1838–1927. 2. Feminists—United States—
Biography. 3. Women—Suffrage—United States—History. 4. Suffragists—United States—
Biography. I. Title.
HQ1413.W66F75   2004
305.42´092B—dc 22   2004041893

Contents

Chronology of Events

January 19, 1870	Woodhull, Claflin & Co., Brokers, open for business
April 2, 1870	Woodhull declares herself a candidate for the upcoming presidential election in the *New York Herald*
May 14, 1870	First issue of *Woodhull & Claflin's Weekly*
January 11, 1871	Woodhull presents her "new departure" Memorial to the House Judiciary Committee (Majority Report rejects, January 15, 1871)
May 11, 1871	Woodhull speaks before the National Woman Suffrage Association (NWSA) Meeting in New York
May 15, 1871	Roxanna Claflin brings charges against Colonel Blood for alienating the affections of her daughters Woodhull and Tennessee Claflin, and the family appears in Essex Police Court
July 1871	Section Twelve of International Workingmen's Association (IWA) forms with Woodhull as leader
August 11, 1871	Claflin nominated for Congress in the Eighth Congressional district in New York
September 1871	Theodore Tilton publishes *Biography of Victoria C. Woodhull* in the *Golden Age*
September 12, 1871	Woodhull elected president of the American Association of Spiritualists (AAS)
November 7, 1871	Woodhull and Claflin attempt to vote
November 20, 1871	Woodhull delivers her free love lecture, "The Principles of Social Freedom," at New York's Steinway Hall
December 17, 1871	French and Anglo-American sections of the IWA parade in honor of the martyred French *communards*

December 30, 1871	Marx's Communist Manifesto published in English for the first time in *Woodhull & Claflin's Weekly*
February 17, 1872	Thomas Nast publishes the Mrs. Satan cartoon in *Harper's Weekly*
February 21, 1872	Woodhull delivers "Impending Revolution" speech before IWA sections and others at New York's Academy of Music
March 12, 1872	Karl Marx and IWA General Council temporarily suspend Section Twelve, pending confirmation at the International Congress, the Hague, September 1872
May 11, 1872	Equal Rights Party convention nominates Woodhull and Frederick Douglass for president and vice president
May 28, 1872	IWA General Council formally announces break-up of Spring Street Council
June 3, 1872	Frederick Douglass's home in Rochester destroyed by fire
June 13, 1872	Claflin elected colonel of African-American militia, the Eighty-Fifth Regiment of New York
June 22, 1872	*Woodhull & Claflin's Weekly* temporarily suspends publication until November 2, 1872 issue
July–August 1872	Woodhull and Claflin evicted and homeless
September 2–9, 1872	The Hague Congress of the IWA formally suspends Section Twelve
September 10, 1872	Woodhull verbally exposes Beecher before AAS delegates in Boston, who reelect her for second term as president
November 2, 1872	*Woodhull & Claflin's Weekly* publishes Beecher and Challis exposures
November 3, 1872	Woodhull and Claflin arrested by federal marshals under 1872 postal law

March 3, 1873	Congress approves new federal obscenity legislation, known as the "Comstock Law"
June 27, 1873	Woodhull and Claflin found not guilty in federal obscenity trial under 1872 code
September 16, 1873	AAS (now Universal Association of Spiritualists, UAS) in Chicago, reelects Woodhull for third term as president
October 1873–February 1874	Woodhull lectures in the west
March 13, 1874	Woodhull and Claflin found not guilty in Challis libel suit
May–June 1874	Woodhull lectures in far west and California
August 22, 1874	Plymouth Church Committee investigation exonerates Beecher of all charges of impropriety
August 24, 1874	Theodore Tilton files charges against Beecher for alienation of his wife's affections
September 1874	UAS reelects Woodhull for fourth term as president
September 1874–June 1875	Woodhull lectures in the west, popularizing the Beecher-Tilton scandal
January 11, 1875	*Tilton v. Beecher* civil trial begins
June 2, 1875	*Tilton v. Beecher* trial ends in a hung jury
September 1875	UAS reelects Woodhull for fifth term as president
September 1875–June 1876	Woodhull lectures in west, south, and northeast
June 10, 1876	*Woodhull & Claflin's Weekly* ceases publication
September 1876	Woodhull resigns from UAS
October 8, 1876	Woodhull divorces second husband Colonel James Blood
November 1876–February 1877	Tilden/Hayes election. Hayes agrees to "southern compromise"; federal troops withdraw from south
August 1877	Woodhull and Claflin depart for England

Introduction
Victoria Woodhull, Sexual Revolutionary

Early in 1870, two women opened for business on Wall Street. In a deluge of publicity, Victoria Claflin Woodhull and her sister Tennessee Claflin demonstrated that women could establish and successfully run a business, even in a man's world of stock speculation. No one knew much about them, except that they appeared to be unfazed by controversy. They seemed accustomed to public life; they said they had pursued a series of careers, from acting to magnetic healing and fortune telling. They had also privately speculated in stocks and claimed a stunning $700,000 profit on "Black Friday" the previous autumn. They even had some experience in women's politics: Woodhull had attended a suffrage convention in Washington the year before. The opening of Woodhull, Claflin, & Company, however, marked their elevation to the national public stage. Across the country, newspapers called them the "Bewitching Brokers" and spread word of their sensational financial debut to the nation at large. It was the beginning of a tradition for Woodhull and Claflin, in which they dramatized the tensions inherent in women's public lives, and made spectacles of themselves for political effect. They dispensed with the protection of respectability and soon learned that speculation over their sexual lives dominated their reception in the popular press.[1]

Woodhull, Claflin & Company, Brokers, directly confronted the traditional gender roles that made public life controversial for women in 1870. Though men, particularly Woodhull's second husband Colonel James Blood, conducted the firm's day to day business, as owners the sisters were trailblazers for women's economic power. They called their company "the first firm of Female Brokers in the World," according to one reporter who emphasized the sisters' conscious defiance of the status quo. "No women had ever been stock or gold brokers," said Claflin, according to a *New York Courier* reporter, who quoted her in characteristically pithy language. "Wall Street was taboo to petticoats. . . . [But] we did not intend to let our petticoats interfere with anybody, or take up any more room in the street than the other brokers' trousers." They were not the first women to speculate on Wall Street, but their vocation as brokers was a first in the disreputable world of high finance, where even male brokers bore the stigma of immorality. Woodhull and Claflin challenged the notion that a female broker was improper because she performed public work in mixed company, unprotected in a world of men.[2] As the *Courier* reporter quoted Claflin: "Why shouldn't [women] just as well be stockbrokers as keep stores and measure men for shirts? We couldn't see why."[3]

Publicity, Woodhull later revealed, was a primary goal in establishing the firm. She hoped "to secure the most general and at the same time prominent introduction to the world that was possible." The opening brought attention but it also brought public debate over the propriety of women in male spaces like Wall Street. It was a novelty for Wall Street brokers who came to visit the firm; it was a sensation for the crowd of men who reportedly pressed their faces to the glass outside.[4] Brokering was a business that most people thought unsuitable for women. Even one supporter of women's work cautioned, "women could not very well conduct the business without having to mix promiscuously with men on the street, and stop and talk with them in the most public places; and the delicacy of woman would forbid that." Precisely because of its challenge to the idea of woman's delicacy, women's rights activists saw the opening as a harbinger of change. Wall Street had too long excluded women, Susan B. Anthony wrote in her paper, *The Revolution*, because of the "bad habits of Wall Street men who stare at every woman on the pavement except the apple sellers." The new firm established a precedent; Woodhull and Claflin, Anthony predicted, would "stimulate the whole future of women by their efforts and example."[5] As a dramatic event that defied convention, the opening of Woodhull, Claflin & Company became a lightning rod for sexual politics in 1870.

Popular media tended to recast the opening as a sexualized spectacle; daily and weekly papers, seeking to shock and entertain their readers, used Woodhull and Claflin as sensational news copy. Illustrated sporting newspapers were probably most effective in making the sisters notorious. *The Days' Doings*, for example, used the full battery of visual stereotypes to make the firm analogous to a brothel. A cover image (Figure 1) exaggerated the sisters' sexy (for the time) postures and their proximity to male clientele, and thereby questioned their morality. Another such image (Figure 2) depicted Claflin in an aggressive stance and bold stare that mirrored contemporary images of streetwalkers. The short skirts, more a reflection of the artist's imagination than their actual clothing, revealed the sisters' ankles and

No. 91—Vol. 4. NEW YORK, FEBRUARY 26, 1870. Price 10 Cents.

Figure 1. This cover image of Woodhull and Claflin in a men's sporting newspaper shows the sisters in suggestively curved postures. The men crowd Woodhull and Claflin and gaze directly upon them to indicate a lack of proper respect. The placement of the hand of the man on the left emphasizes Claflin's moral ambiguity: is he merely gesturing, or is he actually touching Claflin's thigh? The visual codes in this cover illustration established the sisters as sexually available. *The Days' Doings*, February 26, 1870.

calves in popular shorthand for "fast" women. Only the third image (Figure 3), with a more respectable parlor setting, suggested the artists' difficulty in representing the novel firm, but even its genteel imagery resembled depictions of high class brothels. The accompanying text exaggerated the strangeness of the female brokers, and diminished the political significance of the opening itself. The presence of Woodhull and Claflin on the cover of the illustrated sporting news sexualized the firm, and easily eclipsed any political agenda.[6]

Other commercial illustrations reinforced this interpretation of the firm. A cover woodcut image in the Wall Street paper (Figure 4), the *New York Evening Telegram*, showed the sisters sitting in an open carriage and wielding a horsewhip, two visual markers of "fast" or immoral women. In 1874, the brothel imagery, complete with sensual touching and open bottles of alcohol, became embedded in Wall Street lore in Matthew Hale Smith's *The Bulls and Bears of New York* (Figure 5). In this way, popular illustration of the brokerage firm set a tone that persisted in the sisters' subsequent

THE FEMALE BROKERS OF THE PERIOD.—THE TELEGRAPHIC APPARATUS AT THE ESTABLISHMENT OF WOODHULL, CLAFLIN & CO., 44 BROAD STREET, NEW YORK.—SEE PAGE 136.

Figure 2. Short skirts, exposed feet and ankles, and bold postures mark the new brokers as fast women in this second sporting illustration. A humorous reference to the sisters' "telegraphic apparatus" reminds the reader that their direct gazes on the men are immodest. *The Days' Doings*, February 26, 1870.

ventures in public life. It became the recurring theme in the strange political career of Victoria Woodhull. She would frame a spectacular event in the language of social principles; media coverage would then reinterpret it as a titillating spectacle. Woodhull survived these disparaging interpretations thanks to her skill in turning scathing media commentary into publicity for her struggle for social change. Put another way, she took her status as a disreputable woman, and converted it into a political asset.

Woodhull's public transformation from notorious woman to celebrity challenged Americans to come to terms with the full meaning of sex equality. She was not the most gifted female politician, though she was one of the most powerful speakers of the time. Her contribution was to act out the period's most extreme positions on a public stage. From 1870 to 1876, against the political backdrop of Reconstruction, she used a range of tactics to demand opportunities denied to women on the basis of their sex. As a broker, editor, public speaker, presidential candidate and celebrity, she

Figure 3. A third image of the brokerage house offers a more respectful and genteel presentation of the business. The lack of conformity in these three depictions (Figures 1–3), appearing in the same sporting newspaper issue, indicates the sisters' social ambiguity and the novelty of the new firm. *The Days' Doings*, February 26, 1870.

[handwritten margin note: Woodhull advocates for women's social equality]

insisted that women and men be held to the same standards in public life. She made her biggest mark on the period's popular culture, because she enacted spectacles in national media for the average person that challenged contemporary notions of gender and class. As a woman who surrendered her own privacy, and whose life was grist for the sensation-mongering press, she made the exposure of others' secrets a powerful tool of social change.

The Strange Career of Woodhull and Claflin

Victoria Woodhull and Tennessee Claflin were children of the Second Great Awakening. They were the seventh and ninth children born into a large, transient family on the old Ohio Valley frontier. Their father was a miller and part-time confidence man who, neighbors believed, once burned his

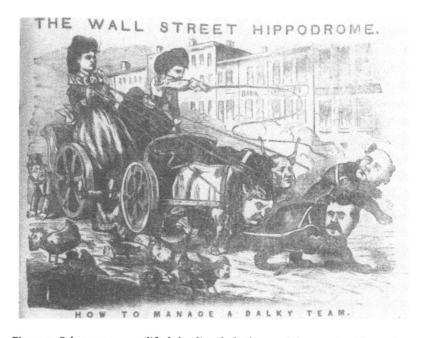

Figure 4. Other papers amplified the disorderly theme of the sporting illustrations. Here, Woodhull and Claflin drive the bulls and bears down Wall Street. The open carriage, the whip, and their violent conduct were visual shorthand for disorderly women and prostitutes. Their cruel treatment of the men in the image includes an obvious reference to castration, suggesting that the sisters' presence on Wall Street threatens masculinity itself. *New York Evening Telegram*, February 18, 1870.

own mill for the insurance money. Their mother was a Methodist enthusi-ast spiritually reborn during religious revivalism of the 1830s. Born in 1838 and named for England's new queen, Victoria was an odd, visionary child who believed herself destined for greatness. Her parents married her off at the age of fourteen to a doctor named Canning Woodhull. Because of her husband's alcoholism, young Victoria largely supported their two children with her practice as a medical clairvoyant. Meanwhile, her parents capital-ized on the "magnetic" powers of Victoria's little sister Tennessee, seven years her junior, by hawking her through the old Northwest as the "Won-derful Child" clairvoyant and cancer healer. The nature of their business ventures frequently brought controversy to the family. Tennessee's inability to cure one woman's cancer brought a manslaughter suit in 1864. A year later, when a reunited Victoria and Tennessee practiced clairvoyance in Cincinnati, neighbors, suspecting them of prostitution, ran the family out of town. Later that year, Victoria's clairvoyance business in Chicago shut down, this time on charges of fraud. The family supplemented such failures with

Figure 5. The symbolic codes of prostitution persist in this 1874 depiction of the "bewitching brokers." One sister appears to promote their newspaper; the books and desk in the background indicate an office setting. However, the physical touch-ing, the lewd expression of the man, and the alcohol on the table are suggestive of the brothel. Matthew Hale Smith, *The Bulls and Bears of New York* (1874). Courtesy of the American Antiquarian Society.

lucrative traveling medical tours through the west in a covered wagon, which filled their coffers and gave the sisters firsthand experience in human nature and the art of salesmanship.

By 1866, the family had moved to St. Louis, where Woodhull operated a business as a clairvoyant healer in a local hotel. There a Civil War veteran named Colonel James Harvey Blood, who had heard of Woodhull as a "most brilliant literary character," consulted her professionally and won her heart. Woodhull obtained a speedy divorce from her first husband (though she retained his last name), and married Blood in 1866. To evade his first wife (and two children), Woodhull and Blood embarked upon another tour in the covered wagon. It was in Pittsburgh, Woodhull later claimed, that she decided the family's next move: in a vision, the Greek orator Demosthenes told her to move them all to New York City. In 1868, Woodhull, Blood, her two children, her sister Tennessee, their parents, and an assortment of siblings and relations settled at 17 Great Jones Street in New York. With the aid of Tennessee's magnetic healing skills, they gained the trust and financial backing of Cornelius Vanderbilt. In January 1870, with his help, Woodhull and Claflin opened the first women's brokering business on Wall Street—the start of a career of "firsts."[7]

Her stock market opening was surprising for a woman in 1870, but Woodhull aspired to greater things. That April, she nominated herself a candidate for the 1872 presidential race. Within a month she and her sister launched a journal, *Woodhull & Claflin's Weekly*, which quickly became a pioneer of radical thought. She developed political connections with Radical Republican Representative Benjamin Butler from Massachusetts, and in January 1871 presented a memorial to Congress on behalf of woman's suffrage, becoming the first woman to address a Congressional committee. She shocked and fascinated audiences with candid speech on the subject of free love, a loosely defined ideology that meant anything from easing the divorce laws to abolishing marriage altogether. She headed a section of the International Workingmen's Association (IWA), and protested with the organization in the streets of New York. She and her friends sought to unite disparate reform groups into a single political organization called the Equal Rights Party. In 1872, the party nominated Woodhull for president with Frederick Douglass as her running mate.

The consequences of this radical nomination came swiftly: she lost her home, her paper, her means of earning a living and Vanderbilt's backing. In frustration, and to demonstrate her ideology of a single sexual standard, she spoke out against a number of prominent men, notably the nationally beloved Brooklyn pastor Henry Ward Beecher, who had, she claimed, committed adultery with the wife of one of his closest friends. The Beecher exposure eclipsed her presidential bid, and she faced harassment and jail for obscenity and libel charges for the accusations. Fighting these charges left her financially crippled. Over time, however, the legal action against her became an asset, and she became a celebrity in her own right as the victim of excessive federal persecution. She spent the next four years popularizing the Beecher story and her evolving ideas about sexuality on the national lecture circuit to large and increasingly enthusiastic audiences. In 1876 she divorced Colonel Blood, and a year later she sailed to England, lecturing successfully in several English cities. At one such lecture she met a younger scion of an old British banking family, James Biddulph Martin. She married him in 1883 and lived the life of an English gentlewoman until her death in 1927.

This book focuses on Woodhull's American heyday, from 1870 to 1876, when she became a symbol of the period's radical sexual politics. It examines not her life but rather a series of media events she launched to challenge the existing social order. Social activists migrating toward the Democratic Party hailed her as a renegade populist, a victim of church and state, and welcomed her attacks on the declining radicalism of the Republican Party. Conservatives saw her as an incarnation of evil, and disparaged her as "the Woodhull" and her supporters as "Woodhullites." Woodhull's repeated acts of political theater gave her unusual prominence and make her an instructive, and heretofore unrecognized, period marker for Reconstruction. Along with the social activists who promoted her, she struggled to shape the course of Reconstruction's political culture even as it scripted her actions and limited the arena in which she could promote radical change. The popular press singled her out as a sign of the times, a "folk demon" representing perceived threats to the established social order. In response, she used the tools of popular media to turn her notoriety into social and political power. Her transformation from notorious woman to celebrity illuminates the gendered political landscape of the early 1870s. She is, in effect, a barometer of the political culture of Reconstruction.

Recovering Victoria Woodhull

Generations of Americans have found Woodhull fascinating. During the twentieth century, Woodhull's biographers have confronted and contributed to her story, as well as her elusiveness as a historical subject. Biographies, biographical novels, documentaries, plays, a musical, and chapters in volumes about American "originals" perpetually add—or invent—new twists to the Woodhull story.[8] At the same time, Woodhull remains curiously absent from mainstream historical narratives. Despite all the retellings of her story, it is ironic that, after a lecture by her most recent biographer, a member of the audience asked the speaker, "Why have we never heard of Woodhull before?"[9]

It is nearly impossible to recover Woodhull as a historical actor in her own right. Her own personal papers are fragmentary and heavily edited. We will never know for certain who really wrote the lectures, speeches, letters, and articles attributed to her. They were almost never written in her own hand, and she later repudiated many, saying they had been written without her knowledge or consent. Some contemporary observers said that Woodhull could barely write, and that she did not have the education, breadth of knowledge, or grasp of the language necessary to produce the writings that appeared over her name. On the other hand, many others credited her with a powerful gift for extemporaneous speech on a wide variety of subjects. Whether these conflicting assertions are accurate or an indication of contemporary prejudice remains unknowable and, perhaps, unimportant.[10]

The question of authorship arises from Woodhull's unusual status as a female politician at a time when women were all but barred from political leadership. It also reflects the scruples of contemporary political radicals who worried about the dishonesty in crediting Woodhull for other people's work. Most historians and biographers agree that anarchist Stephen Pearl Andrews wrote the words to her famous lectures, with help from others (including her husband, Colonel Blood, who frequently wrote letters and editorials attributed to Woodhull, and even signed her autographs). It was not an uncommon practice. Fifty years later, her associate, anarchist Benjamin Tucker, remembered with shame being given credit for a speech he delivered to the New England Labor Reform League in 1873 that had been written by someone else; he referred to this, and most of Woodhull's lectures, as "humbug" and "fraud."

Speakers were often selected for their appeal to particular audiences, regardless of authorship. This explains the choice of a nineteen-year-old (Tucker) to address a major convention: he was selected for his appeal to younger radicals. Similarly, radical thinkers like Andrews deliberately chose Woodhull as the mouthpiece for their ideas. Perhaps they suspected their views would get a better hearing (or a wider audience) coming from a woman. Former abolitionists, reorganizing after the Civil War, looked for new faces to appeal to newer, younger, constituencies. Like many modern presidents, whose speeches are the products of committees and focus groups, Woodhull spoke the words in the public realm, and lent her name to the many letters to the editor, speeches, and articles attributed to her. She was a willing and effective voice for reform. Her importance lay in her power to move an audience and her courage to express ideas that defied more conventional views.

The lack of traditional historical sources makes the "authentic" Woodhull tantalizingly difficult to find. Her closest associates, among them the most radical social reformers of the time, left little documentation about Woodhull. Her influence on more respectable social reformers was so poisonous that their own papers conspicuously omit reference to her.[11] To make the historian's task still more difficult, Woodhull spent decades revising her life story. Her most explicit account of her early life is highly suspect, because she dictated it for the public eye, and continually updated and revised this account in her paper, *Woodhull & Claflin's Weekly*.[12] Her subsequent marriage into old English money, which funded a new series of autobiographical pamphlets in Britain, further complicates her account. She published several edited autobiographies before her death in 1927, and she left a provision in her will for her daughter Zula Maud to rewrite her life story yet again.[13]

Woodhull's historical obscurity stems in part from her social origins. To modern interpreters, she may seem like yet another middle-class suffrage woman in crinoline; to her contemporaries, however, she was anything but respectable. Her first biographer, Emanie Sachs, relied heavily on the impressions of well-connected suffrage activists, to whom Woodhull had always been an outsider. "I do not believe Mrs. Woodhull was ever an important factor either in this country or in England," Carrie Chapman Catt advised Sachs in 1927. "Her life was chiefly valuable as demonstrating that a reformer can entirely queer every effort she makes by getting too far ahead of the average trend of public opinion, or entirely off the beat." Harriet Stanton Blatch, daughter of Elizabeth Cady Stanton, likewise cautioned Sachs that "Mrs. Woodhull's life would probably not repay study" as she was "never active in suffrage." For Blatch, Woodhull's 1871 memorial to the House Judiciary Committee on behalf of suffrage "began and ended her suffrage activity." The suffrage historian Ida Husted Harper concurred. "Only a little handful of suffragists in New York City knew Mrs. Woodhull," she wrote. "I never saw her. She flashed in and flashed out, was handsome and brilliant and ignored the conventional morality."[14] The discomfort of these prominent suffrage women reflected in part a social position closed to Woodhull, but probably also their awareness of the way popular media used such figures to discredit their movement.

A few of Sachs's sources looked beyond the media version of Woodhull and Claflin and gave them credit for their courage in defying convention. "They represented an unpopular cause," Joseph Greer, who knew the sisters slightly, told Sachs in 1927, "and like nearly all pioneers they paid the penalty in misrepresentation." Others agreed with this view. "I know so well what it cost any woman to take any forward step, in those days, that my hat is off to every one of them," wrote Grace Ellery Channing-Stetson, who was barely in her teens during Woodhull's heyday. A playwright and friend of Charlotte Perkins Gilman, Channing-Stetson had little patience for the young, modern women of the 1920s. The flapper generation, in her view, shirked responsibility and spurned the vote that previous generations had struggled for decades to secure. Instead, they wallowed in materialism and incapacitated themselves with high heels and extreme diets. "They even think they have discovered Sex—which we knew all about three generations ago and did not think we had invented then."[15]

True to its times, sex rather than responsibility was the focus of Sachs's biography, *"The Terrible Siren"*. Writing in the commercial, sexualized climate of the Roaring Twenties, Sachs unearthed the old stories and scandals to produce a muckraking biography that appeared in 1928, a year after Woodhull's death. Sachs rightly questioned Woodhull's adopted British respectability and criticized her for her hypocrisy in denying free love, but also reduced her to a ridiculous figure. The Red Scare and attendant dismissal of reform in the 1920s made it easy to trivialize Woodhull, her paper, and the radicals who supported her. The book's widespread popularity thwarted Zula Maud Woodhull's dying wish to have her mother's biography written in a more favorable light. Sachs's lively, scurrilous biography became the master narrative on Woodhull for the next forty years.[16] Subsequent biographies through the McCarthy era represented the sisters as lunatics, eccentric icons from the annals of Americana. Antagonism for the American left and tacit adherence to the new domesticity made Woodhull into a cartoonish foil for the post-World War II American woman.[17]

It took the reemergence of feminism to challenge *"The Terrible Siren"*. In 1959, Eleanor Flexner questioned the notion that Woodhull singlehandedly put women's suffrage back half a century. Feminist scholarship of the 1960s and 1970s highlighted the sisters' brokerage business as a milestone for women. Woodhull also began to resurface as a major player in the struggle

for women's equality. Two collections sidestepped the question of prove-
nance and published the articles and speeches that bore Woodhull's name as
if she had written them herself.[18] More recently, a new focus on the political significance of the "New Departure" theory has revealed how this argument for woman suffrage, developed by activists in the late 1860s, gained
national publicity by Woodhull's memorial to Congress in early 1871.[19] Woodhull's connection to international socialism has resurfaced in new studies
that show her in a broader role in that movement than previous scholars of
socialism had allowed.[20] These looks at the 1870s reveal that Woodhull had
important interactions with the period's radical political movements.

In the wake of second wave feminist scholarship, three new biographies shed new light on Woodhull's remarkable life. The first to appear, Lois
Beachy Underhill's *The Woman Who Ran for President* (1995), is a thoughtful recovery of Woodhull as a political actor and thinker in her own right
with strong connections to other social radicals. Underhill also tackles the
difficult question of Woodhull's authorship; she goes so far as to analyze the
handwriting on autobiographical notes written, she says, by Woodhull herself. Underhill's discovery of these notes through the Holland-Martin family (descendants of Woodhull's third husband, John Martin) is a major new
source of historical information about Woodhull, particularly her life after
her marriage to Martin. Two other biographies published in 1998 offer fascinating interpretations of Woodhull's impact on her contemporaries. One,
by journalist Mary Gabriel, salvages extensive newspaper coverage from the
period in a way that illuminates several episodes of Woodhull's life, particularly her relationship with the International Workingmen's Association.
Barbara Goldsmith's biography, on the other hand, celebrates a more sensational reading of Woodhull reminiscent of *"The Terrible Siren"*, but rightly
focuses on the centrality of Spiritualism to Woodhull's influence and popularity. Together, the three biographies round out Woodhull as an individual,
and clarify her relationships with notable personalities of the 1870s.[21]

Woodhull the person, however, can only partly explain her historical
significance; it is as a phenomenon that she most influenced the period. For
example, her exposure of Henry Ward Beecher was a watershed event in the
nineteenth century. The ensuing Beecher-Tilton scandal sent shock waves
through contemporary views about personal life and religious faith. Richard W. Fox has argued that the scandal reflected shifting popular ideas about
intimacy, marriage, sexuality and divorce. Its significance far transcended
the actors themselves. Beecher and the Tiltons, like Woodhull and Claflin,
were merely dramatizing prevailing views in a turbulent moral climate. It

was a media event that fed off popular fascination for celebrity. It also provoked a religious controversy within the Protestant faith; as Altina Waller shows, conservative Protestants saw in it a way to halt what they saw as creeping liberalism among their flocks. Contemporary responses to the three principal actors were also revealing; many assumed Beecher's guilt, yet found in Tilton an easier scapegoat, while his wife Lib Tilton gradually retreated into obscurity and (temporary) blindness.[22] Thanks to Woodhull's exposure, the scandal left a lasting impression on contemporaries.

This study attempts to place Woodhull in the larger context of the trial she set in motion. Her decision to expose Beecher, a spontaneous act apparently made on her own initiative, had profound consequences. It galvanized conservatives to act against what they saw as runaway social freedom that threatened to gain great commercial power. As Helen Lefkowitz Horowitz argues, Woodhull was on the cusp of a new sexual framework emerging in the nineteenth century that saw sex as essential to a full and happy life. As this view gained popular currency, formidable opposition arose to silence the open discussion (and sale) of provocative ideas and devices (like contraception). Young Men's Christian Association activist Anthony Comstock capitalized on conservative disgust with Woodhull, and her very public accusation against Beecher, to enact a strict federal statute in 1873 called the "Comstock Law." As the new law's chief enforcer, Comstock oversaw public, commercial discourse about sexuality and contraception. Nevertheless, Woodhull's flamboyant defiance meant that questions of sexuality entered contemporary discourse. Comstock slowed but did not halt the gradual liberalization of views about sexuality and reproduction. As Andrea Tone demonstrates, obscenity law often failed in the courtroom, as juries and judges downplayed the crimes of publishers and commercial contraceptive manufacturers in recognition of popular usage. Comstock was successful, however, in censoring the most outspoken sex radicals, and Woodhull was his big target.[23]

New scholarship on nineteenth-century sexual reform movements shows the strategic alliances and choices of far-flung activists as they faced the growing shift away from reform. Many radical reformers in Reconstruction had cut their teeth on the Spiritualist movement, which gave women a forum where they could meet, organize, and speak before mixed crowds of like-minded individualists. A small subset of this amorphous non-organization was an uncompromising network of sex radicals who saw the sexual liberation of women as the key to all other reform. Many independent-minded women, particularly in the midwest, found the ideas of the sex radicals compelling.[24] Woodhull tapped into their broad-based network, as well as their local organizations and associations; her connection to these activists helps explain her popularity in rural areas of the country. Sex radicals demanded plain speech on the subject of human sexuality; they continually struggled to make simple, nonprovocative, scientific information about human physiology available in the public sphere. Woodhull brought this information into the realm of popular culture.

Woodhull's revolution was cultural; she brought the ideas of sexual hygiene activists into the commercial public sphere. This, in turn, depended on her personal transformation from a notorious object of scorn to a popular celebrity. Over the six years studied here, Woodhull became one of the modern world's first celebrities. Her longevity in the public eye was the key to her fame—to paraphrase Daniel Boorstin, she was "known for [her] well-knownness." Woodhull's well-knownness was a fluke of timing; she came to prominence in the midst of a graphic revolution and used its tools to further her fame. Graphic media took off after the Civil War. Popular images gave Americans easy access to popular spectacles, and created a perpetual demand for new visual stimuli. Woodhull satisfied this hunger. As a favorite subject in men's sporting news, she reached a mass audience in poses ranging from prostitute to public teacher to entertainer. Such popular illustrations, though they tended toward the satirical, made her ubiquitous; her image became a metaphor for radical social critique that could not be fully disregarded. Woodhull catered to the public desire for flamboyant individual figures by staging dramatic public events, by courting newspaper attention, and by selling publicity photographs and lithographs to fans. Celebrity, as David Marshall notes, is a function of consumer culture, but also promises democracy by advertising the notion of possibility. Woodhull and her "rags-to-riches" story—as well as the populist message she drew from it—probably appealed to Americans' need for hope in a turbulent era of social and economic change.[25]

Notorious Victoria Woodhull

This study seeks to reconcile competing views of Woodhull and Claflin as sex radicals and sexual objects in sporting news. The story begins with representations, particularly illustrations in the sporting press. Historians have only begun exploring the realm of cheap illustrated news.[26] The use of sporting papers as sources poses a formidable research challenge. They were both sensational and cheap, which made them less likely to be preserved than the average commercial newspaper. Despite the relatively high circulation they enjoyed, two of the three most popular sporting papers were not preserved in complete sets for the early 1870s. *The Days' Doings* (New York) is the only such paper still available in a complete run for these years. Frequent references to this paper in contemporary sources name it almost interchangeably with the *National Police Gazette* (New York) and the *Illustrated Police News* (Boston); I take it as a representative of its kind, though I do supplement it with available copies of the other two major sporting papers.

Historians have overlooked Woodhull's extensive coverage in the sporting news, yet this was precisely where her notoriety took hold. In 1870, people across the nation knew that Woodhull was not respectable, because her image was on the covers of the men's newspapers displayed in newsstands, cigar shops, barbershops, and barrooms. Papers like the *National Police Gazette* and *The Days' Doings* regularly reported on "the Woodhull" and used her to sell papers. Catering to a male clientele, the papers were part of the social coming-of-age—an initiation ritual—for young men, who read them in public, exclusively male environments. Their pages showcased feisty and often violent women in ways that emphasized their bodies and sexual availability. In the three years following their brokerage debut, *The Days' Doings* featured Woodhull and her sister more than any other celebrity or event.[27] Typical renderings gave the sisters shortened skirts and suggestive postures. Such visual cues denoted "fast" women and marked them for viewers as sexually depraved.[28] Woodhull's very public life made her prime fodder for such papers. Regardless of the content of stories about her or even the actual depictions of her, her regular presence in the sporting press classed her as a notorious and disorderly woman;[29] portrayal in such papers made her as sexually suspect as the other women who appeared in the same pages.

In the 1870s, there was a growing commercial market for distorted, sexualized representations of women in the popular men's sporting newspapers like *The Days' Doings* and the *Police Gazette*. As the images from the brokerage opening suggest (Figures 1–5), they were more than neutral renderings of "authentic" scenes; they conveyed complex meanings through the arrangement of the players in the frame. Commercial illustrators in the nineteenth century, like those producing images for the popular *Frank Leslie's Illustrated Newspaper*, created a partial view of reality. As Joshua Brown demonstrates, narrative and technical strategies made illustrations dramatic and visually striking, but also constructed or reinforced stereotypes about class, race and gender.[30] That paper's tawdry cousin *The Days' Doings* (also produced by Leslie), and other sporting papers, were less subtle because more specialized: they offered white male spectators sensational narratives of women's duplicity, fallen women doomed to prison or death, and other fables of women's subordination. These visual tableaux depended on and reinforced negative stereotypes of women. Woodhull's presence in such a forum established her disreputable social standing, even as it brought her fame.

Tennessee Claflin exaggerated her sister's notoriety in sporting news, because she was if anything less respectable than her sister. Woodhull's sponsors frequently promoted Claflin as a surrogate for her older sister. Together, the sisters came to embody a cultural radicalism that arose not only from their daring sexual politics, but also from the coded class and gender positions they represented. Claflin would mirror Woodhull's actions during these years. They ran the stock brokerage business jointly, Claflin ran for Congress after Woodhull ran for president (unofficially, and neither was elected), and she also published and spoke about free love. The twinning of the sisters is not surprising in a nation that was, at the time, obsessed with twins and duality. It is informative to view the sisters as they appeared in contemporary sporting news, with Woodhull as the representative public woman, and Claflin as her more rambunctious alter ego.[31]

What is interesting about Woodhull is her insistence that her reputation, especially the sensational version filling the pages of the sporting press, was irrelevant to her ideas. She was attempting to create a new definition of public womanhood in the nineteenth century, when political activism was still a rather controversial activity for respectable women. This was not a new feature of women's public lives: before the Civil War, critics used sexual innuendo to discount female activists ranging from Quaker abolitionists to free thinkers like Frances Wright, regardless of their actual behavior; even after the war, critics sexualized women's rights advocates to discredit them.[32] There were two reasons for this. First, many believed that, without the protections of home and family to keep her chaste, a woman in public would become immoral. In addition, the challenges by female activists to women's subordinate, dependent role in the traditional family aggravated this fear; their ideological challenge to woman's domestic nature left them vulnerable to speculation about their sexual lives. Women who were sex radicals explicitly discussed questions of sexuality and reproduction. As the daily labor paper, the *New York Standard*, put it in 1871 "How is it that woman's rights, and shrieking for suffrage, and women speaking in public, always seem to be inseparable from nastiness?"[33]

Woodhull and the social radicals in her network sought to make accusations of nastiness irrelevant to the lives of public women. Words alone, they believed, would never change women's position in society. Only individual acts of defiance in local situations would force people to recognize the artifice behind what everyone thought of as "normal." Dress reformers—women who risked ridicule, harassment, or jail by wearing pants in public—knew this well. Many made personal sacrifices to further the cause of women's equality. Sex radical Laura Cuppy Smith, for example, offended her neighbors by walking through town with her pregnant, unwed daughter to defy the double standard that blamed the woman for the mutual offense of extramarital sex.[34] Woodhull and her supporters were for a time determined to do whatever it took to eradicate social inequality. From small acts of defiance to civil disobedience, Woodhull demanded that her contemporaries recognize their own preconceived notions of women's nature as nothing more than social constructs.

In styling herself a public woman, Woodhull sought a female analogue of the public man of politics. This was a hazardous undertaking. The common usage of "public woman" literally meant a street prostitute, and conservatives deliberately blurred the distinction between the two. Most public work for women at the time had immoral connotations; even middle-class women who ventured into public occupations, such as sales clerks, were open to suspicions of sexual profligacy.[35] The ideal of a strict division between public and private spheres had great power in the nineteenth century to define class and gender privilege. Many women led public lives, but often faced negative consequences that ranged from open taunting to covert criticism. Sex radicals located the heart of the problem in private relationships. Public men rarely faced negative consequences for illicit sexual behavior; women's private transgressions, by contrast, infiltrated their public status. Woodhull's exposure of Beecher's sexual secrets in 1872 asked society to judge a charismatic public man on the same terms that it judged a public woman. According to the sex radicals, true equality demanded that scurrilous gossip be equally relevant to women and men, or irrelevant to both.

Woodhull was at first unfazed by her notoriety; after all, she invited the reporter from *The Days' Doings* to her hotel, and she must have known how coverage in such a paper would appear to the public at large. The fact that she welcomed this publicity suggests that she was less sensitive to the hazards of public life than more respectable women. As a traveling healers, stage performers, and professional clairvoyants, she and Claflin were accustomed to public scrutiny. They may have had no conventional status to lose, in fact; there is conflicting evidence that the sisters may also have been occasional prostitutes, but even without that stigma they were far from respectable in the commercial northeast.[36] To nineteenth-century readers, their flamboyant brokerage opening, as evidence of their penchant for media coverage, signaled their lack of delicacy; they deliberately flouted the decorum required of ladies. They dined, for instance, without a male escort at New York's fashionable Delmonico's Restaurant at a time when such behavior marked them as prostitutes.[37] When Woodhull declared herself a presidential candidate in April 1870, and stood before a congressional committee to present a memorial on behalf of women's suffrage the next January, she showed the world that she was not ashamed of being seen. When her private life became the subject of public criticism, she used the criticism as evidence of hypocrisy in high places. When newspapers linked her sexual nonconformity to her political ambitions, she made sexual liberation the cornerstone of her revolution.

Woodhull's political performances exposed her to public scorn, but she appeared less anxious to deny accusations against her morality than to insist that they should not matter. In this sense her actions transcended the older choice women faced between seclusion and exposure. She "made a spectacle of herself," to use Temma Kaplan's formulation, as a tool of social protest. Political allies, from sex radicals to women suffragists to socialists, used her example to mobilize constituencies and to dramatize the contradictions that made women's political life so fraught with tension to begin with. Social movements chose—even welcomed—Woodhull as a leader, attracted by her public flouting of convention. They applauded her disruptive inversion of power and legitimacy in the public sphere. Woodhull was an unruly woman who both galvanized support and antagonized opposition; she dramatized a comic upheaval of the sexual order, yet in the process significantly altered that order. Both heroine and folk devil, her disorderly conduct celebrated revolution and stimulated a sizeable conservative reaction.[38]

Victoria Woodhull and Her Sexual Revolution

Not all revolutions succeed unequivocally. In the 1870s, Victoria Woodhull staged a series of revolutionary events to challenge the existing social order, and eventually participated in the reaction against her earlier views. This study traces the waxing and waning of the sexual revolution Woodhull embodied for her contemporaries. The four chapters encapsulate four significant episodes of her career: (1) the early effort to forge a consensus about women's sexual oppression; (2) the attempt to mobilize a broad constituency through acts of political theater; (3) a program of civil disobedience against laws designed to stifle opposition to the sexual status quo; and (4) the popularization and coincident taming of her radical critique of the social order. Woodhull's story sheds new light on the intertwining of radical political movements in the 1870s. Her revolutionary program coincided with Radical Reconstruction; by 1876 both movements were in decline.

Chapter 1 describes the early phase of her political activism, in which Woodhull and a small group of radical freethinkers attempted to forge a consensus based on what they called "the Principles of Social Freedom." Social freedom was a polite euphemism for a philosophy the press dismissed as free love. It held that social, cultural, and religious control over sexuality was harmful to society, and particularly to women. Woodhull attempted to unite a coalition that included socialists, sex radicals, and women's rights activists. Her organizing principle was that women's inequality stemmed from their economic dependence on men: marriage was a form of sexual slavery for women through which women exchanged sexual and maternal labor for economic security. She argued that exaggerated sexual differences, including prescriptions about woman's proper place, reinforced the subordination of women. Sex radicals backed Woodhull to promote the idea that women should cast off the unnatural bonds of marriage as a first step toward liberation. Controversy fragmented the fragile coalition, and by 1872 only a small cadre of social radicals endorsed Woodhull's Principles and her politics of defiance.

Chapter 2 provides an in-depth look at Woodhull's nomination for president of the United States. This was a deliberate act of political theater designed to shake up popular notions about race and gender. When delegates of the Equal Rights Party nominated Woodhull for president of the United States at their convention in May 1872, with Frederick Douglass as her running mate, they wanted to send a symbolic message of universal rights to the world. Amid the political backlash against Radical Reconstruction, however, the press cast the nomination in highly sexualized and racist tones, revealing deep-seated resistance to the idea of universal rights. Woodhull was the national spokeswoman for social freedom (free love). Douglass, on the other hand, was the national spokesman for social equality (civil rights). He supported the controversial Civil Rights Bill, which sought to provide African Americans equal access to public institutions, including transportation, accommodations, courts of law, and public schools. His opponents accused Douglass of promoting interracial "mingling." Douglass, not consulted before the convention, rejected the place on Woodhull's ticket, but not before the nomination had generated satirical and racist press commentary. Because of their respective positions on sexual and social equality, the Woodhull/Douglass nomination laid bare the growing miscegenation hysteria of a critical election year. Vilified in the press, Woodhull turned to a more accessible and effective method of getting her message across.

Chapter 3 explores Woodhull's use of "exposure" as a political tool, and a form of civil disobedience. Late in 1872, Woodhull exposed the nation's most prominent Protestant minister, Henry Ward Beecher, for allegedly committing adultery with the wife of his good friend Theodore Tilton. The scandal allowed conservatives to discredit a generation of reform movements, from abolition to woman suffrage, that Beecher represented. The public "outing" of Beecher and a few other respectable men put the principles of the sex radicals into practice, and posed a dramatic challenge to sexual hypocrisy and the existing social order. At the same time, the Beecher exposure triggered the antagonism of moral crusaders, notably Anthony Comstock. He had both Woodhull and Claflin arrested repeatedly under obscenity legislation that he strengthened in the process with their punishment in mind. His relentless pursuit of the sisters crippled them both socially and financially. The questionable grounds of his actions, however, gradually generated popular backlash against the moral authoritarianism he represented. To dramatize the sexual double standard, Woodhull deliberately challenged Comstock and the federal government to act against her. Sex radicals used the Beecher scandal and Comstock's actions to stimulate open debate on taboo social questions, including prostitution, adultery and divorce. Woodhull's persecution in 1872–73 prompted anarchists and free lovers, as well as general commentators throughout the country, to question the rise of Comstockery. Her exposure and the subsequent popularization of the Beecher scandal marked the beginning of the end of the period's revolutionary potential.

Most historians leave Woodhull after the Beecher exposure. Chapter 4 recovers from historical obscurity the last three years of Woodhull's American career, during which she popularized and simultaneously tamed her radical social critique in a new incarnation of her family's traveling show. From 1873 to 1876, Woodhull earned a small fortune spreading her version of the Beecher scandal. To the delight of sex radicals, Woodhull's canny performances on the lecture circuit brought the notion of the single sexual standard before large audiences nationwide. But the popular appetite for her lectures, and the commercialization of Woodhull's political message, coincided with the declining popularity of universal rights activism. Beecher was just one of several discredited Republican stalwarts during these years, and their shaming was yet another blow to the party's moral authority. As Republicans during Grant's second term eschewed the more extreme possibilities for racial reform, by 1876 Woodhull likewise abandoned her most controversial positions. Her later lectures replaced the abstract ideal of total sexual liberation with a more palatable notion of maternal "sexual science." This deeply religious and proto-eugenicist argument for sex education, for the benefit of the race (initially the human race as a whole) became the underpinning of her later eugenics work in Britain in the 1890s. Woodhull's retreat from her radical positions of 1872 coincided with the end of Radical Reconstruction, as well as the declining fortunes of international socialism and woman suffrage.

Many sex radicals were disappointed when Woodhull abandoned their most radical principles and sailed for England in 1877. Their most unconventional, powerful, and dramatic spokeswoman had apparently betrayed them to occupy herself whitewashing her own reputation. Hindsight suggests that their criticism was misguided, if not unfair. Reaction against Woodhull was both personal and political in nature, a backlash against both the woman and the liberal humanism she represented. Woodhull herself ultimately participated in this backlash. People expected impossible, contradictory things of Woodhull. Because she was one of very few women willing to take radical positions on women's sexual rights in the public sphere, activists pinned extravagant hopes on her success. They wanted both the unlettered populist heroine from the Ohio frontier and the female scholar; the downgraded prostitute and the chaste reformer; the hero of the working man and the champion of bourgeois capitalism. It is not surprising that people wanted all this from Woodhull; she offered all these versions of herself to the public at different stages of her career. She was the ultimate performer, dramatizing every possibility of women's advancement on the public stage. In the end, she personally underwent the reaction against a revolutionary historical moment.

Early women's rights activists faced a host of obstacles inconceivable to male political contemporaries, invisible to twenty-first-century readers. Many would like to have a female Thomas Jefferson or Abraham Lincoln, statesmen, public speakers, politicians. And they do exist: theoretician Elizabeth

Cady Stanton, fiery rhetorician Sojourner Truth, uncompromising moralist Susan B. Anthony, principled conciliator Lucy Stone. But there was also Victoria Woodhull, and her prominence in contemporary culture makes her significant today. Her ambition and social obscurity enabled her to take risks most respectable women avoided. Stanton shrewdly recognized Woodhull's significance in the aftermath of the Beecher-Tilton scandal:

Victoria Woodhull has done a work for woman that none of us could have done. She has faced and dared men to call her the names that make women shudder, while she chucked principle, like medicine, down their throats. She has risked and realized the sort of ignominy that would have paralyzed any of us who have longer been called strong-minded.[39]

To understand fully the continued, perplexing lag in women's active involvement in public life, it is necessary to appreciate what put it beyond the reach of most women in the past. The historical origins of women's exclusion from the public sphere are starkly evident in the experiences of those who dared to defy conventional wisdom. This book hopes to offer some insight into the resistance of modern political culture to the full meaning of equality.

Chapter 1
"The Principles of Social Freedom"

Ten weeks after the opening of Woodhull, Claflin & Company, Brokers, in 1871, Victoria Woodhull took another swipe at the male monopoly on public life; she nominated herself as a candidate for the 1872 presidential contest. She saw herself as eligible because she embodied the many facets of women's rights activism. In an open letter to the *New York Herald*, Woodhull said:

While others of my sex devoted themselves to a crusade against the laws that shackle the women of the country, I asserted my individual independence; . . . while others sought to show that there was not valid reason why woman should be treated . . . as being inferior to man, I boldly entered the arena of politics and business and exercised the rights I already possessed. I therefore claim the right to speak for the unenfranchised woman of the country, and . . . announce myself as a candidate for the Presidency.[1]

Soon after, Woodhull, along with her sister and a small network of social activists, began publication of a new radical press, called *Woodhull & Claflin's Weekly*. Woodhull used her new visibility and her newspaper to establish a coalition of reformers determined to erase class and gender inequality. Her social critique appealed for the support of activists housed in three distinct social movements: a revolutionary group of Spiritualists known as "free lovers," women's rights activists who sought equal political opportunities for women, and a splinter of labor reformers who sought recognition from Karl Marx's International Workingmen's Association (IWA, the First International). To all three groups, Woodhull offered a blueprint for a new order that was based on a principle she called social freedom.

As a woman in public life, Woodhull regularly collided with gender and class prescriptions restricting womanly behavior. Society tended to see two kinds of women, those who were respectable and those who were not. Those who saw themselves as respectable women generally sought male protection and economic support in marriage and avoided public life: they saw their seclusion in the private sphere, in fact, as proof of their superior class status. Women activists and public speakers sought to challenge this limited view of respectability in a variety of ways, but only a few openly flouted the underlying sexual double standard. Woodhull's apparent failure to shrink from public commentary marked her from the outset as not respectable, but she fought against the tendency to reduce all debate to her reputation. Her strategy, instead, was to call the double standard into question by insisting that her sexual life was irrelevant to her public image unless men upheld the same strict code of behavior they used to denounce her.

[margin note: sexual double standard]

Creating a Reform Coalition

The Sex Radicals

The sex radicals—members of a faction of the Spiritualist movement that contemporaries often dismissed with the more disparaging term "free lovers"—were quick to recognize Woodhull's political significance. Within weeks of the brokerage's opening, anarchist Stephen Pearl Andrews sought out Woodhull's acquaintance; he saw her as an attractive spokeswoman for social reform, and probably helped her to draft her nomination letter to the *New York Herald*. Before the Civil War, Andrews had been an ardent abolitionist, socialist, Spiritualist and women's rights activist. He was widely known for his advocacy of "social freedom," a polite euphemism for the free love movement that had flourished in the radical press and a few experimental communities in the 1850s: Andrews himself had been associated with Long Island's free love community, Modern Times (now Brentwood, New York). In 1853, Andrews published his views—a frank defense of free love and critique of the hypocrisy of conventional marriage—alongside opposing perspectives in a pamphlet entitled *Love, Marriage and Divorce*. He and other sex radicals based their ideology of social freedom on an Enlightenment belief in individual rights as applied to women. He introduced Woodhull to a national network of activists who believed, as Helen Lefkovitz Horowitz puts it, "that sex lay at the core of being"; for them, free love (defined in a number of ways) was the key to all other reforms. Andrews's editorial influence over the *Weekly* brought it an agenda and a following, making it a forum for social freedom as the harbinger of revolution.[2]

[margin note: Stephen Pearl Andrews + free love]

Through the spring and summer of 1870, Andrews and his fellow sex radicals used the *Weekly* to articulate the most extreme claims to women's political and social emancipation. They denied that sex was merely for pro-creation, insisting on women's rights to sexual agency within and possibly even outside marriage. Even among these extreme reformers, there was a wide spectrum of opinion on exactly what free love meant. Some believed that monogamy was the highest possible state, and that individuals should have the freedom to choose a lifelong mate carefully based on spiritual and physical affinity; within the current, imperfect state of marriage, they felt, a woman had the right to refuse her husband sexual access. Others, who might be termed "serial monogamists," wanted to abolish marriage, which they saw as a form of sexual slavery for women, but advocated enduring free relationships based on mutual attraction. Most extreme were the vari-etists, who opposed any social restraints on sexuality whatsoever; only indi-vidual attraction, rather than social sanctions, they held, should dictate the frequency and permanency of sexual partnerships. From its publication, all these strands of the debate over social freedom filled the pages of the *Weekly*; sex radicals like Andrews, Ezra Heywood, Juliet Severance, Olivia Freelove Shepard, Lois Waisbrooker, Moses Hull, and Francis Barry wrote regularly about prostitution, the abolition of marriage, the single sexual standard, and dress reform.[3] Their writing strove to raise consciousness about sexual inequality, to eliminate exaggerated indicators of sexual differ-ence, and to destroy the double standard that forgave men for behavior con-demned in women.

Most sex radicals were also Spiritualists. Spiritualism was a loosely connected movement of Christian nonconformists and freethinkers who believed that the spirits of the dead could, if properly understood and heeded, make a positive contribution to the world of the living. Spiritual-ism empowered the nineteenth-century women's rights movement because Spirit guidance gave female activists the cultural authority to lead public lives.[4] Female mediums and especially trance speakers claimed to channel male spirit voices, which freed them from conventional gender roles, and allowed them to speak in public and instruct audiences in the parlor and on the stage. Spiritualists' emphasis on women's rights posed a very real threat to traditional marriage; the goal was to free women from conventions and appearances (including clothing) that demonstrated their subordination to men. Woodhull's new allegiance to Spiritualists and dress reformers, for example, was evident late in 1870 when she adopted a variant of the reform costume—leggings under a flowing shirt and a man's jacket. All but the most extreme Spiritualists had abandoned the reform dress after the Civil War: sex radicals used such controversial displays of reform dress to exhibit

[handwritten margin note: dif defs of free love]

their struggle for women's complete sexual liberation. They lived their principles publicly and dared the rest of the world to do the same.[5]

Sex radicals believed that hypocrisy tainted the social order and made class and gender equality inaccessible to women. To illustrate this point, they frequently wrote about prostitution, which they saw as a disease, caused by the economic exploitation of women, that "festered in silence." Only equal economic rights for women would cure it. "Remove the causes and the effects will cease," argued a typical *Weekly* editorial. "Give woman employment and you remove her from the need of self-destruction." Desperation drove many women into abusive or exploitative relations with men purely for survival. "We hope all our girls and women will soon be educated up to the standard of preferring the glorious freedom of self-support, even as washerwomen and ragpickers, to holding legal or illegal sexual relations undictated by attraction. *She who marries for support, and not for love, is a lazy pauper, coward and prostitute.*" In advocating social and economic remedies for prostitution, sex radicals went beyond a demand for the vote.[6] By referring to marriage as legal prostitution, they insisted that both groups of women exchanged sexuality for material benefit, but men held up married women as exemplary, and disparaged the prostitutes they secretly visited. This double standard punished women for sexual behavior forgiven in men; silence, sex radicals maintained, only made women more vulnerable to exploitation.[7] Their demand for an open assessment of men's role in perpetuating the social evil became the backbone of Woodhull's free love philosophy.[8]

Beneath these calls for economic equity and sexual openness lay the belief that women, like men, were sexual beings. Prostitution, "the legitimate offspring of marriage and its accompanying errors," was a natural consequence of denying women's sexual agency. "Women, for no other crime than having followed the dictates of a natural appetite, are driven with fury from the comforts and sympathies of society," a *Weekly* correspondent insisted. Most provocative here was the assertion that society's denial of a woman's natural appetites essentially forced her into prostitution. The idea that women experienced sexual desire—even if it led them astray—contradicted more palatable claims of victimization offered by earlier reformers. The assertion of female sexual agency undermined the Victorianism of some pre-Civil War women's reform movements: as spiritual rather than physical beings, the argument said, women would purify political corruption.[9] Woodhull's insistence on female sexual agency, but more important, her determination to end the silence on the subject, scorned the idea of women's moral superiority to men. Instead, she insisted that both sexes be held to the same standard: a moral order that shielded men and condemned women for the same act was not worthy of protection. Only honest scrutiny of social problems could bring about their solution.

The Woman Suffrage Movement

Woodhull's social activism also had a political bent, evident in her self-nomination for president, which attracted her to the woman suffrage cause. She forced the connection in January 1871, by presenting a powerful suffrage Memorial to the House Judiciary Committee. It was one of Woodhull's few public ventures that garnered respectful treatment in illustrated news (Figure 6). The Memorial encapsulated a recent shift in legal theory on women's right to the vote. Suffragists had divided in 1868–69 when the Fifteenth Amendment, which had granted federal protection of the vote regardless of race, left women out of the franchise because the Fourteenth Amendment referred to citizens for the first time as "male." Most woman suffrage activists saw no other option than to pursue a "Sixteenth Amendment" enfranchising women. Woodhull's Memorial brought national attention to a legal strategy known as the "New Departure." Ignoring the word "male," it argued that the Fourteenth Amendment had indeed made women citizens (by virtue of being born in the United States), and demanded Congressional action to enforce women's right to vote. The New Departure gave suffrage women a way to mend fences following the heated racialized debate over the Fifteenth Amendment. It also offered them an appealing route to the vote by direct action at a local level that would avoid the tedious and probably doomed attempt to pass a separate amendment.[10]

Suffrage women were both intrigued and repelled by Woodhull's flamboyant public life. Even members of the more militant wing of the suffrage movement, the National Woman's Suffrage Association (NWSA), were reluctant to attend Woodhull's Memorial: her visibility in illustrated sporting news like *The Days' Doings* made her anything but respectable. NWSA leaders Susan B. Anthony and Elizabeth Cady Stanton were hard pressed to persuade Connecticut suffragist Isabella Beecher Hooker to attend Woodhull's presentation. Hooker, a new member of the NWSA, hoped to give the movement an aura of respectability, but Woodhull's financial and political resources soon overpowered Hooker's genteel reservations. When Woodhull repeated the Memorial before the suffragists' convention later that day, she also pledged $10,000 to the cause; while the money never explicitly appeared in the organization's coffers, it is possible that she contributed as much in kind by publishing the *Weekly* and circulating other literature for woman suffrage. NWSA leaders tapped Woodhull for copies of the Memorial and the Judiciary Committee reports it generated to spread the word about the "new departure." Such potential contributions to the movement, particularly her willingness to speak publicly for an unpopular cause, made Woodhull too powerful an asset to ignore.[11] Trance speakers had long proved attractive spokeswomen for suffrage, and Stanton saw in Woodhull a new charismatic figure on the rostrum. "Neither Anna Dickinson nor Kate Field ever [thought] enough of our movement to make a speech on our platform," Stanton wrote to a friend soon after meeting Woodhull, referring to the two most popular female lecturers of the period. Woodhull's potential to publicize the cause proved hard to resist.[12]

Women opposed to suffrage seized on Woodhull's new prominence in the movement to discredit the idea of the woman's vote. For these anti-suffrage women, Woodhull was the perfect illustration of the dangers that

Figure 6. Woodhull achieved a political coup for suffrage by obtaining a hearing with the House Judiciary Committee for her suffrage Memorial. Here she holds the attention of the Representatives as well as the suffragists who were initially reluctant to hear her. Claflin is seated at the right of the image. This depiction, much more respectful than those found in the sporting papers, was intended for a middle-class family audience. *Frank Leslie's Illustrated Newspaper*, February 4, 1871. Courtesy of the American Antiquarian Society.

public life posed to women's special status as guardians of domestic virtue. Their paper, *The True Woman*, saw Woodhull's unsavory reputation as eroding women's respectability. "While some good, but misguided women, have, doubtless from the best of motives, embarked in this [suffrage] cause," wrote the editors, "we have, of late, witnessed with great surprise, an affiliation between them and others of more than doubtful lives, who by throwing off all feminine delicacy, have gained a bad notoriety. This fact proves the dangerous and downward tendency of the doctrines of these free thinking women." Woodhull, these anti-suffrage women insisted, epitomized the "dangerous and downward" slide of suffrage women to infamy.[13]

In May 1871, Woodhull's notoriety became even more burdensome for pro-suffrage activists when her personal life became a public scandal in New York's Essex Police Court. Woodhull's mother brought charges against Woodhull's second husband, Colonel Blood, for "alienating the affections" of daughters Victoria and Tennessee, apparently because he had supplanted

Woodhull's priv life becomes a scandal

Figure 7. Tennessee Claflin's squabbling in police court with sister Mary Sparr over mother Roxanna Claflin's affections placed the family in the disorderly category. The humorous expressions of the male bystanders provide visual cues that invite comparable responses in the (largely male) readers. *The Days' Doings,* June 3, 1871.

their parents and drawn them into the realm of social radicalism. Newspapers underscored the family's coarseness, evident for these editors both in the bizarre charges and the "shameless effrontery" with which the sisters "bore the inquisitive glances of the crowd" when they appeared in court. Other signs of their lack of respectability were the unusual facts that Woodhull was divorced and sheltered her first husband, Dr. Canning Woodhull (an ailing alcoholic) under the same roof with her current husband Colonel Blood (to whom she may not have been legally wed). *The Days' Doings* depicted the family engaged in public sparring in the courtroom as a crowd of amused male spectators looked on (Figure 7). Lurid headlines like "Tennie and Vic" and "Blood Will Tell," and disreputable revelations of her family background showcased Woodhull as a vulgar public woman. As the *Cleveland Leader* put it, her

brazen immodesty as a stock speculator on Wall street, and the open, shameless effrontery with which she has paraded her name in circus-bill types at the head of her newspaper as candidate . . . for the Presidency in 1872. . . . [A]ll this has proclaimed her as a vain, immodest, unsexed woman, with whom respectable people should have as little to do as possible.

The public disgrace imputed to her Essex Police Court appearance was fodder in the hands of the respectable press. By virtue of an unconventional background and a failure to shrink from public scrutiny, Woodhull reinforced the idea of the shameless public woman.[14]

The timing was unfortunate. The story burst into print just as pro-suffrage women were preparing for their annual May conventions. Woodhull's personal scandal unleashed controversy over sexuality and public life for women, or sex in politics, as popular commentary put it. Novelist Harriet Beecher Stowe channeled her objections to Woodhull into her novel, *My Wife and I*, serialized in her brother Henry Ward Beecher's *Christian Union*. As one of Stowe's characters put it, women like Woodhull cut "the very ground from under the whole woman movement; for the main argument for proposing it was to introduce into politics that superior delicacy and purity which women manifest in public life." According to Stowe, Woodhull's notoriety seemed to prove that women would have a negative impact, for it jeopardized the moral purity, and thus the class status, of suffrage crusaders. In illustration, the fictional female editor Audacia Dangyereyes bore all the hallmarks of a fast, slangy woman, from her direct stare to her exposed ankles (Figure 8). "If Mrs. Woodhull was a real lady, she would refuse to hold office," one disenchanted suffrage advocate wrote to Isabella

Beecher Hooker soon after this appeared. "A repentant Magdalen I can accept—even in office and before the world—but a woman who 'glories in her shame'—never!" In spite of resistance from within the movement, Woodhull, along with other sex radicals like Frances Rose McKinley, promoted woman suffrage in acts of public theater, such as testing the "new departure" theory that women could vote by going to the polls that November (Figures

THE ADVANCED WOMAN OF THE PERIOD.

Figure 8. Harriet Beecher Stowe lampooned the "public woman" in her portrayal of Audacia Dangyereyes, a minor character representing Woodhull and Claflin, in her serialized novel *My Wife and I*. In this image, a slangy, improper Dangyereyes sits on the edge of a table like a man and gazes directly into the shocked eyes of narrator Harry Henderson. Harriet Beecher Stowe, *My Wife and I* (1871). Courtesy of the American Antiquarian Society.

9–10). Her visibility continually linked woman suffrage to her questionable life and provocative theories, and became a tangible thorn in the side of the movement. It was difficult for suffrage women to enjoy the benefits of her celebrity without seeming to endorse her radical social critique.[15]

The International Workingmen's Association

By summer 1871, Woodhull hoped that her class and gender critique might prove more attractive to a third constituency, the international socialists. She was not the first suffragist to connect women's inequality to their lack of financial independence; Susan B. Anthony, for one, had worked with the Labor Reform League and frequently addressed the subject of women's work in the *Revolution*.[16] Most labor activists, however, worked through male-centered organizations devoted to the interests of single trades or crafts.

Figure 9. Acting upon the new departure theory in the women's suffrage struggle, Woodhull and Claflin attempt to vote in New York on election day in 1871. Her ballot was refused, Woodhull later claimed, because the Democrats who controlled the polling stations feared that women would vote for the Republican ticket. *The Days' Doings*, November 25, 1871.

International socialists, under the auspices of the International Workingmen's Association (IWA), were alone in promoting large-scale collective actions in the early 1870s. (The IWA was at the time the only national labor organization in the United States not devoted to any single craft.) The IWA had formed in 1864 to promote international labor solidarity as a crucial weapon in the war against capital. The American branch had strong roots in the German trade union movement: the first section in America formed in 1867 out of the German General Working-Men's Union, and officially became Section One of the IWA in December 1870. Friedrich Sorge, a German immigrant whom Philip Foner has called the "Father of modern socialism in America," led Section One. American radicals, ranging from Spiritualists and sex radicals to former abolitionists and labor reformers, formed several sections of what Timothy Messer-Kruse calls the "Yankee International." By early 1872, the IWA peaked with an estimated five thousand members in

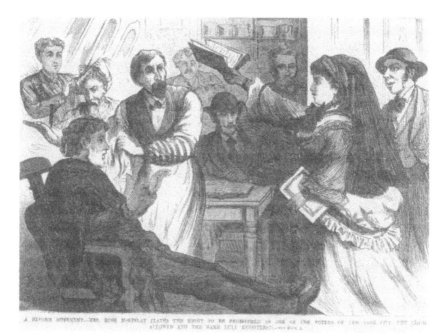

Figure 10. Free lover and suffragist Frances Rose McKinley also asserts her rights under the new departure theory of suffrage, and succeeds in registering to vote. She is shown with the upraised arm of the "strong-minded woman." In this image, McKinley literally invades the male world of the polling station, the barbershop, a novelty evident in the consternation of the patrons. *The Days' Doings*, November 25, 1871.

roughly thirty sections.[17] Between 1871 and 1872, Woodhull was instrumental in both the movement's growth and its subsequent decline.

Woodhull, Andrews, and other sex radicals formed Section Twelve of the IWA in spring 1871, on the heels of her family scandal in Essex Police Court. They hoped that Internationalists would prove more courageous than suffragists in supporting their interpretation of social freedom. Offering her services as a lecturer, and making available her paper (*Woodhull & Claflin's Weekly*), offices, and staff to the IWA, Woodhull swiftly took on a leadership role in Section Twelve. To Sorge's disgust, the commercial press soon used Woodhull to disparage the American IWA as a whole. From June through August 1871, Woodhull and her fellow social radicals promoted Section Twelve as uniquely situated to steer the course of the entire IWA in America, a position that put them immediately into conflict with Section One. In Woodhull's favor, Section Twelve had strong connections to the American left. *Woodhull & Claflin's Weekly* gave Section Twelve unique access to English-speaking radical public opinion: in 1871 it was the IWA's only English language press in America. That summer, Section Twelve translated, printed, and distributed Marx's defense of the Paris Commune (probably at Woodhull's expense), *The Civil War in France*, while the *Weekly* published articles sympathetic to the Commune and the International alongside arguments for dress reform and women's rights. By August, however, Section Twelve had come to blows with Sorge and the German American leadership of Section One, who were appalled by such a flagrant connection between the IWA and free love.[18]

Events that September made the Woodhull connection even more onerous for the IWA's Section One. That month popular editor Theodore Tilton published a biography of Woodhull, at her dictation. Tilton's biography, he later claimed, was a price he paid to prevent Woodhull from revealing a personal scandal involving his wife and popular minister Henry Ward Beecher. In the biography, Woodhull's frank disclosures, revealed in a rather ludicrous mixture of showmanship and disingenuousness, gave credit to Spirit influences for her rise to prominence. She claimed their powers as clairvoyants and magnetic healers had allowed her and Claflin to secure the backing of railway magnate Cornelius Vanderbilt to finance their brokerage house. Illustrated sporting newspapers like *The Days' Doings* depicted the biography in scathing images that mocked her Spiritualism and exaggerated her family's vulgarity (Figure 11), while popular news reports emphasized Woodhull's connection with the IWA. Sorge and Section One immediately responded to the threat Woodhull posed to his vision of the IWA as a manly

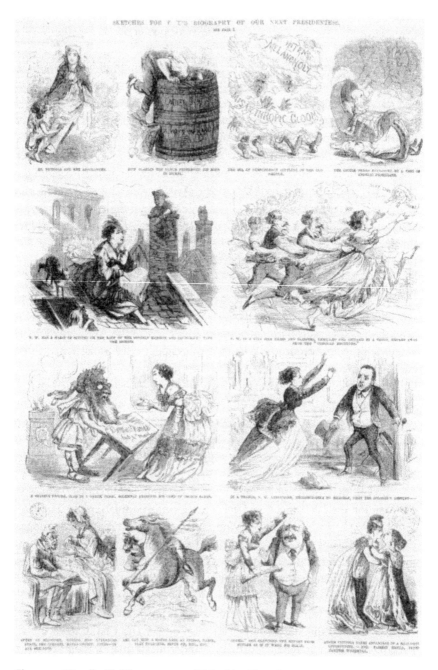

Figure 11. Woodhull's life story, as published by Theodore Tilton, provided much amusement to *The Days' Doings*. Here the sporting newspaper mocks her candid revelations to Tilton, including her claims that she had been attended by spirits since infancy, and her ambition to rule America as the twin "Victoria" to the Queen of England. *The Days' Doings*, October 7, 1871.

workers' organization. As the press excoriated Woodhull's biography, Sorge quickly worked behind the scenes to convince Karl Marx and the IWA General Council in London to reject Section Twelve's petition to lead the American IWA.[19] International socialists did not agree with Woodhull that sexual slavery was the underlying cause of social evils like prostitution; like the suffragists before them, they feared Woodhull's potential to discredit their movement.

The Principles of Social Freedom

The Tilton biography's emphasis on Spiritualism was not accidental: Woodhull had commissioned the pamphlet to solidify her position among sex radicals in the Spiritualist movement. Its focus on the role of Spirit powers in shaping her destiny was good advertising for the movement's only national organization, the American Association of Spiritualists (AAS): that same September, delegates found copies of the biography on their seats at the eighth annual convention of the AAS in Troy, New York.[20] Sex radicals apparently dominated the convention; they found Woodhull's speech captivating, and elected her, over a few objections, the organization's president for the following year. Her Spiritualist opponents, however, felt that she had manipulated the organization, and immediately protested that she was ineligible for election, and even that she and her friends had stuffed the ballot box (claims vigorously denied by officials monitoring the election). Critics said that she was using Spiritualism as a vehicle for her own ambition. Behind these technical concerns and accusations lay a longstanding tension over the place of free love in the movement. Woodhull's election as AAS president divided Spiritualists into three camps, represented by three competing newspapers: opponents published their criticisms in Chicago's *Religio-Philosophical Journal*, moderates debated her leadership in Boston's *Banner of Light*, while fervent supporters found voice in *Woodhull & Claflin's Weekly*. As the controversy raged in the Spiritualist press, Woodhull, Blood, and Andrews prepared to bring the entire debate before the public, in a speech (delivered by Woodhull) fully explicating the meaning of social freedom.[21]

Woodhull presented this lecture, entitled "The Principles of Social Freedom," on November 20, 1871, at New York City's Steinway Hall. It was probably the most frank defense of social freedom before a public audience in American history. She intended that the lecture would answer her critics and unify her coalition around the theme that sexual slavery was the basis of women's inequality. Placards advertising the lecture billed it as her vindication, designed "for the express purpose of silencing the voices and stopping the pens of those who . . . persistently misrepresent, slander, abuse and vilify [Woodhull] on account of her outspoken advocacy of, and supreme faith in, God's first, last and best law," namely social freedom or free love. Placards cautioned, however, that those seeking scandalous behavior in the free love lecture would be disappointed, for "the advocacy of its principles requires neither abandoned action nor immodest speech."[22] These disclaimers only underscored the lecture's sensational content and the speaker's notoriety: she was a celebrity by virtue of her reputation and her unconventional views. A vast and boisterous audience turned out to hear her speak.

Woodhull had spoken before crowds in the past, but the size and commotion of this audience was intimidating. Her notoriety made the spectacle particularly risqué, as it allowed people to assess, and even confront Woodhull in person. A rowdy audience waited impatiently and with much commotion for the lecture to begin, while Woodhull waited backstage for Henry Ward Beecher, who had agreed to introduce the lecture as part of a deal to prevent her from revealing the alleged relationship between him and Elizabeth Tilton. When Beecher failed to show, Theodore Tilton finally agreed to introduce Woodhull, using chivalry as an excuse once it became apparent that no other man would do so. "I was told she was coming upon this stand unattended and alone," Tilton told the crowd to hisses and applause. Woodhull's courage in facing the unruly crowd, to deliver a lecture on a subject widely believed to be morally improper, established her credentials among sex radicals and reform lecturers. Her vulnerability as a woman before a disorderly crowd became an asset: her poise and energy won her several ovations.[23]

The message of the lecture—"one sexual standard for all"—combined several strands of social radicalism. As a generation of sex radicals had done before her, Woodhull demanded remedy for the sufferings of women under the abuses of "legalized prostitution," or marriage. The American Revolution had justly put an end to religious and political despotism, Woodhull told the audience; only social tyranny remained. Marriage, sanctioned by law and church, was the agent of this social tyranny, but its roots lay deeper, in the economic inequality of women. This analysis of social relations led inevitably to a critique of "respectable" conventional marriage. Natural attraction was the only reliable guide to human emotion, Woodhull insisted. Law alone could not protect morality: "I honor and worship that purity which exists in the soul of every noble man or woman, while I pity the woman who is virtuous simply because a law compels her." In fact, she argued, law itself made people dishonest, for "*all* persons whom the law holds married against their wishes find *some* way to *evade* the law and to live the life they desire. Of what use, then, is the law except to make *hypocrites* and *pretenders* of a sham respectability?" The hypocrisy of the current situation, in other words, was what she deplored.[24]

Furthermore, she argued that economic inequality fueled the sexual double standard that punished women and excused men for the same sexual acts. "The *veriest systems of despotism* still reign in *all* matters pertaining to social life," Woodhull claimed. "Caste stands as boldly out in this country as it does in political life in the kingdoms of Europe." Society held prostitutes in contempt, even as it upheld the respectability of the men who visited them: "there are *scores of thousands* of *women* who are denominated prostitutes, and who are supported by *hundreds of thousands* of *men* who should, for like reasons, also be denominated prostitutes, since what will change a woman into a prostitute must also necessarily change a man into the same." A dearth of economic alternatives forced women into marriages and then made them support a system that degraded less "fortunate" women:

I have heard women reply when this difficulty was pressed upon them, "We cannot ostracize *men* as we are compelled to [ostracize] *women*, since we are *dependent* on them for *support*." Ah! here's the rub. But do you not see that these *other* sisters are *also* dependent upon men for *their* support, and *mainly* so because you render it next to impossible for them to follow any *legitimate* means of livelihood? And are only those who have been fortunate enough to secure *legal* support entitled to live?

Women were thus complicit in the very system that kept them subordinate to men. They valued only legally sanctioned unions and dismissed as despicable their less fortunate sisters, "the only difference between the two being in a licensed ceremony, and a slip of printed paper costing twenty-five cents and upward." Class differences among women prevented honest assessment of a system where respectability hid the exploitation of prostitutes.[25]

"Social freedom," Woodhull told the audience, was the only logical solution to such social tyranny. "The sexual relation must be rescued from this *insidious* form of slavery," she said. "Women must rise from their position as *ministers* to the passions of men to be their equals." The only way to achieve this goal was to give women the educational benefits enjoyed by men, and train them for purposeful economic lives independent of marriage.

"They must be trained to be *like* men, permanent and independent individualities, and not their mere appendages or adjuncts, with them forming but one member of society. They must be the companions of men from *choice, never* from necessity." As such, women should determine sexual relations, and seize control of maternal functions, through abstinence if necessary. Noting that most women entered marriage without any knowledge of sexual relations or human physiology, Woodhull insisted that women be properly educated in the workings of their own bodies. Only open discussion and education could properly prepare women for safe and harmonious sexual lives. Women must demand this change to liberate themselves from social tyranny.[26]

The lecture was an effort to link three fractious and divided communities around a single cause and one charismatic figure. Few, however, took the "Principles" to be an articulation of serious social theory. Such a controversial subject, presented by an infamous speaker, was unlikely to find respectful consideration in the press. The most controversial aspect of the lecture was the extreme individualism inherent in Woodhull's argument. "And to those who denounce me," Woodhull told her audience at one point, "I reply: 'Yes, I am a free lover. I have an inalienable, constitutional and natural right to love whom I may, to love as long or as short a period as I can; to change that love every day if I please.'"[27] In this statement, Woodhull went beyond the bromide of "monogamist" sex radicals; when she claimed the right to change lovers at will, even daily, she took the theoretical extreme of the free love cause, known as "varietism."

Woodhull's contemporaries interpreted this statement as a spontaneous response to audience heckling, and therefore an "authentic" reflection of her own views. In fact, it was likely the product of Andrews's thinking on individual sovereignty in sexual relations, and it appeared within the text of the speech itself, later sold in pamphlet form. Andrews took the "varietist" position that social freedom meant unconditional freedom from any restraints or conventions in intimate relations, whereas Woodhull's own views, to judge from her later statements, were probably closer to the serial monogamist position, at least in theory. She spent the next few years backpedaling from this extreme position on free love. But regardless of whether this statement was written by Andrews or Woodhull, this application of "rights" here appealed overtly to civil libertarians on the fringes of social reform. What mattered was that Woodhull—a woman—gave voice to such a controversial idea on a public platform. It was certainly newsworthy: it was the most frequently cited passage of the lecture. In that single statement, she became the byword for sex radicalism and a target for conservative defenders of the "traditional" family.[28]

The event proved even more spectacular when vocal opposition to Woodhull's argument emerged from the balcony, in the voice of her own sister, Utica Brooker. Brooker disrupted the lecture, standing up to demand that Woodhull explain what was to become of illegitimate children born of free love. Woodhull tried to quiet her sister by inviting her on stage to debate the question: when Brooker declined, police intervention forced her to resume her seat (Figure 12). This public demonstration gave the press more evidence of the coarse family displays that dogged Woodhull's public persona. In fact, Brooker's objection to Woodhull's "varietism" was part of the free love debate: it is even possible, given the family's expertise in showmanship, that the interruption had been planned in advance to bring out the question and allow Woodhull to score rhetorical points. Instead, the media exaggerated the spectacle, its nonconformist audience of free lovers, and "the fast young men about town, who had come for the fun of the thing," at the expense of any principles Woodhull articulated. Inflammatory media coverage effectively stifled any rational discussion on the merits of "social freedom."[29]

Woodhull and her supporters responded to scathing press commentary with even more defiance of social hypocrisy. They countered the public outcry following the Steinway Hall lecture with threats to expose the private free love practices of "respectable" critics. Tennessee Claflin, for example, in a letter to the *New York Sun*, criticized Horace Greeley's recent editorial in the *New York Tribune* on a new Infant Asylum. She noted his hypocrisy of calling the Asylum a model of "a Christian institution," when the institution's purpose was to rear the babies born out of wedlock to women of "respectable birth." In other words, said Claflin,

society first damns the woman, and charges as a crime on her the beautiful and natural facts of maternity, and then organizes an institution for the express purpose, and connives with her to evade the law, and impose a lie on the same society which has condemned her; and this organized falsehood and hypocrisy is praised by the Tribune, which pretends to be horrified at free love, as a "noble Christian charity."

Two weeks later the *Weekly* published a muckraking letter from a woman who ran a brothel in New York. This self-confessed "Madam" offered to give Woodhull two ledgers containing "the names and residences and some of the incidents of each visit" of the "male prostitutes" (as she called her clientele).[30] Both threats directly confronted sexual hypocrisy and demonstrated

Figure 12. Woodhull and master of ceremonies Theodore Tilton, on the stage at the left, fail to silence the heckling of one of Woodhull's sisters, Utica Brooker, during Woodhull's controversial free love speech at Steinway Hall. Police intervention to silence this sisterly disturbance, as well as the raucous crowd in the background, reinforce the disorderly woman connotations. *The Days' Doings,* December 9, 1871.

the centrality of sexual openness to Woodhull's definition of social freedom. Her critics had cornered Woodhull—and her allies—into defending a principle of social revolution through the exposure of hypocrisy.

A Fractured Coalition

The Steinway Hall lecture fragmented Woodhull's constituencies, one by one. The first to go were the international socialists. Woodhull's public promotion of social freedom terminated relations with Sorge and Section One of the First International. Advance rumors of the lecture prompted Section One to set up a new American council behind Woodhull's back. The new council dismissed her social critique underlying the "free love" question as the work of a few bourgeois enthusiasts and excluded any mention of

Figure 13. The mock-funeral march of the American International Workingmen's Association in honor of the martyrs of the Paris Commune became the march of Woodhull and Claflin in popular press renditions. The image gives precedence to Woodhull's controversial Section Twelve, names Claflin as the flag-bearer, and emphasizes the proximity of the women to the African American militia. More reliable reports place Woodhull and Claflin in a carriage near the back of the march. *The Days' Doings,* January 6, 1872.

women's issues from the IWA agenda. "All this talk of theirs is folly, or worse than folly, and we don't want their foolish notions credited as the views of this society," one member of Section One declared. "This nonsense which they talk of, female suffrage and free love, may do to consider in the future, but the question that interests us as working-men is that of labor and wages." The new council inaugurated a "two-thirds rule," holding that two-thirds of the members of any IWA section must be wage laborers, a decision that favored participation by workers in trades and crafts but largely excluded reform-minded women.[31]

The exclusion of Section Twelve from the new council coincided with Woodhull's increasing celebrity as a leader of the International. That December, commercial newspapers highlighted the presence of Woodhull and Claflin at the IWA funeral parade for the Communards (recently executed by the Thiers government in France), for example. Planned by French sections in collaboration with Section Twelve and others (over the opposition of Sorge and Section One) to protest continuing suppression of radicals in Paris, the march was a political spectacle whose message was the principle of universal rights. The Skidmore Light Guard, a Black militia unit, led the procession, followed by a group of women on foot; political refugees from Cuba and France; French, German, Swiss, and Bohemian sections of the International; and finally Irish nationals. Several additional symbols of universal rights were evident, notably three men—a French, an Irish, and a Black man—who marched with linked arms in a prominent place. As many as five thousand marchers gathered in Cooper Square (at Eighth Street), and marched down Third Avenue into the Bowery, west on Great Jones Street, up Fifth Avenue to Thirty-Fourth Street, down Sixth Avenue to Fourteenth Street, Union Square, where the marchers dispersed after circling the statue of Lincoln. Illustrations of the march appearing in *The Days' Doings* and the less flamboyant *Frank Leslie's Illustrated Newspaper* (Figures 13–14) both centered on the presence of Woodhull and Claflin, particularly their close proximity to the Skidmore Light Guard, when in fact the sisters rode in carriages at the back.[32] Such illustrations inflated their importance to the IWA in a way that equated its economic goals with extreme social radicalism.

Woodhull's media prominence, along with growing evidence of grass roots support for Woodhull among unskilled laborers in early 1872, may explain why her section refused to cede leadership of the American IWA to Section One. She delivered a popular lecture called "The Impending Revolution" that February, which compared the wealth of a few capitalist entrepreneurs at the expense of workers with the wealth of slave owners before the Civil War. Thousands flocked to the lecture—even the critical *New York Herald* reported that six thousand attended, with as many more turned away for lack of seats. Woodhull's revolutionary message, and the audience's enthusiastic response to her calls for an uprising of the disenfranchised workers, generated extraordinarily negative commentary in the commercial press.[33] "Personally Mrs. Woodhull is of no possible consequence," the *New York Times* editorialized. "Still, her periodical exhibitions of bitter language upon the platform attract numbers of idle people, among whom are some whose ignorance and envy fit them to receive her folly as though it were words of wisdom." The *Times* was particularly concerned with her power to incite class unrest. "She is . . . capable of mischief in inflaming the unthinking hostility of the poor to the rich, and in fostering, in the minds of the working men who applauded her last Tuesday night, the conviction that capitalists have no rights which working men are bound to respect."[34]

Woodhull's uncompromising anticapitalist statements in the lecture made her an attractive spokesperson for downtrodden workers in early 1872. In March, fifteen hundred unemployed workers rallying in Tompkins Square spontaneously began chanting Woodhull's name.[35] Four days later, workers responded enthusiastically to her lecture at an anniversary gathering in honor of the Paris Commune.[36] However, Woodhull's popularity had the opposite effect on Marx and the General Council in London, who decided that March to take Sorge's advice and provisionally suspended Section Twelve from the IWA, pending approval by the International Congress

Figure 14. This image, which appeared in a family illustrated paper, includes the catafalque in the march. It also emphasizes the juxtaposition of the African American militia and the women marchers, giving Claflin the shortened skirt of the "fast" woman. Figures 13 and 14 demonstrate the fictional quality of illustrated news in the 1870s, which relied on often unreliable press accounts as sources, and allowed its illustrators great artistic license. *Frank Leslie's Illustrated Newspaper*, January 6, 1872.

in the Hague the following September. Although she continued to advocate the positions of the "Yankee International," the IWA's leadership seemed determined to sever all connection with Woodhull and Section Twelve.[37]

The Steinway Hall lecture likewise sowed division in the ranks of the woman suffrage movement. Catharine Beecher, perhaps the most influential critic of Woodhull's influence, recast her longstanding opposition to woman suffrage by appealing to suffragists' class interests and respectability. "Can any Christian woman sanction in any way the efforts of such a woman?" she demanded in public print as rumors of Woodhull's coming "social freedom" lecture circulated in Hartford, Connecticut. Woodhull's "past character and history," said Beecher, have "not been favorable to the cultivation of feelings of delicacy and propriety."[38] Woodhull's public endorsement of social freedom allowed anti-suffrage women to show that public women like Woodhull were dangerous threats to the respectability of the suffragists. Woodhull embodied, in fact, the central dilemma of activism for women. Media coverage of suffragists was rarely flattering; a typically disparaging illustration (Figure 15) appearing in *The Days' Doings* in February mocked the "raid of the strong-minded" women, one wielding the inevitable raised umbrella, on the Senate Judiciary Committee, then reconsidering the Woodhull Memorial. Woodhull's connections came with the price of notoriety. As Abigail Duniway, editor of moderate suffrage paper *The New Northwest* put it, however unsavory Woodhull might be as an associate, she was "the only woman who can get the ear of the men who have usurped our rights, and women must speak through her until they get into power." Woodhull's celebrity was both an asset and a liability.[39]

The most vivid illustration of this dilemma appeared in the famous "Mrs. Satan" caricature, which depicted Woodhull as a demon (Figure 16). Drawn by Thomas Nast, the best-known political cartoonist of the 1870s, Woodhull stood in the foreground, complete with horns, wings and claws resembling the demon Apollyon in John Bunyan's popular Christian parable, *Pilgrim's Progress*; she held a sign that read "Be Saved by Free Love." In the background, a wife and mother, overburdened with a drunken husband and countless small children, rejected Woodhull and her teachings and piously turned away to face her hard lot. The cartoon's overt message was negative: faced with the temptation of social freedom, the struggling mother tells Woodhull that "I'd rather travel the hardest path of matrimony than follow your footsteps." Perhaps unintentionally, however, the heavy burdens of the wife and mother illustrated some of the reasons why women's emancipation was necessary. Its irony was obvious to women's rights activists when they saw it in 1872. As pro-suffrage Martha Coffin Wright wrote to Elizabeth Cady Stanton soon after it appeared, with warm regards for Stanton's sick daughter, "you must strengthen her all you can, for the inevitable burdens in store for her, if the choice is such as Harper describes in that cartoon." As Wright saw it, "Mr. Nast proved a little too much in that picture."[40]

Suffrage leaders of the NWSA, particularly Stanton and Anthony, publicly supported Woodhull's social critique and the idea of a single sexual standard, even though they disagreed privately about the wisdom of associating with her. Stanton dismissed charges of Woodhull's immorality as irrelevant: "When a woman of this class shall suddenly devote herself to the study of the grave problems of life, brought there by profound thought and experience, and with new faith and hope struggles to redeem the errors of

Figure 15. The "strong-minded women" overrun the Senate Judiciary Committee, then considering Woodhull's Memorial on the Fourteenth Amendment. Frenetic postures, upraised arms, umbrellas, and eyeglasses designate the women as political agitators. Senator Carpenter's helpless fear lends the scene a humorous, satirical note. *The Days' Doings*, February 17, 1872.

Figure 16. Published after her free love speech at New York's Steinway Hall, this image established Woodhull as a folk devil. Her clawed wings resemble those of the demon Apollyon in John Bunyan's *Pilgrim's Progress*, a religious fable enjoying renewed popularity in the 1870s. Like Bunyan's hero Christian, the wife in the background willingly shoulders heavy burdens (in her case, a drunken husband, many children, and poverty) and resists the temptation of an easier path that Woodhull offers. *Harper's Weekly*, February 17, 1872. Courtesy of the American Antiquarian Society.

the past by a grand life in the future, shall we not welcome her to the better place she desires to hold?" Stanton saw no practical reason to deny the movement access to Woodhull's newspaper, powerful connections with the New York media, and network of social radicals. Anthony likewise made a strong public defense of Woodhull, on the ground that women should not be held to a higher standard than male politicians. "I was asked by an editor of a New York paper if I knew of Mrs. Woodhull's antecedents," Anthony told the NWSA convention in January 1872. "I said I didn't, and that I did not care any more for them than I do about those of the members of Congress. Her antecedents will compare favorably with any member of Congress." Anthony strenuously objected, however, when trance speaker Addie Ballou, who sat upon the NWSA platform, rushed down to the floor to nominate Woodhull as a candidate for president of the United States.[41]

Privately, Anthony thought Woodhull was bad for the movement. She was frustrated that Stanton courted the controversial connection in spring 1872 by helping Woodhull and the sex radicals develop a platform for the "Grand Combination Convention" planned for that May.[42] Unlike her friend, Anthony became increasingly convinced as she toured the Northwest that winter and early spring that Woodhull was a political liability. Facing declining audiences and insufficient cash receipts throughout the tour, Anthony spent considerable effort clearing up the misconception of many on the west coast that woman suffrage meant free love. She was also personally opposed to the notion of free love, particularly the varietism Woodhull had promoted at Steinway Hall. As she commented in her diary, Woodhull "was the first woman man had succeeded in fashioning to his own ideal—so that she theoretically accepted man's practical theory of promiscuity or change." Anthony, who saw varietism as a male-centered philosophy that ignored possibly dire consequences for women, saw much to fear in Woodhull's public declaration of social freedom.[43]

To "Shock the World to Its Very Center"

Spiritualists, those most likely to be sympathetic to Woodhull's unconventional views, similarly divided over the question of Woodhull's leadership. The *Religio-Philosophical Journal* editor, S. S. Jones, provided a forum for Spiritualists who supported women's rights, marriage reform, and free thought, but rejected Woodhull's revolutionary application of the "principles of social freedom." Many objected, as had the suffragists, to varietism itself. Moderate Spiritualist Emma Hardinge-Britten, for one, dismissed Woodhull's views for failing to consider the fate of children born out of wedlock. Moderates also worried that Woodhull's notoriety would erode the fragile reputation of Spiritualists in the eyes of mainstream Christians, the press, and the public at large. Correspondent Hudson Tuttle voiced the concerns of many readers when he wrote to the *Journal* early in 1872:

Her notions of love and the marriage relation are the most objectionable, as they place in the hands of our enemies a powerful weapon to wield against us, inasmuch, I regret to say, as she is endorsed, as far as I have noticed, by the spiritual press, and also stands elected President of the association of Spiritualists.[44]

Sex radicals countered this criticism by noting Spiritualism's long association with social freedom. Dr. Juliet Severance was blunt: "Talk of freedom as a cause of impurity in social life. Nonsense! It is the only means by which purity becomes possible." For Severance, Tuttle's criticisms denied Spiritualism's inherent challenge to conventional morality. "What is the ground of complaint? Simply that she advocates social freedom. Is that any thing new for Spiritualists?" Severance demanded. "I admit that in clear, forcible argument, in earnest, fearless advocacy, she excels any of us who have preceded her, but that she has advanced any more radical ideas on social life, I deny."[45]

The popular Spiritualist organ, the *Banner of Light*, sought the middle ground, hailing the controversy over Woodhull as a means to promote debate on the free love question. Without fully endorsing her views, the paper remained true to the movement's heterodoxy, and encouraged readers to study Woodhull's entire lecture (which it reprinted on the front page), not just those portions published, out of context, in the popular press. In February 1872, the *Banner* gave Woodhull extensive space to defend herself, printed a flood of letters in her favor, and offered readers a running debate on the front pages on the meaning of "social freedom." Elderly Spiritualist E. S. Wheeler, for one, defended her election, by pointing out that Woodhull gained little by association with Spiritualists. "American Spiritualists have not done a great deal to enlarge the 'opportunities' of Victoria C. Woodhull for enunciating her 'peculiar views,'" Wheeler wrote.

With a powerful journal in her hands, with wealth at her command, with faith "to remove mountains," with an intellect and inspiration to teach philosophers and statesmen, and a consecrated eloquence to enchain the hearing of the people, she assumed the service of the Spiritualists of America and the world. . . . She might have *shunned* unpopularity by refusing to become identified as a Spiritualist in so public a manner.[46]

The *Banner* also printed a spirited defense of Woodhull by trance speaker Laura Cuppy Smith, who said that "social reform is hazardous work, and we want no cowards. We are ready to walk through martyrdom, if need be, for this holy cause."

Lois Waisbrooker agreed: as she explained in her regular column, men and women were answerable only to the Spirits, or to what she called the "court" of science, for their actions. Spiritualists ran the danger of becoming "as tyrannical as any other class of people" if they succumbed to the scruples of the "respectable;" it was not a movement for those who shrank from conflict. "When they come to feel the spirit of the above, they will not shrink from the discussion of any question," said Waisbrooker. "If they can't stand the fire, then let them go."[47] Spiritualism gave Woodhull an irrefutable defense for her controversial actions. The faith of its adherents in Spirit guidance was both a strength and weakness for the movement: it allowed widely dispersed individuals to take part in a collective identity based on a phenomenon—Spirit manifestation and control—that was not easily verified. Woodhull benefited from this uncertainty; the unruly guidance of the Spirit world, she insisted, dictated all of her uncompromising positions on social issues. She was merely the instrument of a higher cause:

I have no personal cause to maintain. I propose to obey, so far as in me lies, a guidance superior to my own knowledge; and that guidance commands me to speak, and I speak. I cannot yield my allegiance to it; and if its mandates carry me where Spiritualists cannot follow, let them not say that I desire to commit them to anything but the truth.[48]

Supporters likewise challenged skeptics who questioned Woodhull's Spirit influences. "Once deny that Joan of Arc or Mrs. Woodhull have been inspired by spirits," as Charles Holt put it, "and, by the same process of reasoning, I will convict of fraud every inspirational medium on earth." Spiritualism, such arguments revealed, was on shaky ground when it sought to purge its ranks by making respectability and scientific proof criteria for membership. Sex radicals blamed conservative Spiritualists for dividing a movement that should be strong enough to support any radical views, as orthodoxy of any kind was antithetical to the movement. "Brother," Holt chided Hudson Tuttle in an open letter, "let us have no more bickering. The Orthodox world is laughing at us."[49]

Predictably, *Woodhull & Claflin's Weekly* aired the most extreme positions raised in Woodhull's Steinway Hall lecture. Here correspondents debated the full implications of social freedom with Woodhull and the

Weekly's editorial staff, in a series of letters and articles through the spring of 1872. Many of these writings elaborated upon the evils of marriage. Marriage gave men the legal power to force women to submit, said E. S. Wheeler: "Being a chattel, a thing, a possession, a piece of goods, it is requisite that the landlord and owner use his own, and somehow get the value out of that which is his," he said. Mary Leland likewise condemned marriage as a "religio-civil institution which binds woman soul and body, and delivers her over to tyranny and lust, to go when her master says go, to come when he says come, to bear children in sorrow and disgust, to be parlor ornament or kitchen drudge as her lord may fancy." Like other sex radicals, Leland looked to "new methods of relating the sexes which shall banish pain and slavery and secure harmony and happiness."[50] Such writers fueled Woodhull's conviction that she spearheaded a revolution in social mores.

Exactly what this sexual revolution should accomplish was a point of lively dispute. As it had done before Steinway Hall, the *Weekly* published a range of perspectives that sought to distinguish "free love" from promiscuous "lust." In response to a reader's concerns, the *Weekly* clarified the theory of varietism: "If it be ever proper to change our love; if we may conscientiously ever do it; if indeed we may rightfully love more than once during the whole course of our life, it must follow that there is none but a natural limit to the right to change." That March, Frances Rose McKinley's lecture on free love, published in the *Weekly*, supported this view. "In a perfect condition of society," McKinley stated, "special loves which jealously demand the entire consecration of one to the other will be almost unknown." Other writers explained the difference between social freedom, loosely defined, and promiscuity implicit in Woodhull's system. As Spiritualist lecturer Sarah Somerby saw it, "A true free lover can never be promiscuous in the sexual relations. That is the very thing they are fighting against. They are the only ones who see clearly that what is by the world called marriage is a system which forces people into adultery and promiscuity." Veteran sex radical Henry Child agreed that Woodhull was misunderstood: "*She* stands convicted of advocating love, *pure* love to all humanity—they of legal prostitution."[51]

Not all *Weekly* writers accepted these views; a few warned that sex radicals underestimated the potential dangers, specifically to women, arising from the common understanding of free love, particularly from the theory of varietism. Spiritualist Lucinda Chandler cautioned, "*Perfect liberty* or freedom (used to express liberty), is and can be only through *perfect obedience to the highest quality of being*." She did not endorse the new framework emerging among sex radicals that "the 'sexual union' is an overwhelming necessity of human beings." On the contrary, she believed that sexual excesses led to many kinds of social evils, including children born without strong parental protection, and the spread of disease. Chandler struggled to reconcile the competing problems of freeing women from the tyranny of marriage while preventing their exploitation by a male-oriented varietist system. Like many sex radicals, she fell back on two solutions: true love, freed from the crass considerations of money and power over another, and sexual education. "More knowledge," Chandler believed, "a higher standard of manhood and womanhood, of the obligations of wedlock involving requirements of the highest purity and reverent regard for personal rights, and of the responsibilities of parentage, will tend to secure a higher standard of marriage."[52]

While they differed on specifics, most *Weekly* correspondents agreed on the need accelerate the war in the name of social freedom. A typical writer urged Woodhull to "unmask the batteries, expose the enemies' works, and success will crown with unfaiding [*sic*] laurels, all noble defenders of the truth." When one correspondent asked Woodhull, "When in your lecture upon social freedom, you remark that you have a right to change your love every day if you wish, do you not make an extravagant and useless expression?" the question offered a timely opportunity to explain her motives. "It is time, in the advance of the ages," Woodhull responded, "that the broadest freedom should be proclaimed. It was necessary that the whole false fabric of society should be shocked to its very center." Echoing Chandler, Woodhull's rejoinder blamed the current "low state" in sexual relations on poor education and lack of knowledge that only complete openness could cure. "I shall never cease to lift my voice," Woodhull's response promised. "Therefore, I say: Proclaim it long and loud, that every one is free, and that nobody has the right to rule over another, even as to love." Two weeks later, another writer echoed Woodhull's words, encouraging her to use her radical views to "shock the world to its very center."[53]

Such extreme endorsements of social freedom and sexual openness, particularly in light of Woodhull's own vulnerability to scrutiny and gossip, help explain what many contemporaries saw as a low phase in her activist career. Many reformers who complained of Woodhull's visibility in the movement, she knew, had indiscretions of their own (including adultery and divorce) to hide from view. To explode the myth of "respectability" among her critics, Woodhull (or her associates) printed mock-ups detailing these transgressions under the *Woodhull & Claflin's Weekly* banner. In return for silence, they demanded financial support for the free love cause endorsed by the private actions, if not the public statements, of respectable reformers. Woodhull maintained that the threats were merely part of her social critique that saw prevailing sexual mores as disproportionately beneficial to the ruling classes, and especially men. Most recipients, however, interpreted them as blackmail. When Susan B. Anthony heard of it from friends who had received such threats, for example, she became determined to oust Woodhull from the NWSA.[54] Woodhull's principles of social freedom had led her toward the abstract notion of exposure at any cost, alienating a wide range of middle-class reformers along the way.

By spring 1872, Woodhull's "Principles of Social Freedom" rallied the most unconventional social activists to her defense. Their next effort to "shock the world" was to be a political gathering scheduled for that May at New York's Apollo Hall, which they promoted as a "Grand Combination Convention," to bring together prominent activists from across the spectrum of socialists, Spiritualists, and woman suffragists. Woodhull's extreme views on social freedom had stripped her following of all but the most radical activists, who began preparations for an act of political theater designed to engage the most radical promises of Reconstruction. They planned it as a spectacle of defiance of the current political situation that would stimulate further revolutionary acts. Collectively, they hoped that the Convention would generate significant public dialogue in a critical election year.

Chapter 2
"A Shameless Prostitute and a Negro"

On May 10, 1872, at 8 o'clock in the evening, 668 delegates of the newly founded Equal Rights Party, from twenty-two states and four territories, invited Victoria Woodhull to come forward and share her views on the party's radical platform, adopted earlier that day. She took the stage to uproarious applause, and congratulated the delegates on their political daring. "From this Convention will go forth a tide of revolution that shall sweep over the whole world," she promised the cheering delegates. And revolution was needed: "Go where we may in the land," she said, "there we see despotism, inequality and injustice installed where there should be freedom, equality and justice instead." How could there be equality of opportunity, Woodhull asked, when one-eighth of the population was functionally illiterate, when the rich hoarded wealth and corrupted politicians? For her extremism, Woodhull offered no apology. "Shall we be slaves to escape revolution? I say, never! I say, away with such weak stupidity! . . . I say, let us have justice, though the heavens fall." Her words electrified the political radicals in the audience, who unanimously chose her as the party's candidate for President of the United States; they then selected Frederick Douglass as her running mate, a man who represented both "a principle and an idea."[1]

How we interpret this scene today depends on how seriously we take the Equal Rights Party delegates in their choices. If we listen to their words, they meant the two nominations to shock and instruct the nation on the full meaning of universal rights. The party welcomed controversy, and fully expected the interracial Woodhull/Douglass ticket to stimulate national dialogue about the period's racial and sexual politics. The goal was to force the major parties to address the political aspirations of historically marginal groups—African Americans and women—and thereby further the party's agenda of universal rights. In the growing conservatism of the period, however, the press responded with ridicule and exaggerated the sensational aspect of the candidates, with one paper dubbing them the "piebald" ticket. A year after the Paris Commune had aroused elite fears of revolution, the nominations gave papers a shorthand way to conflate a broad spectrum of reform thought with the actions of a radical few.

The party's political coupling of one of the century's most disreputable white women with one of its most respectable black men was more a provocative gesture than a bid for electoral success. Woodhull, thirty-four years old at the time, was by virtue of her age (and possibly her sex) disqualified from assuming office as president. Douglass, who was not consulted beforehand, never seriously considered the nomination. As an act of political theater, however, the event revealed a significant undercurrent in the cultural politics of 1872. At the time, the raucous press reception suppressed the Convention's egalitarian message, and later, Woodhull's eugenics work in the 1890s came to overshadow the latent idealism behind the joint nomination.[2] Without ignoring Woodhull's later views, it is instructive to view the Woodhull/Douglass ticket as the effort of a group calling themselves the National Radical Reformers to address the most pressing social questions of Reconstruction—racial and sexual equality. Planned as a spectacle of universal rights, the nominations forced latent biases about race and gender into sharp relief.

Tensions were running high in 1872 political culture; it was a pivotal year in Reconstruction politics. Since the late 1860s, the Radical Republican Congress had passed sweeping civil rights measures that were based on the notion of human rights: the 14th and 15th Amendments, the Civil Rights Act, the Force Act, and the Ku Klux Klan Act all offered protection for the rights of formerly enslaved men. The KKK Act, for example, passed in April of 1871, allowed federal prosecution of acts of intimidation that prevented a citizen from the exercise of his rights, especially voting. Taken together, these measures reflected the commitment of Radical Republicans in Congress to the principle of civil rights. Many reformers saw these new precedents as a sign that a philosophy of universal rights would soon extend to women and workers as well.

By 1872, however, popular support for active federal intervention in local affairs was in decline. That year, the presidential race became hopelessly confused when the Democratic Party chose Horace Greeley, longtime Republican, editor of the *New York Tribune*, and well-known abolitionist before the war, to run against incumbent Republican President Ulysses S. Grant. Greeley's surprising nomination on the Democratic ticket came about when he joined a group of "Liberal" Republicans who decried the expanded role of the federal state and alleged widespread corruption in their party; they united briefly with moderate Democrats in an attempt to regain the presidency. Northern Democrats hoped that their alliance with Liberal Republicans would moderate their party's image as the party of slavery, and attract black votes. Greeley's candidacy was doomed to failure; despised by conservative southern Democrats and denounced by most northern Republicans, he stood little chance of winning. When Grant won an enormous popular majority in November, Greeley acknowledged that he was the "worst beaten man" ever to run for president.[3]

The Equal Rights Party's nominations of Woodhull and Douglass revived the universal rights promise of Reconstruction, even as mainstream Republicans, under Grant, were backing away from the principle. In fact, the 1872 election signaled the death of Radical Republicanism in national politics, and foreshadowed the demise of Reconstruction. The defection of Greeley's Liberal Republicans to the Democrats only underscored the declining power of Radical Republicans to maintain popular support for federal protection of rights. After the election of 1872, the distinction between parties on a national and local level increasingly became one of race, with the Democrats frequently running open white supremacy campaigns. The Liberal revolt probably forced the Republican Party to retreat from Reconstruction and adopt a more corporate image, a move the party eventually justified with the popularization of social Darwinism and laissez faire capitalism.[4] The Woodhull/Douglass nomination demanded renewed political commitment to universal rights. While it failed in that regard, its reception in popular media laid bare deep underlying resistance to full equality.

Miscegenation Hysteria in 1872

One thing that made the Equal Rights Party nominations of Woodhull and Douglass so provocative was their deliberate challenge to the growing fear of miscegenation, or race mixing, typically imagined by white conservatives as rape. The successful (albeit temporary) enforcement of the Ku Klux Klan Act deterred political lynching, but white supremacists found that the federal government was unlikely to stop them from punishing alleged social crimes, like rape.[5] Northerners who objected to the lynching of a man for exercising political rights tolerated (or ignored) the same lynching when it was justified as retribution for an attack on a white woman. Southern racists pitted the "purity" of white womanhood against the "bestial" nature of the black man as a new rationale for lynching, which developed into a powerful mechanism for social—and political—control. During Reconstruction the "pure white woman," one of the central fictions of the antebellum southern aristocracy, became a more inclusive symbol, available to a broader compass of white women. Lynching was a strategy among Southern Democrats to reassert political control, drawing its power from the new racial stereotypes that Republicans in Congress were unwilling or unable to confront.[6] Lynching, justified by racists as necessary to prevent interracial attacks, evolved into a terror campaign that effectively disenfranchised whole communities of freedmen. Interracial rape hysteria was a powerful mechanism for rolling back the civil rights gains of Reconstruction.

The nomination of Woodhull and Douglass contradicted the emerging stereotype of the black rapist who, allegedly seeking revenge, violently attacked white women.[7] It was not that opposition to interracial sexuality was new: before the Civil War, pro-slavery commentators used accusations of "amalgamation" or racial mixing to discredit abolitionists and other political opponents.[8] What changed was the widespread idea that such interracial alliances were violent rather than voluntary. Northern Democrats invented the term "miscegenation" during the final months of the Civil War in 1864 and gave the word salacious connotations to use against the Republican Party.[9] The new term was used almost exclusively to denote the sexual pairing of a black man and a white woman; despite anti-miscegenation laws, white men in relationships with black women rarely faced punishment.[10] The myth of the black male rapist simplified long-standing miscegenation fears by erasing voluntary white participation in race mixing and simultaneously justified violent retribution against the alleged rapists. Lynching consequently became integral to the establishment of white supremacy in the New South.[11] Thus the Equal Rights Party choice of Woodhull and Douglass constituted a bold rejection of prevailing racial views.

The party hoped that the Woodhull/Douglass nominations would provide a way to bridge the divide between suffrage women with civil rights activists that had developed in the political struggle over the Fourteenth and Fifteenth Amendments in the late 1860s. White women had been a crucial part of the abolitionist movement, but after the Civil War advocates for black civil rights and women's rights became hopelessly divided over the passage of these amendments. Tensions arose in Kansas in 1867 over the question of suffrage in the new state's constitution. A faction of the state Republican Party hostile to black suffrage introduced a joint suffrage measure, which linked black suffrage to woman suffrage and doomed both propositions to defeat. As a result, woman suffrage activists Elizabeth Cady

Stanton and Susan B. Anthony felt increasingly betrayed by the Republican Party, and even accepted the support of racist demagogue George Francis Train, who funded their paper *The Revolution.*[12] Stanton also resorted to racial justifications for (white) women's political claims. In an 1868 speech on the dangers of the exclusion of women from Fifteenth Amendment, Stanton defended a young white girl on trial for the infanticide of her baby that resulted (she claimed) from a rape by a black man. "With judges and jurors of negroes," Stanton warned, "remembering the generations of wrong and injustice their daughters have suffered at the white man's hands, how will Saxon girls fare in their courts for crimes like this?"[13] Such divisive political rhetoric in the name of women's rights, from a seasoned reformer like Stanton, reveals the fault lines of the race and gender politics in the postwar period. The universal citizenship symbolized in the Woodhull/Douglass nominations, the Equal Rights Party (rather naively) hoped, offered a unifying principle to reunite divided and embittered reformers.

Frederick Douglass was no casual choice for a vice presidential candidate; he was nationally famous for his advocacy of "social equality" (what we now call civil rights) and its application to public spaces like transportation, schools, churches, cemeteries and juries.[14] The cornerstone of the social equality debate during the campaign spring of 1872 was the public school system, which in turn raised the controversial question of mixed schooling. Douglass and other well-connected black families pressured Radical Republicans to support mixed schooling, and late in 1871 Senator Charles Sumner of Massachusetts included the provision in his Civil Rights Bill. The controversial bill was hotly debated in the Senate in April and May 1872, and spilled over into newspapers. "Its mixed-school clause is the one which excites the greatest repugnance," insisted one Democratic paper:

Democrats from all over denounce it. Southern Republicans make wry faces and shake dubious heads whenever it is breached. . . . The whites are singularly unanimous in their opposition, while the colored people are holding nightly mass-meetings, passing innumerable resolutions, memorializing Congress, and . . . in many cases regarding the passage of the bill as something which dare not be refused.[15]

Most states practiced de facto segregation of schools, and few white taxpayers tolerated mixed schools; the bill threatened an upheaval of a particularly personal kind, one that even most white Republicans did not welcome. Opponents used taxation as their nominal excuse for rejecting public education, but thinly disguised miscegenation fears gave the debate its psychological power. Mixed schools existed in some state constitutions, but more often in law than in practice. Mixed schooling legislation in Louisiana, for example, included punitive measures against white families who resisted integration by boycotting the public schools. But white rioting crushed the Louisiana experiment and foreshadowed a persistent opposition among southern whites to interracial public schooling.[16]

In May 1872, Douglass vocally defended the Civil Rights Bill—sometimes known as the School Bill. As the U.S. Senate debated the subject, Douglass warned that "designing educated white men" were exploiting differences between poor whites and blacks. "Educate the poor white children and the colored children together," Douglass insisted, "let them grow up to know that color makes no difference as to the rights of a man; that both the black and the white man are at home; that the country is as much the country of one as of the other, and that both together must make it a valuable country." Even his white Republican colleagues in the press reproached Douglass for his support of mixed schooling. As the *New York Republican* put it, "we do not believe in mingling the black and the white children in one school. We do not think the mingling is good for either race. God intended that the negro should be with the negro in society, as He intended the white should be with white." Douglass rejected such views:

We do favor the "mingling" of white and black children in common schools as affording the best means for a common education. *The "mingling" of colored and white, to which the Republican objects, has been a fact for generations in this country.* . . . Abundant evidence [in the form of "colored people of mixed blood"] exists in our midst of the desire on the part of whites to mingle with the blacks.[17]

White men had frequently coerced black women into sexual alliances during slavery—many slaves, including Douglass himself, had white fathers. Most Americans, however, preferred to ignore this; despite Douglass's efforts, mixed schooling was eventually dropped from the Radical Reconstruction program, in no small part because Democrats played on the fears of Northern Republicans of its potential to promote miscegenation.[18] For all his work to clarify the concept, white supremacists had made Douglass's idea of "social equality" (or civil rights) synonymous with interracial sex.

Victoria Woodhull was no idealized "pure white woman"; she was by 1872 the "Apostle of Free Love"—the national spokesperson for "social freedom." She had become the press's favored representative of the women's suffrage campaign, after spending two years shocking New York and the nation with her willingness to bear the standard for unpopular causes. Her stock brokerage firm on Wall Street, her political actions for woman's suffrage and on behalf of the IWA, made her a visible and controversial public figure. Her vocal defense of prostitution and advocacy of free love were widely known. During the six months prior to the nomination, Wood-hull had brought the free love cause to national attention in a series of speeches, notably the "Principles of Social Freedom" speech given at Stein-way Hall in November 1871.[19] Sporting illustrations had made her, and her unconventional audience, notorious. For example, Boston's *Illustrated Police News* portrayed Woodhull as a hard-faced woman on a platform of men (Figure 17), while innocent young girls in her audience appeared vulnerable

Figure 17. This early sporting illustration image is a rare depiction of Woodhull lecturing on the "principles of social freedom." The image scorns Woodhull as "the apostle of free love upon the rostrum," giving her the hard face and short hair of the "strong-minded woman." The text exaggerates an unconventional audience: "Strong minded women with angular limbs and sharp features, sat by the side of blooming girls too young to realize the atrocious teachings of the chosen apostles of free love, while long haired Spiritualists and dashing young men about town mingled in the crowd, with mothers, who should have been at home, and wives forgetful of their domestic duties." *Illustrated Police News*, January 18, 1872. Courtesy of the American Antiquarian Society.

to the influence of morally suspect sex radicals. She brought to the nomination, in other words, negative associations about the "long haired men and short haired women" who supported her.

Her activities also stimulated racialized commentary. The commercial press viewed her political activities on behalf of women as indicative of the negative influence of universal rights on the political system. In 1872, illustrated newspapers, in fact, depicted her activism as promoting race mixing. One famous drawing from *Harper's Weekly* showed her attempt to vote in November 1871 against a backdrop of racial types (Figure 18) that reminded viewers of the revolutionary potential of universal rights activism. *The Days' Doings* portrayed Claflin's activities as the hostess for the weekly Cosmopolitan Club in starkly racist terms (Figure 19). Woodhull and Claflin defied convention and promoted sexual revolution as part of a broad-based political agenda. Her nomination with Douglass explicitly exacerbated conservative fears about the racial implications of her revolution.

Figure 18. Even more moderate illustrated newspapers worried about the social threat posed by universal suffrage. This image of Woodhull's attempt to vote gives her the posture of the "strong-minded woman." By depicting the well-dressed African American man and the soft-hatted Irishman at the left and left-of-center, the image reminds readers of the racial threat posed by universal suffrage. *Harper's Weekly*, November 25, 1871. Courtesy of the American Antiquarian Society.

A PLACE WHERE MEN AND WOMEN OF THE MOST
DIVERSE STATIONS IN LIFE MAY MEET—IN FACT
A REPUBLICAN COURT.

Figure 19. *The Days' Doings* had previously linked women's suffrage to
amalgamation. This image lampooned Claflin's political aspirations for the
Cosmopolitical Club in the summer of 1871. In this segment of a larger series of
satirical images of Claflin, she presides over an admiring, racially heterogeneous
crowd. *The Days' Doings* (detail), July 22, 1871.

The Woodhull/Douglass Nomination

Party organizers, primarily sex radicals and Woodhull's remaining allies in the "Yankee International," planned their Equal Rights Party convention to bring a variety of reform groups together for unified action against the prevailing political parties. The decision to hold the convention opened a festering rift between activists who favored political action and those who did not. The fact that the call for the convention appeared in Woodhull's paper reinforced suspicion among conservative Spiritualists that she was using the movement as a vehicle for her own ambition. For the first time, the Spiritualist *Religio-Philosophical Journal* devoted its front pages to the Woodhull controversy. Editor S. S. Jones attacked her directly, denouncing her person, her presidency of the AAS, and her free love ideology next to her letter inviting Spiritualists to the convention, on the paper's front page. He sarcastically justified his "personal remarks," on the grounds that "Your position and the tone of your article compels us to forget that your sex differs from that of General Grant, or any other distinguished aspirant for the presidential chair." No decent Spiritualist endorsed the coming convention, in Jones's view. "Your persistency in advocating what contains grains of truth, in a manner to shock the highest sense of propriety, has given you a notoriety unenviable;" notoriety, he suspected, was the sole reason for the convention. "Your public career evinces the fact that you are an adventurer, seeking notoriety," Jones wrote, "without regard to the question whether your sentiments accord with or shock the public moral sentiments." Jones's criticisms would haunt him that November, when Woodhull exposed him as an adulterer along with Henry Ward Beecher. For the moment, however, he rallied conservative opposition to Woodhull's leadership of American Spiritualists.[20]

The Equal Rights Party convention reintroduced an old question for Spiritualists: should they create their own party or remain formally separate from politics? Members of the movement had no common political orientation, though most were amenable to reform issues; particularly in the midwest, Spiritualists drew members from a range of political positions, from ex-abolitionists who leaned toward the Radical Republicans to old Free Soil Democrats who resented any control by eastern elites. Some Spiritualists, however, found the idea of a separate political party intriguing, and even the moderate Spiritualist paper, the *Banner of Light*, expressed cautious enthusiasm for the convention.[21] As the *Banner* recognized, the Equal Rights Party convention tapped into widespread frustration among radicals with the existing political choices. The Republican and Democratic parties are "both in the process of disintegration," the paper said that March. "They need recruiting from entirely new sources. Their old dogmas and schemes are worn out." It was a popular sentiment among radical reformers that spring. Sex radical Anna Middlebrook saw the convention as an antidote to political apathy; "we will use our influence to turn from office those *traitors* that profess but do not *practice* Republican or Democratic principles."[22]

Critics, however, saw no place for political activism in the Spiritualist movement. "Spiritualism, as I understand it, is infinitely above the petty strife of party, faction, or even nationality," wrote Spiritualist Hudson Tuttle, "and to narrow it to any issue, to cast its fate with any party, however strong, is to seal its doom."[23] Organization, for many Spiritualists, was anathema to the anti-authoritarian tendencies of the movement, even when dedicated to reform. This was particularly the case as the convention appeared to be the work of the Woodhull-controlled American Association of Spiritualists and American sections of the IWA, both of which moderate Spiritualists wanted to avoid. As an alternative to the national association, moderates advocated robust local organizing instead of a top-down national body. Real Spiritualism, said medium Susan C. Waters, had no leaders.[24] "No one disputes the right of Mrs. Woodhull or any other person to project and carry on as many reforms as they can find baskets or budgets to hold them," Spiritualist D. A. Eddy wrote, "but when [they make] the bold, unblushing attempt to make Spiritualism a *packhorse*, I . . . shall object." Opponents blamed Woodhull's upcoming convention for the new tensions wracking in the movement and in the spirit world. "Before this *disturbing* element (the Woodhull excitement) made its appearance," as Eddy saw it, "there was a greater amount of harmony, concert of action, and union of purpose, existing in the spiritual family, than had ever been witnessed before in the history of the world." Debate over the convention was so heated that veteran free love advocate and freethinker Austin Kent urged his colleagues to part amicably. "If Spiritualists are soon to divide—as is claimed by some, though I do not believe they are—let them shake hands and part, not quarrel and separate."[25]

On the eve of the Equal Rights Party convention that May, it was not only the Spiritualist movement that was in danger of fracturing. Woodhull's tenuous connection with several sections of the First International was also on the verge of breaking. Even as she courted workers' support at the New York Labor Reform League on May 6, other sections of the Yankee International questioned the political activism and public display anticipated at the upcoming convention.[26] Pro-suffrage women had the most difficulty separating their own convention from the Equal Rights Party convention; calls for both had appeared side-by-side in *Woodhull & Claflin's Weekly*, with prominent suffragists, including Susan B. Anthony (without her consent), listed as supporters of the new party idea. Anthony and others wary of Woodhull's influence and notoriety were determined to take back control of the NWSA convention, at least, from Woodhull's charismatic leadership. On the evening of May 9, when Woodhull began one of her inspirational speeches on the stage of the suffrage meeting to invite suffragists to the Equal Rights Party convention the next day, Anthony had the gas lights turned out to silence her.[27]

The next day, Equal Rights Party delegates adopted a radical political agenda. They engaged in a series of speeches, debates, and committee sessions designed to unite civil rights activists, suffrage women, sex radicals, and international socialists around the overarching principle of universal rights. Slogans decorating the walls favored strong national support for social and economic rights. The platform, adopted late in the afternoon, demanded universal suffrage and citizenship, but also a strong welfare state that nationalized employment, education, land, and inheritance. Together, the platform's twenty-three planks promoted social, racial, and economic equality. Radical at the time, many of the provisions formed the backbone of Progressivism and entered mainstream politics with Franklin D. Roosevelt's New Deal in the 1930s.

Woodhull's uncompromising call for revolution that evening (excerpts of which appear at the opening of this chapter), according to eyewitnesses, suited the jubilant mood of party delegates. Her delivery "animated her hearers to a high degree of enthusiasm," sex radical Alfred Giles later reported to the *Banner*. "The audience was intensely alive. Expectation gleamed from every eye." In the excitement following Woodhull's speech, several delegates sprang to their feet to address the convention, but before they could speak a man referred to as Judge Carter (probably Spiritualist lecturer, Hon. A. G. W. Carter of Cincinnati) leaped onto the stage, shouting "Mr. President!" until allowed to address the delegates. "The time for words has passed," Carter said: "We want action." As delegates shouted their approval, he nominated Woodhull as the Equal Rights Party candidate for president of the United States. All accounts agree that the audience went wild at this point, cheering, shouting, men throwing their hats in the air, women waving their handkerchiefs. After several minutes, when the crowd grew quieter, the presiding officer, Judge J. D. Reymert, announced that a motion had been made and seconded, and asked those in favor to say "aye." Once again the delegates cheered uproariously for several minutes, seemingly unanimous in their choice of Victoria Woodhull as their presidential nominee. With apparent reluctance, Woodhull returned to the stage and thanked the party for the honor: "I feel it more deeply and sensibly since I have stood before the world so long, sometimes receiving its approval, but oftener encountering its rebuffs," she said. She accepted the nomination, and promised to carry the party's radical principles "into governmental practice."[28]

The vice presidential nomination was somewhat more controversial. After the excitement of Woodhull's nomination had subsided slightly, sex radical Moses Hull stood and nominated, as the Equal Rights Party candidate for the vice presidency, "that true friend of human liberty, Frederick Douglass." A former slave and powerful advocate for Negro rights, Douglass was the perfect symbol of the party's commitment to universal rights, Hull said. This nomination immediately sparked a heated debate on the convention floor: given Douglass's vocal support for President Grant's reelection, delegates proposed a number of alternatives with equally sound reform credentials, including Ezra Heywood, Benjamin Wade, Robert Dale Owen, Theodore Tilton, and Wendell Phillips. Many papers noted that, in the confusion that followed, one "indignant" man proposed Sioux leader Spotted Tail for the honor, "as the Indians had possession of this country before the negroes." Once put to the floor, however, the motion to nominate Douglass received support from more than two-thirds of the delegates, who evidently thought him necessary to the ticket's symbolism of universal rights. If Douglass refused the nomination, a delegate moved that "some colored man be substituted in his place."[29] This sentiment suggests that delegates chose their two candidates more to express the Equal Rights Party's support for race- and sex-blind equal rights than with any concrete plans to get them elected. When Judge Reymert closed the convention two days later, he called the two candidates "representatives of womanhood and manhood; they are true types of America. Personally, they are true and honest and capable. Our country will be happy indeed, when she shall so far triumph in equal rights as to prove her justice to the woman and the man, without distinction and prejudice."[30]

The two nominations underscored the convention's radical agenda; like the International Workingmen's Association march for Paris Commune martyrs in December 1871, the nominations encapsulated an ideal of universal rights. Sympathetic commentators felt that the convention marked an important historical moment. The *Banner* moderately praised the event, where "all shades of radical thought found representation upon a universally free platform . . . . [that] represents, in certain ways, the convictions of many honest reformers." Extremism, the paper acknowledged, had its place in political contests, if only to shock the mainstream out of its apathy: "To the cold, calculating conservative the utterances of the enthusiastic iconoclast may appear volcanic in character, but both classes are necessary in community to preserve the equilibrium." Others who attended agreed that the convention made a powerful statement; as one delegate reported to his IWA section in Philadelphia, the nominations arose from the spontaneous feeling of the convention as a whole, which he found particularly surprising given the heterogeneous body of reformers assembled. He felt the excitement it generated would have great potential to stimulate new sections to form in the name of universal rights. For some socialists and sex radicals, the convention and its nominees inspired new momentum for organizing efforts.[31]

Responses in the Popular Press

This close look at the Equal Rights Party's nominations of Woodhull and Douglass reveals that they deliberately combined the issues of social freedom (sexual rights) and social equality (civil rights). Not surprisingly, however, the nation's press saw the event differently. Reception of the nominations in the press reveals the new power of miscegenation fears to derail the quest for racial and sexual equality; mocking coverage quickly discredited the convention delegates and nominees. Most political papers emphasized the unorthodox behavior of the sex radicals and socialists who attended, dismissing them with the time worn epithet of "long haired men and short haired women." The Democratic *New York World* coverage was probably the most extreme in this regard:

There were women and men, and those who, so far as dress and appearance went, might be classed with either sex . . . the two sexes approached each other more nearly than in any other peculiarity, the faces of the women presenting a hard, angular, masculine expression, while those of the men . . . wore an expression which gave them an appearance bordering on the feminine. In the matter of hair, too, there was a striking resemblance, the men growing their hair as long as possible, while the women cropped theirs almost to the usual masculine shortness.

Commercial papers followed this lead. Illustrated sporting news coverage emphasized the unorthodox appearance of the delegates (Figure 20). "Unsexed" as they were, the *New York Herald* also used sly depictions of the young female delegates who supported free love to paint them as sexually depraved.[32]

The racial composition of the ticket generated even more derision in commercial newspapers. A satirical *Herald* editorial ran under the headline "The Highly Colored Human Ticket for the Presidency—the Free Love Communist Candidates in the Field":

The first place on its ticket is devoted (*place aux dames!*) to the fair sex, and, to make the contrast more forcible, the second fiddle is handed, to draw it mildly, to a male brunette. Considerable doubt was expressed in the Convention as to whether the venerable and colored Fred Douglass could stand on the platform beside the young and painted creature in petticoats . . . .It may be objected that Victoria Woodhull had long ago nominated herself for the Presidency, and her endorsement for the candidature might be considered as a "put-up job;" but with regard to the Vice President, expectant or desired, the case is different. There can be little doubt that the position has been thrust upon him, and it remains to be seen how the representative black man will act under the circumstances.

Figure 20. The Equal Rights Party nomination of Woodhull and Douglass for president and vice president at the "free-lovers convention" generated this depiction. Short-haired, hard-faced and disorderly, the women in the foreground, as well as the "long haired men" surrounding them, pose a contrast to the barbershop audience of the illustrated sporting news. *The Days' Doings*, June 1, 1872.

The Democratic press seemed torn over whether to disqualify Douglass on the basis of his blackness or his respectability. As the *New York World* put it, Douglass was "very well qualified to be the ideal 'respected fellow-townsman' whom the convention agreed in chiefly hating. We really do not see why a convention in behalf of chaos should spoil its work and make a distinction in disfavor of Mr. *Douglass,* as it is clear that it did make that distinction solely on the grounds of his race and his color."[33] That this symbolic goal was a deliberate choice of delegates escaped almost every editorial assessment of the event.

For many Democratic commentators, the Woodhull/Douglass ticket was just a sideshow in a bizarre election year, no more ridiculous than Horace Greeley's Liberal Republican candidacy on the Democratic ticket. In Douglass's home town, for example, Rochester's *Democrat and Chronicle* urged Greeley to be chivalrous and step out of Woodhull's way: "Mr. Greeley has now an opportunity to be gallant as well as wise," the paper wrote sarcastically. Greeley probably would lose his constituency to Woodhull in any case, the paper noted, for "it is an obvious fact that Mrs. Woodhull is a more popular candidate than he. A very large majority of the equal rights branch of the liberal-Democratic anti-tyranny party are in favor of Mrs. Woodhull." *Pomeroy's Democrat* of New York was disgusted with all the presidential tickets; Greeley's and Woodhull's nominations were equally outrageous. "In a fair toss up, Victoria, the Woodhull, has won her right to the pole, so let her and Douglass, Viccy and Freddy, have a fair start, and get off well together." The other two candidates, President Grant and George Francis Train, only proved that the candidacy was open "for anything and everything but Democrats!" Some Democrats, outraged at their exclusion from the election, suggested that Woodhull's candidacy had been orchestrated to benefit Grant's reelection by fragmenting the opposition.[34]

But the Woodhull/Douglass ticket was, for most commercial papers, ludicrous on its own merits. The *New York Evening Telegram* dismissed the Equal Rights Party platform as standing for "free love, woman's suffrage, women's rights generally, animal magnetism, Spiritualism, psychology, mormonism, and all the other isms, and creeds, and doctrines that can be gathered together to shock the moral sensibilities of society." Like most New York papers, it ignored any greater objectives of the party. "This party being actuated by a sort of don't-care-a-d[amn]dativeness will make the most noise in the campaign, and will contribute no small share of the fun." As the *Philadelphia Inquirer* put it, "these semi-lunatics who met in New York do not set upon the principle that whatever is, is right, but upon the much broader suggestion, that 'whatever ought to be is.'" Telegraphic news dispatches echoed these scathing local reports. "The Radical Reformers adopted a wonderful Constitution," read an Associated Press dispatch: "Mrs. Woodhull and Fred. Douglas [sic] were then nominated President and Vice-President, amid great confusion. . . . Convention broke up in an uproar." Many papers ignored this dispatch, though they ridiculed Woodhull's lengthy letter to the press announcing her acceptance of the nomination. Papers that did reprint the telegraphic report of the convention added editorial spin. The *Charleston Daily Courier*, for example, dismissed the Equal Rights Party platform as "Women's Rights, Free Love, and the total depravity of men."[35] Such disparaging commentary exaggerated the ticket's unconventional nominees, while it excluded its political platform, and most likely deterred potential supporters.

This is particularly evident in the language used to dismiss Douglass by association with Woodhull and Claflin. An unlikely "brutish rapist," the press instead used his nomination as second fiddle to Woodhull to feminize Douglass. The *New York Herald*, for example, labeled him a "male brunette." Perhaps more tellingly, the racist *Pomeroy's Democrat* satirically accused the women suffragists (assumed to make up the Equal Rights Party) of committing an "outrage" (common parlance for rape) upon Douglass by subordinating him to a woman. This comic reversal of the paper's standard black male/white female rape scenario reduced the party's convention to the ridiculous. A later issue elaborated on the comic aspect of the Woodhull/Douglass pairing with a woodcut image (Figure 21) of Woodhull and Douglass in the costume of minstrel performers, complete with stage-prop horses, with large booted feet showing below.[36] These costumes likened Woodhull and Douglass to white men in blackface (and a dress), seeking only to entertain. The minstrel imagery gave the paper a clever shorthand to subvert the revolutionary symbolism of the nominees.

References to miscegenation, veiled or overt, put the Woodhull/Douglass nomination firmly and finally beyond the pale of respectful commentary. The *Philadelphia Inquirer* called the nomination "peculiar" in its "somewhat strange combination of a white woman and a black man." The *New York Evening Telegram* dubbed the nominations the "Dolly Varden Ticket," comparing it to a boldly contrasting dress fabric by that name, popular that summer. "For President, Victoria C. Woodhull, young white woman; for Vice President, Fred Douglass, old black man. This is a large and

Figure 21. Appearing in the racist *Pomeroy's Democrat*, this crude woodcut image lampoons the Woodhull/Douglass ticket. Decked out in costume horses, with heavily booted feet below, Woodhull and Douglass appear as minstrel performers rather than politicians. Adjacent text links the image to a violent episode at the home of Cornelius Vanderbilt (see Figure 22). The costumes and the venue they invoke suggest that Woodhull is not a woman, and that Douglass is not a black man, but rather that they are white male entertainers in costume. *Pomeroy's Democrat*, May 25, 1872.

COMMODORE VANDERBILT'S BLACK COACHMAN AND HIS WHITE AFFINITY.

Figure 22. This sporting illustration indirectly linked the Woodhull/Douglass nomination to the unrelated story of a violent episode at Cornelius Vanderbilt's home. The image falsely implies that the "Negro Coachman" was guilty of a violent sexual assault on a white woman. In fact, the woman was his willing companion and the man suffered a severe beating at the hands of police. *The Days' Doings*, June 15, 1872.

showy pattern with strong contrasts of color." Western newspapers, such as the *Guard* in Eugene, Oregon, dismissed the candidates in the most scathing terms as "A Shameless Prostitute and a Negro." "Which of the candidates on the free love ticket is degraded?" sneered the Democratic *Guard*. "Is Woodhull degraded to the level of a negro, or is Fred. Douglass sunk to that of a common prostitute?" The combination of social and sexual freedom received explicit attention in the *New York Evening Telegram*. "Here is a ticket which beats the most radical conception ever entertained," the *Telegram* noted. "*Free love in front and amalgamation in the rear*."[37]

Omissions in press coverage also shaped perceptions of the Woodhull/Douglass nominations, suggesting widespread editorial bias against fair representation of the candidates. Illustrated sporting newspapers, for example, placed images of the joint nomination among others that made the Equal Rights Party's choices seem disreputable. For example, Douglass did not appear in *The Days' Doings* in coverage of the nomination, in its ratification the next month,[38] or in his rejection of the nomination; the respectable black man was "unrepresentable" in the tabloid forum. Instead, soon after the nomination, *The Days' Doings* distorted an insignificant skirmish under a headline describing a "Bloody Affray" in which "A Frenzied Negro Coachman Attempts an Outrage" on a white woman. The fact that this coachman worked for Cornelius Vanderbilt, who had set Woodhull and her sister up in the brokerage business two years previously, indirectly linked the two stories. The illustration (Figure 22) suppressed the fact that the woman had been the coachman's willing companion, and that he was the victim of police brutality, rather than the reverse. Standing alone, the story suggested a sordid sequel to the Woodhull/Douglass alliance.[39]

Press commentary also inflated political divisions by race and sex. *Pomeroy's Democrat*, in blatantly mocking tones, criticized the women suffragists for insulting Douglass by placing him second on the ticket. "Had the ladies who assembled in such crinolinian wisdom and chignonic superiority in our midst the other day, thought proper to nominate a white man as the number two upon their ticket, no one could have dared to suggest a doubt of their propriety of reserving number one for themselves," the paper commented.

The lovely Woodhull, usually so well-served by the great Athenian as her spirit guide, will have to pay dearly for the insult to the modern Jupiter. Even Greeley will beat her in the Electoral College, for there is not a darkey in the land, from the painted bone-knocker of the music hall, to the rheumatic bone-acher of the plantation, but will rise to resent the insult to their caste done so shamefully upon them by placing the mighty negro Douglass second to a woman; and she, to make the matter worse, a white woman.[40]

The national associations for woman suffrage found themselves linked by association to the nominations; despite the American Woman Suffrage Association rejection of Woodhull as a free lover and Susan Anthony's efforts to silence Woodhull at the National Woman Suffrage Association meeting, most papers referred to the convention as the "woman's rights convention," probably a lingering consequence of the joint call in *Woodhull & Claflin's Weekly*. By ignoring the specifics of the Equal Rights Party platform and delegates, press reception conflated a complex array of reform movements into one, easily dismissed, symbol.

Scathing press coverage intensified tensions between moderate Spiritualists and the sex radicals. Spiritualist Hudson Tuttle had dismissed her a "huckster" since her election as president of the American Association of Spiritualists in 1871; he saw the Apollo Hall Convention as hype, which "pushes her forward on a course of notoriety mistaken for fame." It was probably the inevitable conclusion for outsiders to draw, given the tone of popular reporting. Those who attended, however, saw things differently. "If there are any who doubt the sincerity of those who inaugurated this move," said Spiritualist Mrs. H. M. Slocum, "let me assure them that had they seen the pale faces and heard the earnest utterances of delegates as they . . . pledged the hard earnings of the future in support of this cause, and representing as they did all classes of reformers, from all parts of the country— I say if doubters had seen this as I saw it, they would feel, as I feel, that these people are terribly in earnest." Radicalism was the only possible response to the growing trend toward orthodoxy, Slocum felt, noting recent efforts in New York state to expand the role of religion in state government. "To support the Equal Rights party, is to work in our own legitimate channel, and for principles by which we can stand."[41] It was precisely the creeping conservatism that made sex radicals select Woodhull and Douglass; they wanted to demonstrate their principles in a wide public forum as a means to effect change. Ridicule was hardly surprising in a society that resisted new ideas, and if they were ridiculous, they were deliberately so, and in the name of a worthy cause. "In our progress as reformers we seem, to me, to have reached the second stage of existence, that of ridicule," wrote Julia Milligan to the *Weekly*; "the first, that of persecution, has passed: the third, and last, that of success, *is close at hand*."[42] Their faith in progress buoyed them as they faced public criticism over the controversial nominations.

The Demise of the People's Party

Three weeks later, the Equal Rights Party reconvened to ratify the Woodhull/
Douglass nominations, and restated their goals with an eye to the public's
reaction. After some difficulty securing a hall for the event, the ratification
meeting underscored the universal rights agenda represented by the nominations. Its campaign song was an anthem to the defiance of convention:

If you nominate a woman
In the month of May
Dare you face what Mrs. Grundy
And her set will say?

How they'll jeer and frown and slander
Chattering night and day
Oh, did you dream of Mrs. Grundy
In the month of May?

If you nominate a Negro
In the month of May
Dare you face what Mr. Grundy
And his chums will say?

Yes, Victoria we've selected
For our chosen head;
With Fred Douglass on the ticket
We will raise the dead.

Then round them let us rally
Without fear or dread
And next March we'll put the Grundys
In their little bed.[43]

Even in Douglass's absence, the ratification ceremony showed the party's
determination to confront the period's racial and sexual politics, by loosen-
ing the "Grundys'" stranglehold on acceptable behavior.[44]

The ratification song celebrated equal rights, but also adhered to the
antipolitical stance of many Spiritualists. Shocking the "Grundys" received
far more attention in the song than the actual election of the candidates.
The goal of the Equal Rights Party was to reform the current system by wak-
ing up apathetic bystanders, rather than to replace it with something new.
"There is not a politician in this land who will obtain any high office four
years from today," Judge Carter told delegates at the ratification. "There is

no politics in our new platform. But we shall labor together—both man and woman for the consummation of the object of our ambition—the ballot for both sexes." Moderate critics failed to see the party's radical critique as offering any positive contribution to political life; on the contrary, they were offended by it. Longtime Woodhull opponent J. K. Bailey saw the ratification as "monstrous," because "the object of its work can but be further notoriety."[45]

To deflect such charges, *Woodhull & Claflin's Weekly* clarified the meaning of the Woodhull/Douglass ratification. According to the *Weekly*, Woodhull and Douglass represented the party's goals; "in the ninety-sixth year of the Republic of the United States, they represent classes, who may justly be termed, even yet, the pariahs of our modern system of civilization." By nominating Woodhull, the party "arraigns the despotism over woman as exercised in this Republic." Woodhull was the ideal presidential nominee for social radicals, for "the demand for the personal, social, legal, and political liberties of woman have been better advocated by her actions and in her speeches and writings than by any other woman." By nominating Douglass, the party "proposes to set the seal of the nation on the issues of the war of the rebellion; to exhibit to the world that our people are a unit in the defense of the rights of all mankind; and to reset the Government on the right track." Douglass, "though born a slave . . . has himself achieved both his education and his liberty; . . . has waged a life-long, manful battle for the rights of his race, in which those of mankind were included; . . . has proved that he knows how to assert the liberties of the people, and consequently it is assumed that he knows how to maintain them." These explanations show that Equal Rights Party delegates chose Woodhull and Douglass as ideal representatives, because through their public reform efforts the two candidates embodied their causes.

They were also representative of radical reform because they stood on the margins of mainstream American life: their combination, the *Weekly* insisted, defied conventional sexual and racial stereotypes. In nominating Woodhull and Douglass, Equal Rights Party delegates meant to "hurl a gage of defiance to the despots and aristocrats of Europe, who have long pointed the finger of scorn at our Republic in the matter of slavery, and condemned it as lacking the will to carry out fully the principles of true democracy contained in the Declaration of Independence." Like the Greeley nomination, the Equal Rights Party nominations of Woodhull and Douglass sought to attract the all-important black voter. Although silent on Douglass's feelings about the nomination, the *Weekly* claimed to have the support of black voters. "Several organizations of colored people" including one editor of a Lexington, Kentucky, paper, had, "in the interests of the colored people," visited the party's headquarters to "pledge the support of their vote in his State for Woodhull and Douglass." The Equal Rights Party, the *Weekly* insisted, "alone of all the parties offers to the masses of those once slaves the certain means to political and social equality."[46] Anticipation of support from freedmen gave the party a sense of optimism in early summer.

Tennie C. Claflin reinforced the party's universal rights agenda later that week when she successfully became colonel of the newly combined African American militia regiment, New York's Eighty-Fifth. Earlier in the summer, Claflin had amused many with her bid for the colonelcy of the Ninth Regiment of the New York National Guard following the fatal shooting of its Colonel, James Fisk. The spectacle of a female colonel generated hilarity in the press. Was Claflin, the *New York Times* wondered, "fully prepared to go the length of discarding all pretenses of skirts?"

If she wears even the most abbreviated of skirts, what will she do with her sword? And in what manner does she propose to lead her regiment when marching? If she is mounted, she must either wear the long riding-habit of her former sex, or adopt the trowsers and saddle of the masculine sex, since nothing is more preposterous than an equestrian fringed about with a five or six-inch skirt. It would really seem as though she would be compelled to plunge boldly into the usual dress of other Colonels, supplemented, perhaps, with flowing coat-sleeves and a rudimentary panier, wherewith to remind the world that she is the champion of that sex which has hitherto fought with sharper and lighter weapons than the sword and rifle of the masculine soldier.

The *New York Evening Telegram* suggested that a "good, sensible and serviceable rig would be a double-breasted shad-belly coat, calf-skin breeches, cowskin boots and a Dolly Varden hat. If Miss Tennie would select a mule to ride on, the picture would be more lively and fascinating. Let her try." Such commentary reduced a political gesture to satire and made the whole venture laughable. Illustrated newspapers such as *The Days' Doings* lampooned this attempt in hilarious style, with highly sexualized drawings of "the Female Colonel of the Ninth" (Figure 23). The paper ridiculed Claflin's allusion to Joan of Arc as a model for women's military expertise, and dismissed the whole venture as another pitch for publicity. "As for Joan of Arc, she has been greatly exaggerated by poets and historians," wrote the paper, "and she was never as widely known in her day as is Tennie C. Claflin in hers. Joan of Arc never had her name in the newspapers once, while Tennie C. Claflin's name is in the newspapers all the time."[47]

Figure 23. Claflin's open letter to the Ninth regiment of New York, offering herself as a replacement colonel for the lately murdered James Fisk, received this comic depiction in *The Days' Doings*. In this series of images, a barely dressed Claflin steps into Fisk's large breeches and trades a musket for the umbrella of the "strong-minded woman." Her allusion to Joan of Arc, the salacious potential of her leadership, and, finally, her military incompetence are the subject of broad mockery. *The Days' Doings*, June 8, 1872.

Commentary on Claflin's notoriety did not, however, deter the Eighty-Fifth Regiment, known locally as the "Spencer Grays," from inviting the wealthy broker to be their colonel. Despite opposition from within the regiment, her offer of funds proved irresistible, and she was elected by a margin of three to one. Like Woodhull, Claflin used the controversy surrounding her election to assert a principle of universal rights: she wanted to "show that woman can go to the front." She compared her case to that of freed slaves, on the grounds that she and her family were denied entry into hotels following Woodhull's nomination.[48] Claflin's election as colonel only inflated the satirical commentary in the press, which dwelt upon its racial significance. "The Spencer Grays, a New York military company, fifty strong, color black, beg Tennie Claflin to command them," mocked the *Rochester Democrat and Chronicle*. The *New York Times* saw it as a threat to her racial purity. "Is Col. *Claflin* prepared to . . . exchange the cosmetics of the Caucasian woman for the burnt cork of the pseudo African?" the *Times* asked. "If not, she had better pause before she incurs the expense of six hundred or more uniforms, for she may rest assured that to this blackened complexion she must come at last." The *Evening Telegram* likewise noted that "Tennie, of course, must be uniformed with her command and consequently she must use burnt cork every time she goes on parade."[49] This suggestion of Claflin's inevitable color transformation was another way to use race prejudice to dismiss the potential for interracial political alliance.

Douglass never acknowledged the Equal Rights Party nomination. He was well aware that the competition for the colored vote mobilized all political parties during the 1872 election. He dismissed Horace Greeley's nomination by the Liberal Republicans and Democrats in Cincinnati as a token tribute to the black man and abolitionism. "Not one of the men who voted for Horace Greeley and Gratz Brown as candidates has the remotest idea that they can be elected," wrote Douglass. Democrats were hardly likely to endorse the nominations of Greeley and Brown, and Douglass reminded Republicans that "the Cincinnati movement is only the thin veil to conceal the grim features of the old Democratic Party." More important, Douglass insisted, was Greeley's betrayal of Republican Party principles. Douglass exhorted his fellow black voters not to squander their votes on the Cincinnati ticket.

Colored men are not so rich in political influence and power that they can afford at this time to throw either away upon men who, however excellent, plainly cannot be elected. When we vote now, we should, and will vote for victory as well as for a great principle. The fire is kindled for the colored child's school house in all the gulf states, and the knife of the Ku Klux assassin is ready for the throats of the colored man of the South. Cincinnati holds out no assurance of protection from fire and death. In fact, the Cincinnati movement wrests the colored man's liberty from the custody of the nation, the only power that cares for it, and puts it into the hands of local governments, which would gladly destroy it.[50]

(Douglass's insights appear, with hindsight, prophetic; by 1877, Democrats forced a weak Republican president to withdraw federal protection from the south.) Fully aware of the vulnerability of Reconstruction policies to violent resistance, Douglass put his faith in Grant and the Republican ticket and expanded enforcement of civil rights laws.

African American newspapers conspicuously ignored the Woodhull/ Douglass nominations. In spite of, or perhaps in direct response to, the glee in the Democratic press over the nominations, their silence distanced them from Woodhull and generally reaffirmed their commitment to Grant and the Republican Party. The *New National Era*, for example (the only nationally circulated black paper in 1872), said nothing about the nomination of its former editor by the Equal Rights Party. The *Era* referred to Woodhull only once, in late October on the eve of the election, and then it was in sarcastic reference to the association of the "virtuous Mrs. Woodhull" with the Greeley campaign.[51] Other prominent black newspapers likewise kept silent on the nomination. The Hampton Institute's *Southern Workman* ignored the party's convention, praising instead the virtues of domesticity; the *San Francisco Elevator*, a passionate advocate of mixed schooling, was equally silent. The *Weekly Louisianian* of New Orleans noted the event to ridicule the "wild and visionary pretensions and performances of the recent "Woman's Convention." Below this statement, the paper printed an excerpt from the *New York Independent* that condemned the nomination for "insulting" Douglass by "putting his name on the same ticket" with Woodhull, and dismissed the event as "a little convention of the odds and ends of humanity—men and women who have hung on the skirts of every popular reform, blasé or crotchety reformers." Abolitionist allies preferred that Douglass publicly reject the nomination. "Mrs. Woodhull's convention looked and acted like a body of lunatics," abolitionist Oliver Johnson wrote to William Lloyd Garrison. "Of course Frederick Douglass will take the earliest opportunity to disclaim all connection with such a body, the proceedings of which were utterly beneath contempt."[52] Apparently, the black newspapers decided that mentioning the nominations, even to dismiss them as ludicrous, was a dangerous undertaking; most chose not to dignify the nomination with comment.

Larger political concerns may explain Douglass's curious silence on the nomination. He was already wary of efforts to draw his constituents into Greeley's fold.[53] Douglass attributed his loyalty to Grant and the Republican Party to their vigorous enforcement of the Ku Klux Klan Act, but also rejected the notion that a separate party would benefit black voters. Even before the Equal Rights Party nominations, the black Republican *Weekly Louisianian* rejected the call for a separate party, as "no sensible man advocates a colored man's party. Our strength lies in a union and combination with the most liberal of the two camps."[54] Greeley's comments on racial equality had alienated many black voters; he had argued, for example, that the "colored man" should accept his exclusion by whites on the grounds that one should never force an invitation.[55] Thanks in part to Douglass' mobilization of black voters, Greeley was roundly defeated, particularly in the south. Grant more than doubled his popular majority of four years earlier.[56]

Grant's victory signaled a new direction in national politics. After the 1872 election, Republicans grew wary of the Civil Rights Bill, and particularly mixed schooling. Mixed schooling probably contributed to the decline in (white) Republican voting in Appalachia, and southern Republicans, especially in Alabama, retreated from "social equality" in 1874 in order to attract white votes.[57] The Civil Rights Bill finally passed in 1875, but only after Benjamin Butler, its chief remaining advocate, agreed to drop the controversial mixed schooling provision. It was, in fact, a weak bill with limited enforcement power. The Supreme Court began a sustained assault on the universal rights implications of the Fourteenth Amendment; in a series of decisions, the court curtailed the power of the federal government to dictate the affairs of the states. The Civil Rights Bill shared this fate. Except for the jury provision, an 1883 Supreme Court decision found the Civil Rights Bill unconstitutional with respect to "personal acts of discrimination."[58]

The Woodhull/Douglass nominations, though not central to these national trends, help us see underlying attitudes hidden in this legal and legislative retreat from universal rights. Reverberations from the convention in the presidential campaign demonstrate just how disruptive such an interracial male/female political and cultural alliance appeared in the 1872 election. As summer progressed, the Democratic *New York World* linked Woodhull to Grant by innuendo in the small, but packed, headline (buried on page 5), "*Douglass Objects*: He Does Not Care to Keep Company with Woodhull— Grant Favors Woman Suffrage."[59] The Republicans, on the other hand, used a "colored professor" (in the shape of a blackface (white) performer at campaign stops) to lampoon Greeley by allusion to Woodhull in a campaign skit. This satirical monologue featured an inaccurate, polysyllabic vocabulary and the parody of "black" dialect so dear to the blackface minstrel tradition. In this one skit, the Republican Party distanced itself not only from Woodhull and woman suffrage, but also from the cause of black civil rights: this representative "colored professor" was not meant as an exemplar of an educated black man.[60] Through such performances, the Woodhull/Douglass nomination made the aspirations of woman suffrage and black civil rights easier to dismiss.

As summer waned, enthusiasm for the Woodhull/Douglass ticket evaporated. Both candidates lost their homes: Woodhull and her family were evicted and moved into her brokerage office for a lack of alternatives; Douglass lost his Rochester home of twenty-five years, and a fortune in bonds, to a fire that he blamed on arson.[61] Major reform organizations rejected the new political party. Negative press commentary, in fact, had effectively divided activists into very explicit, issue-oriented camps. For the IWA, preoccupied with orchestrating massive strikes throughout the northeast, the nominations were too unconventional and distracting to be tolerated.[62] As sections abandoned the Yankee International, Marx and Sorge orchestrated the expulsion of Woodhull's remaining allies. Far from appealing to international socialists, the Equal Rights Party nominations in fact gave the International an excuse to refocus on economic rather than social revolution.[63] Woman suffrage activists likewise began to shift from multiple issue organizing toward a single-issue campaign for the women's right to vote. When she doused the lights to stop Woodhull from drawing NWSA women into the Equal Rights Party convention, Anthony congratulated herself on saving the suffragists from disaster.[64] By the fall, the NWSA endorsed the Republican ticket for the presidential race, despite the party's growing reluctance to use federal power to protect women's or other individual civil rights from discriminatory local and state laws. The Republicans' capitulation to the states' rights argument undermined the basic premise of the New Departure strategy, which required federal enforcement of women's rights. It took another half-century of dedicated organizing before suffrage women successfully brought about the passage of a separate Constitutional amendment granting women the vote.[65]

The Equal Rights Party sent a revolutionary message at a turning point in Reconstruction, just as the universal rights principles of Radical Republicans were losing popularity. The mixed schools question, social equality for freed men and women, suffrage for women, and indeed the notion of the suffrage as an inalienable "right," were all casualties of the failure of

Reconstruction ideals to maintain widespread public support.[66] In part this reflected the inability or unwillingness of the Republicans to confront the miscegenation controversy thrust upon them by the Democrats. The abstract ideal of "social equality" had become indistinct from the more immediate (and feared) notion of racial mixing and interracial sex.

The Equal Rights Party's symbolic nominations collided with the emerging miscegenation hysteria; their controversial nature ultimately reduced Woodhull's constituency to extreme sex radicals. Woodhull's next move was to take direct action against the sexual double standard. Late in the summer of 1872, her exposure of Henry Ward Beecher won many sex radicals' grudging approval as a revolutionary act in its own right. However, the Beecher exposure also brought low one of the last powerful symbols of the Republican Party and abolition. The political parties themselves were undergoing a transformation, and activists were torn between their old allegiance to the abolitionist Republicans and their repugnance for the pro-slavery Democrats. Like Woodhull, the social radicals of the Equal Rights Party were drifting away from the Republican Party in its new, business-oriented incarnation. They embraced a philosophy of personal liberty that became, over the subsequent decades, more compatible with the local rule Democratic Party. The Beecher exposure became a significant force in Reconstruction's shifting political culture.

Chapter 3
The Politics of Exposure

In September 1872, Victoria Woodhull took the platform of the annual convention of the American Association of Spiritualists (AAS) in Boston. She intended to deliver her farewell address as the organization's president, bowing to pressure from conservative Spiritualists who thought that she gave the movement a bad name. In fact, the movement was badly divided over Woodhull's leadership. Spiritualist sex radicals, however, were Woodhull's closest friends and staunchest supporters, and they still dominated the association. Just as she was about to speak, she later reported, an "inspiration" overwhelmed her and prompted her to expose the hypocrisy of her critics. Her revelations included the adultery of popular minister Henry Ward Beecher, the sexual debauchery of a Wall Street broker named Luther Challis, and the hypocrisy of S. S. Jones, the conservative Spiritualist editor of the *Religio-Philosophical Journal*. Her logic in turning the tables on her opponents in the three exposures was effective; instead of forcing Woodhull out, the organization elected her president for a second term.[1]

The exposures appealed to sex radicals because they promoted marriage reform and a single sexual standard. The first accused Beecher of having an affair with Elizabeth Tilton, the wife of his good friend Theodore Tilton, editor of the liberal newspaper *The Golden Age* and president of the National Woman Suffrage Association (NWSA). It was not the adultery that Woodhull condemned, but rather Beecher's failure to support free love doctrines that he secretly practiced. Woodhull based her accusations on the private comments of prominent women in the NWSA, notably Elizabeth Cady Stanton and Paulina Wright Davis. The testimonies of such well-regarded women, Woodhull claimed, confirming as they did popular rumor and common knowledge about Beecher, gave her sufficient authority to make her accusations public. Here, she announced, was a known adulterer whose popularity and influence were unmatched in the nation.[2]

Woodhull used Beecher to demonstrate social hypocrisy; her other exposures revealed how men benefited from the sexual double standard.

Her revelations of Luther Challis presented him as a seducer. Woodhull described an evening when she and her sister Tennie C. Claflin had attended, in disguise, a "French ball," the name given to raucous costume parties popular among New York's "sporting" men. As described later by Woodhull's sister, the event boasted "magnificent hussies," an assembly of "three thousand of the best men and four thousand of the worst women." From an adjoining box, the sisters had witnessed the seduction of two innocent young women by Challis and a friend, and had found the girls days later "abandoned in a brothel." The incident, Woodhull told her audience at the American Association of Spiritualists Convention, showed the workings of the sexual double standard. As Claflin put it "there is sufficient evidence to show the world that when women are debauched there must be two parties to the debauchery; and we would ask why they should not both be held up equally to the scorn of the world instead of being called the 'worst women and the best men.'"[3] A third exposure attacked her conservative Spiritualist critic, *Religio-Philosophical Journal* editor S. S. Jones, for supporting a mistress, to demonstrate to Spiritualists "that Jones lives the doctrines he denounces." In this third exposure, Woodhull dared Spiritualist opponents to practice what they preached.[4] The three revelations marked a new stage in her public career; they showed that she was no longer willing to shield men from public scorn that she had long endured.

The Beecher exposure captured the most popular attention and set in motion the most controversial sex scandal of the nineteenth century, known as the Beecher-Tilton scandal. Her exposure of Beecher dramatized the social critique of her allies, the sex radicals: more than merely a spiteful act of revenge, the exposure epitomized their campaign for what they called a "single sexual standard for all." "We are all living more or less under masks," veteran free lover and Spiritualist Henry T. Child wrote in *Woodhull & Claflin's Weekly* early in 1872. "The bubble reputations which we are seeking are too often a cloak for hypocrisy and deceit."[5] For social radicals like Child, exposure was an instrument of morality, especially in the culture of secrecy that characterized the Victorian era.

On one level, Woodhull was practicing a time-honored tradition in American reform circles. Before the Civil War, abolitionists had used the exposure of sexual abuses under slavery to discredit the institution. Beecher himself (a staunch abolitionist) had drawn attention to the moral abuses of the "slavocracy" by staging mock auctions of attractive young African American women at Plymouth Church in Brooklyn: the tactic was designed to shame slavery's defenders by revealing its immoral underpinnings. In publicly exposing Beecher and a few other "hypocrites," Woodhull tapped into the same Protestant tradition of perfectionism, which sought to root out evil, secrecy and hypocrisy, all in the name of moral uplift. Woodhull inaugurated what Richard Wightman Fox calls a "cult of exposure," which contributed to the backlash against Victorianism. Her exposure also followed a reform tradition of revealing what Helen Lefkovitz Horowitz calls "reverend rakes," wayward Christian preachers who became exemplars of religious corruption. Woodhull saw the "ventilation" of the Beecher-Tilton scandal as the social equivalent of the prevailing public health notion that nature's disinfectants, namely sunshine and fresh air, would eradicate disease. She and other sex radicals believed that open discussion of social secrets would eliminate the "filth" that corrupted human relationships. Like the muckrakers who succeeded them at the turn of the century, sex radicals advocated exposure as a tactic to "cleanse the social order."[6]

The public controversy following the exposure helps illuminate the fault lines in the period's class and gender politics. Woodhull's legal persecution in the aftermath of the exposure became, unintentionally, a powerful demonstration of the root causes of sexual inequality. Woodhull and her friends anticipated that some kind of legal action might follow the Beecher exposure: in particular, she knew that printing the story could leave her vulnerable to prosecution for libel (though she felt confident that she could win the suit if it came to court, because she believed the rumors to be true). But she did not expect the intervention of the federal government, or her prosecution under a recently strengthened obscenity statute. The government's involvement imbued the Beecher exposure with social and political significance. It gave Woodhull and her supporters proof that women's subordination by class and gender had the force of government behind it. To emphasize this, Woodhull deliberately challenged the authorities, and repeatedly dared public officials to take action against her in a series of provocative acts. She welcomed every display of unwarranted state coercion against her because it added drama and publicity to her cause.

Sex radicals believed that the Beecher exposure and the subsequent legal and religious controversy offered exciting new populist tools for social reform. Woodhull's "persecution" by local and federal authorities was, they felt, dramatic proof of official hypocrisy in high places. By contrast, social conservatives tolerated questionable legal action against Woodhull as a means to check the reformist power of exposure. Woodhull's strongest adversary following the exposure was Anthony Comstock, the self-styled guardian of Victorian morality. Comstock had been fighting "obscenity" prior to

Woodhull's exposure of Beecher; the event left him with unprecedented federal control over the public sphere. Woodhull's exposures, and particularly her accusations about Beecher (which caused the greatest outcry) made her the first and most notorious sex radical to confront Comstock's ascendancy to power.[7]

The Beecher Exposure

Henry Ward Beecher had long been a household name in the northeast and the nation. He had been pastor of Brooklyn's Plymouth Church since 1847 and had made it into a nationally prominent religious institution. Beecher was the nation's most popular lecturer, and his weekly religious columns appeared in major newspapers across the country. One reason for his extraordinary popularity was his liberal interpretation of the Christian faith. Beecher's "Gospel of Love," as he called it, emphasized both the sensuous beauty of nature and an outpouring of human emotion.[8] "Love is the river of life in this world," he asserted in one characteristic sermon:

Think not that ye know it who stand at the tinkling rill—the first small fountain. Not until you have gone through the rocky gorges, and not lost the stream; not until you have stood at the mountain pass of trouble and conflict; not until you have gone through the meadow, and the stream has widened and deepened until fleets could ride on its bosom; not until beyond the meadow you have come to the unfathomable ocean, and poured your treasures into its depths—not until then can you know what love is.[9]

Beecher was not, despite this suggestive imagery, a free lover; he had long insisted that "the family is *the* most important *institution* on earth."[10] His liberal Christianity had attracted the largest congregation in the country. It proved to be a loyal following: in spite of Woodhull's verbal exposure, that October his parishioners paid extravagant tribute to him on Plymouth Church's twenty-fifth anniversary.[11]

Beecher's popularity had for several years made him the focus for Spiritualists' concern about the personal magnetism of popular religious leaders. Revelations about the "ministerial free love" of orthodox clergymen—the "reverend rakes"—were staple features of the Spiritualist press.[12] Beecher's status as the representative spiritual leader for the age made his actions all the more significant. Spiritualists followed Beecher's liberal interpretation of Christianity very closely, suggesting on occasion that Beecher

IS HENRY WARD BEECHER A SPIRITUALIST?—EXTRAORDINARY MANIFESTATIONS AT PLYMOUTH CHURCH.—THE
REPORTER'S TABLE TIPS AND DANCES IN RECOGNITION OF THE PASTOR'S ELOQUENCE.—SEE PAGE 2.

Figure 24. Henry Ward Beecher appeared in the pages of illustrated sporting news
on rare occasions even before the scandal. This illustration satirically depicts
"Spiritualist manifestations" that were reported in the pastor's Plymouth Church
during his sermon. Spiritualists liked to point out that Beecher's liberal
interpretation of Protestantism was not unlike their own. *The Days' Doings,*
June 8, 1872.

was really a closet Spiritualist. When commercial newspapers, including *The Days' Doings*, spread a story of Spiritualist manifestations in Plymouth Church in December 1871 (Figure 24), Spiritualists invited him to admit his sympathy with the movement.[13] They admired his progressive marriage philosophy and envied his immunity to criticism in the mainstream press.[14] However, Beecher denounced Spiritualism from his pulpit, and Spiritualists blamed his "lack of courage" on cynical commercialism. After his criticisms of the movement, said the *Weekly*, "almost everybody who had admiration for him must have felt a sensible diminution of it." As one correspondent to the moderate Spiritualist press, the *Banner of Light*, summed up Beecher's aversion to their movement, "He may not [admit] that he is a Spiritualist, but he is no less engaged in doing his part in the great work of Spiritualism."[15]

In a more personal sense, he was a logical target for Woodhull's exposure. His prominent sisters, Catharine Beecher and Harriet Beecher Stowe, had publicly denounced and ridiculed Woodhull for more than a year. At first, she retaliated in letters sent to large circulation New York newspapers. "My judges preach against 'free love' openly, and practice it secretly," she wrote back in May 1871. In a veiled threat to Beecher, she continued, "I know of one man, a public teacher of eminence, who lives in concubinage with the wife of another public teacher of almost equal eminence." When the press attacked her following her familial squabble in Essex Police Court a few weeks later, she went farther, alluding to "awful and herculean efforts . . . being made to suppress the most terrific scandal in a neighboring city." Most sex radicals would recognize this reference to Beecher and his Brooklyn church. Theodore Tilton later admitted that he wrote his laudatory (and widely panned) biography of Woodhull that summer to placate her and suppress the scandal.[16]

In the months leading to the exposure, Woodhull suffered extreme public criticism for her views on social freedom; Beecher's refusal to adopt her position on marriage reform was, in her view, hypocritical. Late in 1871, she repeated her threat to expose Beecher unless he personally introduced her controversial free love lecture, "The Principles of Social Freedom." At the last minute, he refused. Tilton presided in Beecher's place and successfully persuaded her not to expose the scandal before the audience. She contented herself with a warning. "If a person believes that a certain theory is truth," she told the audience, "and consequently the right thing to advocate and practice, but from its being unpopular or against established public opinion does not have the moral courage to advocate or practice it, *that* person is a *moral coward* and a *traitor* to his own conscience."[17] Most radical Spiritualists and free lovers in the audience supported this threat of exposure of hypocrisy as a form of social cleansing.

Almost a year passed before Woodhull exposed Beecher on the stage at the AAS convention in Boston. The action was immediately divisive: all but the most radical Spiritualists denounced her. Conservative Spiritualist outrage found expression in the pages of the *Religio-Philosophical Journal.* As one indignant correspondent wrote, "let it be placed upon perpetual record . . . that *not one Spiritualist in one hundred* recognizes the sentiments of *this vile woman* as in the least degree appertaining to modern Spiritualism." Like the mainstream press, the *Religio-Philosophical Journal* suppressed several details of Woodhull's statements (particularly the alleged adultery of its editor S. S. Jones) and attributed the worst motives to her actions. Jones advised his readers to break all ties with Woodhull and the national association. The poor attendance at the AAS convention that re-elected Woodhull president seemed to confirm that the organization lacked broad support among Spiritualists. Noting that only fifty-three votes were cast, of which Woodhull polled thirty-two, Jones scoffed "what a *national* gathering."[18] Getting rid of Woodhull, he insisted, was necessary to put the movement back on course.

In the weeks following her verbal exposure, Woodhull experienced both social isolation and public scorn. Her vulnerability to scrutiny and experience with ridicule probably hardened her to the potential fallout from her exposures. She had no reputation to lose; by virtue of class and gender, she and her sisters faced continual ridicule in ways powerful men could avoid. Illustrated sporting newspapers used almost any excuse to lampoon the sisters, whose images had wide commercial appeal. That October, for example, a characteristic cover illustration from *The Days' Doings* showed Tennie C. Claflin attacking her drama professor as she trained for the stage (Figure 25). This cover illustration used all the usual stereotypes to cast Claflin as a disorderly woman; her exposed ankles and violent demeanor were clear cues to the public viewing her image in newsstands and barbershops. The paper made no effort to disclose the source or public relevance of the story, making it a good indication of the double standard that attended the sisters' public lives.

Far from shrinking from the controversy, Woodhull and her friends decided to expand the scandal's impact by publishing the details of the Beecher and Challis revelations in the November 2, 1872 issue of *Woodhull & Claflin's Weekly.* The paper was immediately controversial, and demand was so high that copies sold for as much as $40.00 each. Woodhull claimed

Figure 25. The sisters' public lives made them public commodities. This cover image, which corresponded to no public event, kept Claflin before readers (and consumers) of *The Days' Doings*, for whom she apparently had significant commercial appeal. Shown here, her attack on her elocution teacher shows both her social aspirations and her inability to govern herself like a "lady." *The Days' Doings*, November 2, 1872.

higher motives than profit, however. The *Weekly* editorialized that true democracy demanded complete openness in social relations, and incremental reforms were ineffectual against the weight of hypocritical society. In the meantime,

men and women tremble on the brink of the revolution and hesitate to avow their convictions, while yet partly aware of their rights, and urged by the legitimate impulses of nature, they act upon the new doctrine while they profess obedience to the old. In this manner an organized hypocrisy has become the tone of our modern society.[19]

Woodhull defended the exposure in both personal and political terms. "It was a paradox which I could not understand," Woodhull explained with some bitterness, "that I was denounced as utterly bad for reaffirming the right of others to do as they did." Her tarnished reputation, in other words, apparently stemmed more from her social position than her philosophy: unlike Woodhull, the Beechers of the world enjoyed the protection of social convention and secrecy.

Exposure of sexual secrets, Woodhull believed, would bring the "revolution" into being. "Had I any right," she demanded, "having assumed the championship of social freedom, to forego the use of half the weapons, the facts no less than the philosophy of the subject placed at my command for conducting the war?"[20] Beecher's visibility, enormous popularity, and permissive Christianity made his exposure an ideal weapon, she felt. Rumored to have seduced many women in his large congregation, he simultaneously enjoyed an untarnished reputation. His own sermons endorsed the ideal of marriage based on mutual attraction; his Gospel of Love, she said, "unconsciously justified all the freedom that he was now condemning, when it came home to his own door, and endeavoring, in the spirit of a tyrant, to repress." Beecher's "moral cowardice" in refusing to introduce her free love lecture at Steinway Hall the previous year, Woodhull insisted, and his pathetic attempts to stop her from publishing the scandal only demonstrated the lengths to which powerful men would go to conceal their true behavior.[21]

The Beecher scandal, in Woodhull's hands, became a byword in social hypocrisy. Here was her social critique writ large. Woodhull claimed she had no personal axe to grind against Beecher himself: indeed, she expressed much admiration for him. She did acknowledge that she had suffered for openly endorsing the behavior that he practiced in secret and denied to the public, that his minions had gone to extreme lengths to castigate her personally and to prevent her from enjoying simple comforts of home and a living.[22] Her own class status made her, she realized, less sensitive to the inevitable fallout awaiting Beecher, and she apologized for the censure he was likely to endure in the coming weeks. But she hoped to prove by this that society had no right to judge individual behavior. If he could remain strong and weather the storm, he would become a better leader for his honesty. "When the first waves of public indignation shall have broken over him," she predicted, "when the nine days wonder and the astonished clamor of Mrs. Grundy shall have done their worst . . . and he finds that he still lives, and that there are brave souls who stand by him, he will, I believe, rise in his power and utter the whole truth."[23]

Woodhull also maintained that Beecher's full disclosures could only benefit ordinary Christians, for "there are other churches just as false, other pastors just as recreant to their professed ideas of morality."[24] Spiritualism, for Woodhull, was the only truly democratic alternative to orthodox religion. The movement's radical individualism made clergy superfluous; it was thus the best instrument for perfecting humanity. Moralizing sermons from hypocritical public teachers could never fix the evils caused by human want and inequality: Spiritualism alone was qualified to become "the Religion of Humanity."[25] Radical Spiritualists agreed, seeing Woodhull as an "instrument" of the "spirit world" to promote the single sexual standard.[26] As Woodhull put it, "Many may deprecate the publication of such facts; but there is no other possible way out of the present social demoralization into which society is declining. *People must be compelled to live just such lives as they want the public to think they live.*"[27]

Exposure as Civil Disobedience

In publishing the exposure, Woodhull and her friends wanted the scandal to have the greatest possible social impact. They knew that society would initially condemn her for exposing Beecher's private life, and they expected to face legal action, specifically a libel suit. "I accept the situation," she wrote in the November 2, 1872 exposure issue of *Woodhull & Claflin's Weekly*, "and enter advisedly upon the task I have undertaken, knowing the responsibilities of the act and its possible consequences." She and her associates worked diligently beforehand to ensure that legal action would not shut down the exposure before the *Weekly* reached its maximum distribution. They arranged for its printing in secret and sent copies to subscribers by mail before distributing them to the newsstands in New York.[28] These actions suggest a concerted effort to get the story to the public, but also an acute awareness that the law was not on their side.

This expectation of legal reprisals recasts the exposure as an act of civil disobedience. As Woodhull put it, in announcing her intentions, "we are prepared to take all the responsibilities of libel suits and imprisonment *with which we are even now threatened* if we unmask, as we certainly shall, one of the most notorious cases that ever existed. Arrests and prisons have no fears for us. . . . We shall simply do our duty, let what may come; and though the duty be a painful one."[29] Woodhull likened herself to William Lloyd Garrison, who in 1830 had served seven weeks in prison for malicious libel when he published an article about a merchant engaged in the illegal slave trade, and who was attacked by mobs for promoting abolition ahead of public opinion.[30] Like Garrison, Woodhull claimed to be secure in her facts, and she welcomed the anticipated prosecution for libel as a means to publicize the extremes of social hypocrisy.[31] More than this, she and her allies knew that legal action taken against them would, in revealing the power of the Beechers of the world, demonstrate the intricate web of forces that constituted "social tyranny."

Circumstances enhanced this strategy beyond their expectations. Beecher did not at first deny the story, nor did he ever sue the sisters or the *Weekly* for libel. Instead, a New York dry-goods salesman named Anthony Comstock, acting in the interest of "public morality," and under the auspices of the Young Men's Christian Association (YMCA), took it upon himself to punish the sisters for the Beecher exposure. In 1872, the renewal of an 1865 U.S. postal law made it a federal crime to send obscene books and pamphlets through the mails. A more stringent New York obscenity law existed, allowing authorities to confiscate "obscene materials." Comstock tried but failed to convince the state district attorney to proceed against the sisters; undaunted, he looked for federal intervention. He obtained a warrant for their arrest under the obscenity provision of the postal code, had federal marshals take them into custody, and imprisoned them in Manhattan's Ludlow Street jail, popularly known as "the Tombs."[32]

Official opinion rushed to sanction Comstock's rather broad interpretation of obscenity under U.S. postal law. At their hearing in federal court, Assistant U.S. District Attorney Noah Davis commented that "the defendants have not only circulated obscene literature, but they have attacked in a most abominable manner the character of one of the best and purest citizens of the United States, and *it is well worth while for the Government of the United States to vindicate him.*" In a like manner, Commissioner Osborne, who presided at the hearing, commented that "this was not only a violation of the law but an outrage upon public morality." Both comments revealed a degree of government intervention in a private "crime" consistent with earlier prosecutions for "obscene libel." Even without sanction from the limited postal code, authorities sought to protect the public morality from Woodhull's exposure. Their determination to protect what they called "revered citizens" set up the next stage of Woodhull's consciousness-raising campaign. What better evidence could be found for the extreme lengths to which powerful men might go to protect their false reputations? Initially, this was her strongest line of defense against prosecution for obscenity. "The idea of the government defending the character of a gentleman," Woodhull's counsel argued at her indictment, was absurd.[33]

Federal prosecution of Woodhull, Claflin, and Blood under the 1872 postal code gave new consequence to their protest against social hypocrisy. No longer was it a simple demand that prominent public men openly support what their private actions condoned. The obscenity indictments revealed the normally hidden mechanisms that promoted class and gender inequality. In addition, they placed Woodhull's campaign for a single sexual standard into a longer tradition of defiance. Dress reformers in the 1850s, arrested and fined under common law for "disturbing the peace" for wearing pants, were well aware of the social power of civil disobedience. A century later, in the early 1960s, civil rights activists who conducted sit-ins at lunch counters segregated (in some states) by custom rather than law likewise faced arrest for violating social norms rather than explicit legal prohibitions. The defiance of the activists dramatized injustices that stayed hidden as long as everybody obeyed "the rules." Woodhull's earlier defiance of convention, such as opening the Wall Street firm and running for president, prepared her for more conscious acts of civil disobedience. The exposure overtly challenged the sexual double standard; the government's intervention helped reveal the social, cultural and legal forces that kept the double standard going.

This strategy initially won few converts; the commercial press, in fact, amplified the official outrage against Woodhull and Claflin. Illustrated sporting papers covering the arrest and indictment used standard visual cues to equate the sisters with hardened criminals. Their shameless demeanors and hard faces in these illustrations, not to mention their radical hairstyles and mannish clothing (Figures 26–30) effectively cast them as criminals. The visual narrative running through these images conveyed a recognizable plot line: arrest on a public street, emerging from a carriage; indictment in court before the curious stares of onlookers; consultation with their attorney before the bars of their cells; and reflection in a humbled, dysfunctional family portrait inside the cell. Their faces and postures in their last appearance in *The Days' Doings*, at the indictment of Colonel Blood, denoted them as harsh, mannish, unsexed women. These five images concluded a story begun in February 1870 with their brokerage opening; the profligate Woodhull and Claflin, they seemed to say, had finally reaped the inevitable rewards of an overly public existence.

Comstock put pressure on the paper's publisher, Frank Leslie, to make sure that *The Days' Doings* did not give them a chance for a new life in visual culture. He obtained an indictment against Leslie's paper late in January 1873 for its publication of "indecent" (though discreet) advertisements for contraceptive devices. "At last, at last!" Comstock wrote in his diary after he obtained the indictment against Leslie. "Thank god! At last action is commenced

Figure 26. Federal marshals arrested the sisters for the publication of the Beecher scandal under the U.S. postal code in November 1872. As depicted here, their short hair, bold stares, and mannish attire, as well as the exposed ankle of one sister, alert readers to their disreputable status. *The Days' Doings*, November 23, 1872.

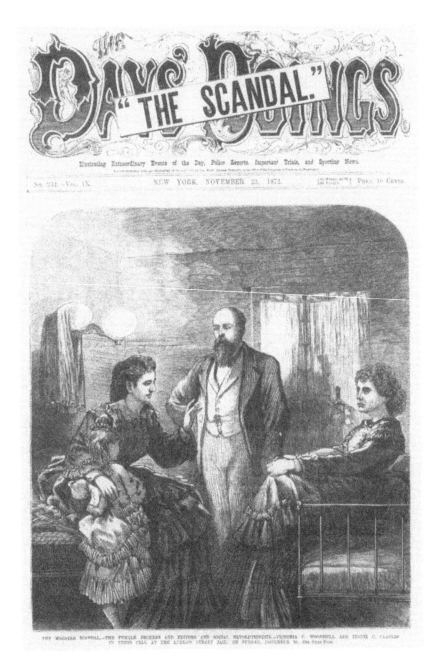

Figure 27. This cover image depicts a disreputable ending to the disorderly career of Woodhull and Claflin. The image shows them, defeated, in "the Tombs," the Ludlow Street Jail, which typically harbored murderers. The sisters, their lawyer, and Woodhull's daughter Zula Maud appear to contemplate a bleak future. *The Days' Doings*, November 23, 1872.

against this terrible curse. Now for a mighty blow for the young." Yet more than advertisements disappeared from *The Days' Doings* pages. Leslie went to extraordinary lengths to placate the anti-vice crusader. In Comstock's presence, he instructed his men not only to refuse all advertisements of "doubtful character," but also to stop producing images of "lewd character." Woodhull and Claflin disappeared from the paper, never to be covered in major illustration again. At Comstock's bidding, apparently, the paper that for three years had featured the sisters more than any other individual or event, erased them abruptly from its pages. All but banned from *The Days' Doings*, they had lost a major source of free, though disreputable publicity.[34]

National commercial newspapers also participated in the distortion of the case. Many reprinted an erroneous Associated Press dispatch asserting that the sisters had been arrested for libel rather than obscenity, and implied that the sisters had invented the story out of malice, or worse, a desire for notoriety. Few criticized Comstock for the arrest. The *New York Herald* was

Figure 28. Celebrated defense lawyer William Howe greets the chastened Woodhull and Claflin in the Warden's Room of the "Tombs." Though depicted as young and attractive, their short, tousled hair marks them as social radicals. The bars on the left remind the readers of their criminality. *The Days' Doings*, November 23, 1872.

Figure 29. Here the hard-faced sisters, again in masculine attire, endure the curious gaze of the crowd in public court. Their watchers appear to be divided between mirth and indignation at their behavior and appear well satisfied with their humiliation. *The Days' Doings*, November 23, 1872.

typical in denouncing the sisters as "women of bold, unabashed front who have flaunted their degradation and lived upon it." Calling the *Weekly* an indecent paper, rumored to be a front for an elaborate blackmail scheme, the *Herald* hoped for a speedy conviction. "To uproot and crush such public enemies is a duty society owes to itself." Woodhull protested against such personal attacks. She contrasted the "system of insinuation and innuendo," evident in such harangues, to her own open and explicit accusations against Beecher, and dared the hostile press to follow her lead and come up with specific charges against her.[35]

After Woodhull and Claflin remained in jail through the month of November without being formally charged, however, some papers began to question the legality of their arrest. As Leslie wrote in his popular family

THE MONSTER SCANDAL.—THE EXAMINATION OF COL. BLOOD, BEFORE JUSTICE FOWLER, THIRD DISTRICT COURT, AS AN ACCESSORY TO THE PUBLICATION OF "WOODHULL & CLAFLIN'S WEEKLY."—see Page 4.

Figure 30. More masculine than ever, the sisters appear in court for the examination of Colonel Blood. Shameless stares, mannish hats, cravats, and hair, and Claflin's unladylike posture (left), render the sisters at their most unconventional. These negative visual codes were apparently not sufficient to discourage imitation, however. Anthony Comstock negotiated with the editor of *The Days' Doings* to prohibit further depictions of the sisters: regardless of future notoriety and court appearances, this would be the last significant image of Woodhull and Claflin in this sporting newspaper. *The Days' Doings*, December 1872.

press *Frank Leslie's Illustrated Newspaper* shortly after their release of from the Tombs, government persecution of Woodhull and Claflin had inadvertently strengthened their claims. Leslie admitted that "it may not be in good taste to publish criminal accusations in detail," but it was the mandate of journalism to expose corruption, particularly when the accused occupied a prominent position in society. Government had no place in such cases, Leslie said. The real threat was "a powerful combination on the part of the Government with, so to speak, *privileged* persons. . . . It was for Mr. Beecher to have remained silent or to have contradicted the charge formally. Else, like any other citizen, he should have invoked the law of libel." Censorship was unacceptable: "Woodhull & Co. have a right to public opinion, and public opinion depends on the press."[36]

Woodhull took up this theme, insisting that sinister motives inspired the official hostility. "Why," she complained, "this is persecution. One of the Sunday papers has published the very same article that we have been arrested for publishing."[37] Sex radicals found this line of reasoning persuasive. Ezra Heywood, whose livelihood and health would be destroyed by the Comstock Law a few years later for his critique of marriage, found the entire situation a mockery of American ideals. "Mrs. Woodhull's articles were a clear, chaste and direct statement of the facts, as she viewed them," Heywood commented. While he thought the exposure misguided, he believed that her arrest should make "every Federal official, from the President on down," ashamed. "Whatever Mrs. Woodhull's views upon social reform or other questions may be," said Heywood, "every friend of impartial liberty should now stand by her; for in her person, the freedom of the press and the freedom of the mails [are] struck down." Woodhull shared this view. As she wrote to the *New York Herald,*

Suppose, Mr. Editor, that some enemies of yours should throw you into a cell for publishing the Challis article, suppress the Herald, arrest your printers, prosecute your publisher, shut up your business office, close all the avenues of press and lecture hall against your honorable defense, would not every land ring with the outrage?

Woodhull appealed to reformers to share her belief that the Grant administration was attempting to suppress "recalcitrant journals" as a means to silence political radicalism.[38]

Concerns about diminishing freedom of speech brought others forward to question the legality of the 1872 postal code. For example, freethinker and iconoclast George Francis Train deliberately challenged its definition of obscenity, by reprinting the entire Beecher story in a new newspaper, *The*

Train Ligue. When this failed to get him arrested, he published a second issue featuring sexually explicit excerpts from the Old Testament. This time, Comstock had Train arrested and thrown into the Tombs, where he remained for five months before the case came to trial, thanks to the decision of presiding judge and Beecher crony Noah Davis to postpone the trial.[39] These confrontations with Comstock, even before he managed to arrange passage of the 1873 statute bearing his name, dramatized his growing power to curtail free speech in the name of public morality. At the same time, they showed the public the high personal cost to individuals who dared to challenge his ever broadening definition of obscenity.

With the *Weekly* suppressed, and Spiritualist newspapers unsupportive of the Beecher exposure, sex radicals sought out other sources of sympathy for Woodhull. Laura Cuppy Smith, finding only scorn in the *Religio–Philosophical Journal* and complete silence in the *Banner of Light*, turned to Horace Seaver's freethinking newspaper, the *Boston Investigator*, for support. Spiritualists had all but abandoned Woodhull, Cuppy Smith reported; only a few personal friends remained to console the sisters in their difficult times. When she inquired about what role the American Association of Spiritualists might take in Woodhull's defense, she learned that the organization's trustees "had requested their Speaker not to visit Mrs. Woodhull, nor allude to her from the rostrum." Dire consequences would arise from this suppression of free speech, she warned, for "woman's emancipation from the thralldom of unjust legal enactment will be retarded by the enforced silence of the brave voice," *Woodhull & Claflin's Weekly*. She took Spiritualist newspapers to task for their failure to recognize the growing threat to the movement:

Is it possible that Spiritualists are growing conservative, sectarian? That in their new-born fear of "side-issues" they wish to limit their speakers and writers to the mere discussion of certain phenomena, important, it is true, but constituting only an introduction to a philosophy so broad that it seems to embrace every branch of reform?[40]

Whether or not they supported the Beecher exposure itself, Cuppy Smith demanded that freethinkers rally against the government's punishment of Woodhull, Claflin and Blood. The *Boston Investigator*'s editor, Horace Seaver, despite his personal distaste for Woodhull's public humiliation of Beecher, reluctantly complied, printing occasional letters from her supporters.

Woodhull's new status as a victim of Comstock's anti-obscenity crusade gave her a new way to rally support from around the country. She exhorted people to continue buying the paper that was the center of the controversy, *Woodhull & Claflin's Weekly*, back in print six weeks after her arrest. Her brokerage firm, now floundering under the burden of the excessive bail bonds, had largely subsidized the paper before her arrest; she could no longer keep the paper going without assistance.[41] "No friend of progressive ideas can afford to be without the *Weekly*," Woodhull said. "It is the only absolutely free paper in the world, besides it will be the only paper in which reliable accounts may be found of the progress of the revolution which is now in reality inaugurated and a bearing upon that revolution—of the important trials which must take place within the coming year."[42] Her personal hardship and the fate of the *Weekly* were inseparable. She called upon activists for a renewed commitment to free speech. "Not only is the freedom of the press threatened by the present prosecution, but so also is the freedom of speech and of the discussion of all reformatory subjects. Five thousand newspapers stand or fall with them; nevertheless, the plaintiffs are left to fight the battle almost alone."[43] It proved a persuasive line of reasoning. "Let us have no 'gag-law!'" belatedly agreed the *Banner of Light*. "Free speech —the unrestricted right to elucidate opinions, however unpopular—is the birthright of all in our American polity!"[44]

In fact, evidence of government censorship helped establish Woodhull as a champion of free speech. At the indictment on federal obscenity charges, both judge and district attorney had emphasized their moral obligation to silence future Woodhulls and Claflins. Similar motives prompted Massachusetts governor William Claflin (no relation to the sisters) to prohibit Woodhull's lecture on the Beecher matter in Boston. Beecher's sister, Harriet Beecher Stowe, probably influenced this decision, but additional motives were evident in Governor Claflin's public comments:

We have enough bad women in Boston now, without permitting this one to come here to further demoralize us. Why, she might even repeat the vile stories about Mr. Beecher, or even attack some of us in Boston. No, sir! This cannot be permitted.[45]

Governor Claflin's comments reveal a desire to protect Beecher not only as an individual, but as a wealthy public man. "She is no better than a panel thief or a common street walker," said the governor, "and I will see that she don't open her vile mouth in the city which was so recently honored by Mr. Beecher's presence."

Woodhull repeatedly reminded the public that Beecher's prominence as a Christian minister made his reputation sacred to his supporters. As she put it, "we have been charged with a crime and confined in jail, and, in the eyes of a thousand sensitive friends, are obscured by a cloud—and for what? We reply for daring to attack hypocrisy in high places." Mrs. E. A. Merriwether, a witness to her speech exposing Beecher before the AAS in Boston the previous September, concurred: "Mrs. Woodhull is making war on rich and powerful men." The sisters' four weeks in the American "Bastille," as Woodhull called it, and the exorbitant bail demanded for their release from prison (estimated in excess of $200,000) showed the world the determination of Beecher's supporters to punish her audacity in attacking one of the nation's most revered public men.[46]

To underscore the government's heavyhandedness, Woodhull deliberately provoked her censors, risking further arrests and fines in order to raise consciousness about her cause. She suspected that the federal government would never attempt to prosecute the obscenity trial; not even the most zealous prosecutor could convince higher authorities that she had been guilty of publishing anything close to "obscene." Instead, she predicted, the government would use the perpetual threat of trial to chasten and silence her. Not content to leave matters in this state of ambiguity, she deliberately prodded the government to act against her:

I give notice here and now, I hope the occasion is a sufficiently public one, that the publication office of Woodhull and Claflin's Weekly is at 48 Broad Street, New York City, and that from that office there will soon be issued and sold to all applicants a revised edition of the suppressed number of Woodhull and Claflin's Weekly, containing the "Beecher-Tilton Scandal," and that within a few weeks there will probably have been sent a million copies of it to every part of the world, so that the whole public shall be my jury and decide whether there is anything obscene in that earnest and all-important statement.[47]

True to this promise, copies were available by application to the *Weekly* office, a fact that left the sisters continually vulnerable to arrest. The government's disinclination to pursue other papers who published the Beecher story supports Woodhull's contention that she and her radical social critique, rather than the alleged "obscenity" of the publication, were the real targets for censorship.

In early 1873, Woodhull began a determined campaign to provoke the government to the greatest possible extent. "The District Attorney can't afford to arrest everybody who says a naughty word," Woodhull jeered, "not even to carry out his assumed new office of protector of the reputation of 'revered citizens.'"[48] The social and political power of the elite was formidable, she noted. Consequently, it was up to the brave few to unearth the government's false positions, one by one. "This shall be done in the columns of the *Weekly* if the liberty of the press is not crushed beneath the hell of despotism that is raised to destroy it," Woodhull promised: "but if this be accomplished, then will the plaintiffs go from city to city, and from town to town, to whole country over . . . and sow the seeds of revolution. . . . *Stop their press they may; but their tongues, never!*"[49] Comstock swiftly responded to this challenge. He learned that Woodhull intended to deliver her suppressed Boston speech at New York's Cooper Union and, using a pseudonym, requested several copies of the exposure issue by mail. Upon receipt of the "indecent" material, he once again invoked the federal obscenity charge. Woodhull faced arrest for obscenity a second time.

Woodhull responded by staging her most dramatic act of defiance. Under subpoena for the second charge, she contrived to deliver the lecture in spite of certain arrest. She learned on January 9, 1873, that she was to be arrested before her speech; forewarned, she and her sister eluded capture and arranged for friends Laura Cuppy Smith and Anna Middlebrook to speak in her place. "But I determined to speak myself," she later wrote. She gained entrance to the hall by disguising herself as an old Quaker woman (even enlisting the aid of one of the federal marshals watching for her arrival at the door). Just as Laura Cuppy Smith was apologizing for Woodhull's absence, an eyewitness reported, the curious figure hobbled to the stage; "there, with an energy and excitement never to be forgotten, threw off her disguise, pushed her fingers through her disheveled hair with tremulous rapidity, and stood before her audience as Mrs. V. C. Woodhull." With great emotion, Woodhull addressed the crowd, according to this witness:

The applause and excitement was at its height, when, fairly hoarse with rage, and almost choking with indignation, she poured forth such a philippic against [Comstock] as to fairly alarm her friends in the audience as to her sanity. She admitted that her health, as well as her reason, was in such a state at that time as to unfit her to deliver her lecture; but, said she, "You have come to hear me, and I shall speak. I was compelled to pass through the doors surrounded by five deputy marshals with warrants in their pockets for my arrest, but I eluded them, thanks to this disguise! And as I am now here, one of the marshals [Crowly] seated at my back has kindly consented that I may go on with the lecture, but when it is delivered I must go to jail."[50]

This witness reported that her performance and arrest were very effective publicity; the New York newspapers were finally "getting restive under the petty acts committed by the blundering officials."

Woodhull's daring lecture at Cooper Union that January provided a bridge between sex radicals and liberal allies. The audience applauded her courage in defying federal authorities, listened to her impassioned speech in rapt attention, and witnessed the marshals as they approached and arrested her, and took her off to jail. Woodhull, who claimed to have anticipated her arrest, went willingly. "Of course I expected this," she later wrote, "and having said my say, with as good a grace as I could command, I surrendered to them." Her decision to lecture deliberately courted arrest to test the obscenity law, and demonstrated the extreme lengths to which her opponents would go to silence her. Her arrest, she felt, proved the government's tyranny to the public at large; it furthered her cause by raising consciousness about the sexual double standard. "I am perfectly satisfied with the results of their cunning," she said. "I hope they are also satisfied, though that they are I very much doubt."[51]

Suppression in Boston and arrest in New York following this performance only increased Woodhull's status as an icon of free speech. Woodhull won a suit against the Boston Music Hall for more than $200 in damages to cover her expenses for programs, tickets and posters, as well as rail fare and hotel charges before the cancellation. Even freethinker Horace Seaver, hitherto unsympathetic to Woodhull's exposure, now issued a more forceful defense of free speech on her behalf.

Mrs. Woodhull has been again arrested and thrown into jail in New York for lecturing. The course pursued towards this woman is either very bigoted or very foolish. It is no crime to lecture, and if she libels any one, let her be tried and punished if found guilty; but to punish her before trial is a mockery of justice. She seems to have frightened the authorities in New York, for they won't allow her to speak or publish; and just so in pious Boston, of course, for we always "follow suit" when bigotry is "trumps" though Music Hall, which silenced her, had to pay damages for so doing.[52]

Such acts, Seaver felt, only demonstrated that the Christian monopoly on public halls in Boston meant that "free speech has little or no chance of a hearing."

Other free speech advocates protested the suppression of Woodhull's lecture in Boston. Liberal Christian minister O. B. Frothingham, for one, defended Woodhull before his congregation, turning their hisses at the outset into reluctant acceptance of his free speech views. The New England Labor Reform League, under the guidance of Ezra Heywood and the organization's president, Colonel William B. Greene, "determined that free speech should be upheld in Boston," according to anarchist Benjamin Tucker. The

League leased the second largest hall in Boston, Tremont Temple, for their convention in February. When word leaked out that Woodhull was to participate, hall owners canceled the contract and were forced to pay damages to avoid a lawsuit. The League evaded Woodhull's banning by taking a number of smaller halls for their three-day convention. As Tucker remembered years later, "The authorities threatened all sorts of interference, but the Convention was held nonetheless." Woodhull not only attended but spoke "four times, including two set lectures, and the authorities were powerless to intervene." If anything, Woodhull's banning in Boston stimulated support and defiance among supporters who admired her for confronting conservative officials.[53]

Free thinkers debated the merits of the Beecher exposure through the spring of 1873. *Boston Investigator* editor Horace Seaver's ambivalence about Woodhull's action aroused F. H. Marsh of Pekin, Wisconsin Territory, to defend her as an agent of religious and social reform. "It matters not whether we agree with Mrs. Woodhull or Mr. Train," Marsh wrote that April, "they have the inalienable right of free speech and a free press, and she should be defended in them. They have violated no law against obscenity, unless the Bible comes under the law; and Christians of course will be slow to admit that, though in the light of reason and common sense the case seems against them." Seaver, however, was still concerned about the truth of the Beecher accusation, and retorted that Beecher, like everyone else, deserved protection from slander, "one of the basest and most contemptible of crimes." Marsh replied that there was no slander in this case: Beecher's protracted silence on the accusations, and his refusal to sue Woodhull, made it clear that her accusations must be true. "If she has told the truth," Marsh argued, "she has committed no slander but has done the world a valuable service in exposing the rottenness of the workings of our social system, and the need for reform."[54]

The Politics of Exposure

The Beecher exposure and Woodhull's defiant performances sheared sex radicals off from the more moderate Spiritualist movement. Spiritualist critics, represented by the *Religio-Philosophical Journal*, were predictably affronted when the Beecher story appeared in print. The paper rejoiced at the arrest of Woodhull and Claflin on federal obscenity charges, quoting a

New York reporter that "Woodhullism is fast dying out, and the signs of a healthier condition of things are evident on all sides." Given Woodhull's verbal exposure of S. S. Jones, its editor, before the AAS a few months earlier, the *Journal's* position was hardly surprising. Conservative Spiritualists used the Beecher exposure as grounds to sever all ties with Woodhull and the AAS. They called for a new mass meeting of Spiritualists because of "the failure of our present National Association to rally the masses under its banner, and of the terrible influence the Woodhull clique is exerting against the interests and opinions of true Spiritualists and their cause."[55] Opposition to Woodhull gave conservative Spiritualists new motivation to reorganize the movement.

Sex radicals saw Woodhull's "persecution" as a political opportunity, a means to achieve women's real social equality. "I glory in your martyrdom," wrote free lover Frances Rose MacKinley, "by means of which the most necessary truths must be established."[56] Sex radicals like Laura Cuppy Smith and AAS Secretary Henry T. Child, remained supportive.[57] Public discussion of the Beecher exposure, sex radicals believed, would make adulterous men as vulnerable to public scorn as their female companions. Angela Heywood used the scandal to illustrate the double standard:

Do people really mean to say that if [Beecher] does not preach what he practices, he is all right? That since Mr. B. is not some poor girl whose reputation is her all, the disclosure of every act of whose life is demanded before she can be trusted, therefore he should be exempt from criticism and exposure? A young man said "I do not think it right to pry into Mr. Beecher's private affairs, but I *should* like to know whether Mrs. Woodhull is a chaste woman; you know they say she lived with two husbands at once!" Those who tenderly fling the mantle of privacy over a reverend eloquent male sinner, in the same breath will ask of a woman, "Is she good?"[58]

Sex radicals hammered away at the notion that gender and class protected the Beechers of the world from shame. "If the crime of Woodhull and Claflin is so great," as one put it, "in publishing the social practices of evangelical and exemplary men, what must be the crime of editors, who publish the acts of the (so called) lower class of individuals?"[59] Even privately, some sex radicals supported the Beecher exposure. Leo Miller, for example, at first skeptical of Woodhull's motives, soon called her "the Joan of Arc in the great social revolution going on in our country and the world, and if few honor her now the next generation will sing hosannas in her praise."[60] For radical Spiritualists, seeking to practice their principles, the Beecher exposure gave the movement new momentum.

Women were subject to more subtle "laws" governing their behavior, sex radicals believed: only by exposing the basic hypocrisy of the sexual double standard could women be made free. The process of exposing this double standard in turn revealed hidden forces, from government officials willing to bend the law to protect revered citizens to newspaper editors eager to condemn her exposure while disguising or downplaying the actions of men. Woodhull believed that powerful men allied against her out of fear that her revolution was gaining ground. "Who is it, then, that tremble when it is proposed to drag these things to the light of God's sunshine so that they may become purified?" Woodhull demanded.

It is the old hoary-headed sensualist, who by his ten years of prostitution has become thoroughly demoralized, and who requires the active stimulus of youth, beauty and purity to rouse his passions. . . . It is your legislators who . . . reduce themselves to the level of brutes, to beat the life out of women, and who support handsome mistresses in splendid style at "*fashionable boarding-houses*." It is your police officials, whose mistresses are the keepers of houses of prostitution, and who share the profits arising from woman's degradation. It is your editors of powerful journals, who, nightly returning from their "rounds of exercise," write pattern articles on morality, and denounce woman agitators as they who would uproot the foundations of society. It is these classes, whom the people have entrusted with the functions of government and who wield the machinery of public opinion, who stand in danger from agitation from the social question.[61]

Until such organized and actively sanctioned hypocrisy as this could be eradicated, she reasoned, women had little chance of achieving real equality.

By June 1873, Woodhull faced two trials: federal prosecution for obscenity under the 1872 postal law and a private libel suit filed by Luther Challis. Both trials concerned language relating to the Challis exposure, which contained the most explicit sexual reference. As the trials approached, she once again provoked government censors by reprinting the entire Beecher story alone (leaving out all other revelations) in the May 17, 1873, issue of the *Weekly*. New indictments quickly followed this action. Woodhull pretended to be mystified by the indictments, as the government had long since abandoned the claim that the Beecher story in itself was "obscene." She was predictably defiant:

We say, bring them on, gentlemen. If five [indictments] are not enough make it seven or ten, or twenty; only suit yourselves, and the better you are suited now, the worse you will be pleased when the fight is ended.[62]

Her intransigence would, she hoped, force the government to demonstrate its own tyranny to the public at large.

Woodhull's martyrdom appeared to be realized on the evening of June 6, 1873, when she collapsed and was presumed dead. Through the day, she had struggled to shore up her legal defense, appealing to newspapers to support her request for a postponement and give her lawyers more time to prepare their evidence. The effort, Tennie C. Claflin reported to the *New York Sun*, had apparently brought on some kind of heart failure. Their struggle to retain legal representation and sufficient bond money to meet perpetual arrest had probably added to the burden, Claflin said. Supporters heard the news with dismay; anarchist Benjamin Tucker, who was at that time slightly acquainted with Woodhull, recalled reading the news "with deepest grief and consternation, mourning less the loss of a friend than the loss of a leader." Cynics reacted to the news with skepticism, calling it a theatrical stunt to win the delay denied by the courts. Authentic or not, the incident proved useful; on recovery she gained a two-week delay for the federal obscenity suit and a postponement of the Challis libel suit until the fall. She also gained some sympathy from unlikely allies. *Pomeroy's Democrat*, long critical of Woodhull, blamed the collapse on her persecution by "incompetent courts." The *Pittsburgh Leader*, still scathing in its indictment of Woodhull's moral character, nevertheless applauded her for training a new scrutiny upon social corruption. "Will the Great Scandal she has raised die with the Woodhull? We neither believe nor hope that it will. The truth is that this scandal has got out of the Woodhull's hands and is now the concern of the church and the nation."[63] Even those who condemned the woman saw the scandal as a way to criticize the abuses of power by the ruling elite.

Consequences of Exposure

When the federal obscenity trial finally came to court at the end of June, it proved disappointing as a test of the 1872 postal code's control over obscenity. Woodhull's and Claflin's legal team came to court prepared to challenge the legal definition of obscenity. The charge was now limited to the single sentence in the Challis exposure—Claflin's accusation that Challis, "to prove that he had *seduced a maiden, carried for days on his finger, exhibiting in triumph, the red trophy of her virginity*." As Train had done, Woodhull's lawyers tested the boundaries of obscenity law. To do so, they produced for comparison an "obscene" excerpt from the Old Testament: "the token of the damsel's virginity." However, the defense prudently presented a backup plan. On the advice of Representative Benjamin Butler, they pointed out that, as written, the 1872 postal code under which the sisters had been arrested applied only to books and printed matter, not to newspapers.[64] When this information came before the court, the judge on this narrow legal ground ordered the jury to rule that the prosecution could not be maintained. On June 27, 1873, the jury found Woodhull and Claflin not guilty on obscenity charges. For free lovers and libertarians alike, it was a Pyrrhic victory, for the definition of obscenity went untested. More important, that March Comstock had successfully secured the passage of a much stronger federal obscenity law, which included newspapers, and he assumed unprecedented federal censorship powers.[65]

Even for sex radicals, exposure and free speech were dangerous organizing principles. If they united supporters, they also inspired the most devastating critique of Woodhull. Joseph Treat, veteran of Ohio's free love community, Berlin Heights, and prior contributor to *Woodhull & Claflin's Weekly*, accused Woodhull herself of hypocrisy. He claimed that Woodhull had prostituted herself and her sisters, particularly Utica Brooker, in times of financial hardship. Treat first made his accusations in a series of letters to sex radical friends in the summer of 1873, and later published them in the pamphlet *Beecher, Tilton, Woodhull, the Creation of Society*. "I have issued this Pamphlet in good faith and kindness to all, with a charity as broad to every one as that I bear myself," Treat insisted. "There is going to be Free Speech in this city of New York. Any attempt to prevent [my exposure], will be already more than Free Speech—will be *Confession*." Woodhull was so troubled by these accusations that when Brooker died of Bright's disease, in July 1873, Woodhull published an autopsy report she claimed proved her sister to have been sexually pure.[66] Treat, like Woodhull, invoked moral principle to justify his accusations; he said he only wanted her to follow her own new standard of sexual openness.

Treat's exposure of Woodhull demonstrated the dangers of principled exposure for its practitioners. The truth of his claims about Woodhull remains mysterious; even sex radicals disagreed on the question. Ezra Heywood and Benjamin Tucker dismissed Treat's exposure of Woodhull as willful falsehood; others defended Treat as a truthful man. The commercial press, always ready to question Woodhull's morality, now depicted her as a woman who advocated harlotry. Many of her new supporters faded from view; her critics became even more vocal in denouncing her.[67] Treat's "exposure" forced Woodhull to defend her reputation while affirming the principle of sexual openness: a difficult task. Gossip circulated that September at the annual Spiritualist camp meeting in Silver Lake, Massachusetts. Woodhull, according to one critic, had great difficulty controlling her anger at the new setback when she addressed her fellow Spiritualists. He described her display of "ugly temper" as being like "some fierce roar of a crazy dragon on the high seas." Her "indelicate expressions" and her revelation of "disgusting details" were so obnoxious, he claimed, that "Young men went away from her harangue with blushing faces."[68]

She confronted the accusation more moderately before the annual convention of the AAS in Chicago in September of 1873, on the first anniversary of her exposure of Beecher. Her critics now felt they had sufficient grounds to oust her from the organization. When one delegate stood and demanded whether the accusations were true, Woodhull denied him the right, as a man, to question her virtue. She rejected the sexual double standard that made prostitutes seem vile while their customers retained respect: unlike men who visited prostitutes, Woodhull argued, "I never had sexual intercourse with any man of whom I am ashamed to stand side by side before the world." She alluded to her financial ruin following arrest and imprisonment. "I knew my paper had to live or I should assuredly be sent to Sing Sing," she told the audience. Consequently, "I went to your bankers, presidents of railroads, gamblers, prostitutes, and got the money that has sent you the paper you have been reading, and I do not think you are the worse for handling it." But she unequivocally refused to address the details of the accusation, instead defending on principle her right to make her own sexual choices, just as a man would. With characteristic bravado, she turned the accusations into principles: "if I want sexual intercourse with one hundred men I shall have it," she declared, with typical audacity. As she saw it, "this sexual intercourse business may as well be discussed now, and discussed until you are so familiar with your sexual organs that a reference to them will no longer make the blush mount to your face any more than a reference to any other part of your body."[69]

Sex radicals, who wanted to complete the trajectory toward sexual openness, once again rallied around Woodhull, and used the new furor over her personal life to decry the growing conservatism of her Spiritualist critics. "We could organize and work together with Catholics, Methodists, Universalists just as well," one disgruntled sex radical put it in the uproar prior to the convention, "Our freedom and efforts would be no less restricted."[70] In a letter read to delegates on the convention floor, radical Spiritualist J. W. Evarts urged those attending to resist the growing trend toward orthodoxy and respectability. "When Spiritualism was more an object of persecution than it is now," Evarts wrote, "and less "respectable," it was braver than it is now, and could defiantly accept the charge of free love and define it as pure love."[71] To demonstrate their solidarity with Woodhull, radical delegates renamed themselves the Universal Association of Spiritualists (UAS), and elected her as president over the vocal protests of several more conservative Spiritualists on the floor.[72] At its first meeting, the Primary Council of the UAS, calling themselves martyrs, made a compact to defy orthodoxy in any form, regardless of personal cost.[73] Over the succeeding decades, Comstock worked hard to ensure that their defiance would be costly indeed.

The truth of Woodhull's allegations against Beecher, like Treat's allegations against Woodhull, will never be known. Woodhull's two sources of information, Elizabeth Cady Stanton and Paulina Wright Davis, eventually insisted that the accusations were accurate. Likewise, Beecher's half-siblings, Thomas Beecher and Isabella Beecher Hooker, privately agreed on his guilt.[74] Beecher eventually denied the story in June 1873, but by then it had already taken on a life of its own.[75] At the same time, powerful financial interests protected Beecher within his own circle. As pastor of the Plymouth Church, editor of the *Christian Union*, and future author of *The Life of Christ* (for which he had already secured a $20,000 advance), Beecher's reputation was too commercially valuable to sacrifice. His personal influence probably diminished somewhat as a consequence of the exposure, but he nevertheless retained a loyal congregation, and enormous audiences on the lecture tour. By contrast, Elizabeth Tilton endured a solitary life, ostracized from society, while Theodore Tilton died overseas, a broken man. The fallout from the Beecher exposure is most significant in its impact on contemporary audiences and its contribution to the renegotiation of power in the waning years of Reconstruction.

Comstock's pursuit of Woodhull and her associates was part of his religious quest to restore "decency" to the public realm. To Comstock this meant guarding the young against any open expression of sexuality, which he called "licentiousness." He was not out to defend Beecher, he insisted— he claimed to have "acted entirely independent of any and all persons" in the case. His main goal, as he saw it, was "*to vindicate the laws* and protect the young of our land from the leprosy of this vile trash."[76] Comstock was not an aberration. He was at the vanguard of a new movement to regulate the public discussion of ideas, whose supporters advocated introducing Christian religious principles into the Constitution.[77] Sex radicals complained that his questionable methods, including trickery and a misuse of personal influence, denied his targets due process rights and remuneration for destroyed or confiscated property. However, many who worried about the consequences of unlimited freedom, epitomized by Woodhull, tolerated Comstock's repressive measures as necessary to protect public morality.[78]

The conflict over the Beecher exposure became a watershed in the history of sex radicalism and free speech. In publishing the story, Woodhull threw down the gauntlet of free love, and Comstock immediately seized the opportunity to do battle with the sex radicals' vocal critique of marriage. His mission was to undo the gains of the sex radicals and their quest for the single sexual standard and, incidentally, to contain the promise of radical individualism and universal rights. His campaign against Woodhull marked the beginning of a campaign against free lovers, and specifically their desire to liberate women from "social hypocrisy." Comstock proved a determined foe against the public discussion of women's sexual rights, even her right to refuse sex in marriage.[79] Women's liberation, either within or outside of the private sphere, he believed, eroded the fabric of social life.

Capitalizing on the outrage over the Beecher exposure, Comstock managed to push through a stronger federal obscenity statute, called the Comstock Law, and became its chief enforcer. Empowered by March 1873 to regulate federal mail, he assumed control over the public expression of controversial points of view. He disregarded the free lovers' faith that individual conscience could regulate human sexuality. Instead, Comstock used his new legal power to strengthen the institution of marriage by silencing its public critics. Ezra and Angela Heywood, Leo Miller, Moses Hull, Benjamin Tucker and Lois Waisbrooker were just a few who tried, for the remainder of the century, to loosen his stranglehold on public debate over sexuality. His censorship powers made the notion of sexual openness both costly and dangerous for decades to come.

Woodhull's creation of the Beecher scandal forced sex radicals to shift both strategy and ideology. It was the beginning of the end of a period of thoughtful debate about the politics of marriage as an institution. Reasonable arguments for sex education and women's nuptial rights became lost in the prosecution of indecent or obscene publications: sex radicals retreated from extreme demands for marriage reform and instead fought for the right to talk about it at all. It was a subtle difference, one that silenced vigorous dialogue on the married state. Social liberals spent more than a century defending speech of any kind, regardless of content. The Comstock Laws left them little alternative.[80]

To evade the new stranglehold over sexuality discourse, Woodhull took to the road, bringing her controversial ideas directly to the public. Beginning with the fall 1873 lecture season, she traveled the countryside, forcing local communities to confront her sexual revolution.

Chapter 4

"Queen of the Rostrum"

In early February 1876, the citizens of Atlanta, Georgia, braced themselves for the arrival of "the celebrated woman agitator of social theories," Victoria Woodhull. Life-size woodcut portraits of Woodhull appeared throughout the city, and advertisements for her upcoming lecture, "The Human Body, Temple of God," filled the pages of the Democratic *Atlanta Constitution*. There was some doubt that authorities would permit her to speak, and the announcement that her lecture would go forward prompted calls for a boycott, on the grounds that "it would not do to encourage her." Many Atlanta citizens disagreed; they decided "to go and hear exactly how terrible were the doctrines which had lifted this woman to such prominence and brought upon herself and her sister such an avalanche of abuse and vituperation, [and] which consigned them to a prison cell." A respectable audience turned out to hear her and by all reports was pleasantly surprised. Far from the coarse display and raucous crowd they expected, listeners found a competent lecturer of "commanding presence," dressed in modest elegance. Holding a copy of the Bible in her hand, the speaker waxed eloquent on the sacred duty of mothers to educate their young about their bodies. The politicians and professional men who attended greeted the lecture with enthusiastic applause; at its close, they invited her to deliver a second lecture on another night. The *Constitution* reporter had reservations about the delicacy of the subject matter, but praise for the speaker. "She is a woman of great ability," he said, "and states her views with singular clearness and force."[1]

Between 1873 and 1876, as this episode suggests, one-time pariah Victoria Woodhull grew increasingly popular, and finally achieved national renown as a commercial lecturer in large cities and one-horse towns throughout the country. During these years she lectured to a cumulative audience approaching half a million people, traveling through the west to California in 1874 and southwest to Georgia, Louisiana, and Texas in 1876.[2] By then, ecstatic audiences applauded her lectures in town after town. As Reconstruction waned, Woodhull capitalized upon her notoriety from the Beecher exposure to promote her sexual revolution, and, not incidentally, earn a substantial income. As a performer, as a woman, and as a political activist, Woodhull was central to the period's complicated sexual politics. Simply by attending, her audiences expressed sympathy for her persecution under federal law, and resisted the moral authoritarianism feeding personal, local, state, and national opposition to her lectures. The market pressures that went with her new celebrity status gradually subdued Woodhull's radical politics, however. Even as she criticized Beecher's sexual hypocrisy, she retreated from the principle of complete sexual liberty, apparently an adaptation to the shifting sexual politics in Reconstruction. Her success in hawking the Beecher story on a national stage was indicative of Reconstruction's declining radicalism, and foreshadowed the emergence of a new political era.[3]

Woodhull's reputation as an agent of extreme sexual politics gave her a competitive edge over other lecturers: a woman talking in public about "social freedom" was something of a novelty act. She was also infamous as the editor of *Woodhull & Claflin's Weekly*, which had become a national forum for the "social freedom" debate. With her husband Colonel Blood at its helm, the *Weekly* welcomed controversial views under the unifying principles of open debate and the single sexual standard. The paper highlighted Woodhull's legal struggles, and pushed the boundaries of free speech, repeatedly testing the right to discuss taboo subjects in public print. As Woodhull toured the country, sex radicals in the *Weekly* promoted teaching girls about sexual matters as a way to prevent their seduction, showcased new works on sexual hygiene, and published recommendations for sex education in schools. The *Weekly* reported experiments in nonmarital alliances, such as Moses Hull's public declaration that he had, with his wife's consent and understanding, committed adultery with Spiritualist Mattie Sawyer.[4] Extreme sex radicals applauded these revelations, while moderates dropped their subscriptions.[5] Audiences attuned to these controversies flocked to hear Woodhull's lectures, which many apparently imagined would be titillating spectacles.

Apart from the controversial subject matter, notoriety and scandal enhanced Woodhull's commercial success. Shrewd marketing of her trials made Woodhull a lucrative addition to many local entertainment rosters.[6] She benefited from new trends in public speaking after the Civil War. The public lecture, once a forum for intellectual enlightenment, had gradually shifted into a venue for popular entertainment. Woodhull was one of a growing number of itinerant commercial lecturers who, after the war, appeared in the opera house rather than in the local lyceum or library hall. The new commercial lecturers, in other words, were performers who entertained more than they educated, shaping popular opinion in increasingly packaged spectacles. At one level, Woodhull appealed to audiences because she satisfied what one contemporary critic called "the popular desire to see notorious or famous people."[7] Her lectures gave post-Civil War audiences a chance to see for themselves just how bad the notorious Woodhull really was.

Woodhull capitalized on her own notoriety, but not without bowing to the demands of the audience. She joined a competitive field of lecturers that included other forceful women like former abolitionist Anna Dickinson and popular educator Kate Field. Women's success in this new marketplace of ideas was undergoing a subtle shift in the early 1870s. Suffragists such as Elizabeth Cady Stanton, Susan B. Anthony, and Lucy Stone had been in high demand immediately following the war, but renewed opposition to women speakers gradually replaced the earlier postwar tolerance. By 1872, none of the suffrage lecturers could command an audience that compared to Woodhull's. Like other women in the new commercial climate, Woodhull was careful not to offend her audience and took pains to appear attractive and feminine. She deliberately contrasted her ladylike manner on stage against her audiences' expectations and proved to be an increasingly resourceful player in what Abigail Solomon-Godeau calls (in another context) "the libidinal economy of commodity culture."[8] Within the strictures of the popular lecture, Woodhull's performance became a sexualized commodity in high demand.

In 1873, Woodhull was also a political spectacle; she epitomized her own anti-authoritarian critique. In spite of her activism in social movements from suffrage to civil rights, Woodhull now embodied a critique of the Republican administration under Grant, and participated in the shifting political mood of the period. Her exposure of Beecher, initially a powerful rejection of the sexual double standard, was just another coffin nail for the Radical Republican agenda for social change. The public humiliation of a man like Beecher, whose political commitment to reform was matched only by his phenomenal popularity and commercial success, encapsulated Woodhull's critique of church and state. Like Brigham Young's nineteenth wife, whose popular lectures about her defection from the Mormon Church helped shame the (Mormon-dominated) Republican Party in Utah, Woodhull profited from a sexualized political scandal.[9] In attending Woodhull's lectures and discussing them afterward, audiences could participate in the humbling of the Republican Party and contribute to the Party's weakening unity and national power. Woodhull's message was nonpartisan, however; she attacked the Democrats with equal fervor, and instead promoted greater individual freedom based on conscience. Woodhull had long endeavored, through a series of spectacles—the free love speech at Steinway Hall, the march of the Communards, the Equal Rights Party nomination—to seize the reins of Reconstruction cultural politics. But it was in exposing Beecher that she left her greatest imprint on the period. The Beecher/Tilton scandal became the media event of the century, and Woodhull's performances were the closest that many remote audiences could come to the national scandal. Woodhull incited popular enthusiasm for the scandal and kept the matter alive in the public mind by giving it an irresistible populist spin.

The Woodhull Lecturing "Machine"

"We can work up the audience, get the people together," wrote Woodhull's husband, Colonel Blood, in 1874, "but it needs her to finish the work. I am afraid it would be an up-hill business to attempt to run the machine without her."[10] Blood, Tennie C. Claflin, Woodhull's daughter Zula Maud, and her mother Roxanna Claflin, all played a role in the traveling Woodhull show from 1873 to 1876. The family's long history in self-promotion and intimate knowledge of the byways of the midwestern states and territories prepared them well for the lecturing marketplace of the 1870s. Before the Civil War, Woodhull's parents had promoted fourteen-year-old Tennessee as a child clairvoyant and operated a traveling family medicine show. Immediately after the war, Woodhull and Blood had ventured forth (under assumed names) in a covered wagon, peddling their own clairvoyance act throughout the northwest. These experiments in showmanship proved a great asset to Woodhull's performances in the Reconstruction-era incarnation.[11] Blood and Claflin were skilled managers for Woodhull's tours, arranging transportation, hotels, advertising, publicity, tickets, and hall rentals before Woodhull's arrival. The irrepressible Claflin was particularly effective as her sister's "advance agent": she was "a one day's wonder to many eager masculine eyes," according to one Dubuque, Iowa, reporter. As a Salt Lake City, Utah, editor put it, Claflin's early arrival "created more of a sensation than the entrance of a first class circus would have done."[12] Woodhull reinforced the circus-like atmosphere on her arrival, granting interviews to local reporters, entertaining old friends and curious new converts at the hotel, and, by 1875, showcasing her sister and daughter as warm-up acts and ticket sellers.

Most of the information about these lectures was preserved in the pages of *Woodhull & Claflin's Weekly*, which proved to be a major asset to the Woodhull show. Careful confirmation and analysis of the clippings published in the paper, compared to less favorable reviews from alternative papers in the same towns, reveals that Woodhull's lectures were significant events that grew increasingly popular between 1873 and 1876. And great care is needed, for Woodhull and her friends developed clever strategies to work the press to their advantage. Perhaps their most effective method was to publish digests of positive press reviews in the *Weekly*; this amplified her themes of political persecution and sexual revolution, and was instrumental to her success in the field. Her lecturing fees kept the paper, never financially self-sufficient, in print; lecture events gave her the chance to distribute (and even sell) the *Weekly* and its message to captive audiences.[13] Press testimonials to Woodhull and her message filled the pages of the paper and inflated her impact on disparate communities throughout the country. They spread advance publicity of Woodhull's upcoming destinations and availability to remote subscribers, and at the same time reassured *Weekly* readers of her reception in other locations. These clippings, as the *Weekly* put it late in 1873, allowed readers to "acquire some adequate idea of the revolution that is sweeping over the Western country." They were particularly effective as advertisements, because they were partial; the prominence of positive reviews overwhelmed those that were less favorable. They also left an imprint in the local press, as their wording gradually filtered into the local reviews.[14]

The abundance of positive clippings was particularly effective in hiding unsuccessful tours from view. A Massachusetts tour planned late in 1873, for example, went poorly, as a result of concerted opposition from local authorities. Anarchist Benjamin Tucker, then nineteen, acted as Woodhull's agent for that tour, at Blood's request. When he arrived in Salem, Massachusetts, he found that the hall owners had decided to close the hall under pressure from civic authorities; only after he returned with page proofs of the proposed lecture—on "Finance"—did he convince the mayor to let ticket sales begin. The delay in advertising proved disastrous, and few tickets were sold; Woodhull decided to abandon the tour. The failure of this short tour may have been the result of location, as her popularity was far greater away from the northeastern establishment. Her emphasis on radical opposition to authority and her class consciousness—the "Lower Million" versus the "Upper Ten"—evident in a show bill from another unsuccessful lecture in Worcester, Massachusetts (Figure 31), found more eager listeners

A Free Press and Free Speech.

VICTORIA C. WOODHULL

WILL SPEAK IN

MECHANICS' HALL,

Monday Evening, Nov. 3, 1873,

At 7½ o'clock. Doors open at 6½.

Reserved Seats secured at Holland's Book and News Stand, 3 Post Office Block.

SUBJECT:—"Behind the Scenes: or, the Relation of Politics to the Industrial and Social Questions."

She will show that all the frauds, corruption and crimes in politics, finance and commerce, from which the country is now suffering, are the legitimate fruits of our system of government, which has been mistaken as republican; and also wherein this country is not a republic. In other words, the lecture will be an impeachment of the government, as the revolt of the early patriots was an impeachment of the English Throne.

Mrs. Woodhull, by her recent efforts, during four days before the National Convention of Spiritualists at Chicago, which elected her President for the third term, wrung from the press of that city the following:

"Victoria Woodhull has risen from nothing to a position on the forum where she stands without a peer. Her intellectual position and vigor are no longer a question of doubt ; in this respect she is above discussion."—*The Chicago Times, Sept. 18, 1873.*

"The lecture in the evening was a really eloquent and exhaustive discussion by Mrs. Woodhull. However her ideas may be regarded, there is no doubt but that she is one of the most active, energetic, able and eloquent speakers that ever appeared in this city."—*The Chicago Tribune, Sept. 19, 1873.*

Admission, - - - - 50 Cents.

"The Lower Million," vs. "The Upper Ten."

(OVER.

The acknowledged Queen of the American Rostrum.

Gag-Law finds No Favor in the United States.

Figure 31. This show bill, from a lecture in Worcester, Massachusetts in November 1873, illustrates some of the early strategies Woodhull used to market her lectures. The populist theme invites an audience to hear stories of church, state, and business abuses. Favorable newspaper clippings reassure readers about Woodhull's speaking ability and the tone and content of the lecture. Woodhull adopts the title "Queen of the American Rostrum." Worcester Broadside. Courtesy of the American Antiquarian Society.

in the midwest than the northeast. She promised her small Worcester audience that she would return and deliver her "social freedom" lecture on another occasion to a much larger crowd, as she had done many times in western cities. Such early failures in 1873 (not highlighted in the *Weekly*) make her later successes more remarkable. Notoriety alone, which she had in abundance in 1873, was not enough to fill houses in some locations; only over time did Woodhull, Claflin, and Blood perfect a highly successful marketing technique.[15]

One effective strategy, evident in her comments in Worcester, was to soften local prejudices by delivering two lectures when possible. Unlike entertainers, who stayed in town long enough to build up a following, the itinerant lecturer relied on reputation and publicity to draw an audience. As journalist and lyceum regular Kate Field put it in 1873, "the lecturer is a creature of mushroom growth, coming up in a night and disappearing the next morning. His career is a constant series of first appearances."[16] Woodhull's primary subject matter made it difficult to secure such first appearances, so she disarmed her critics with a neutral first lecture. These warm-up lectures, which typically focused on finance or politics, demonstrated the breadth of her knowledge while dispelling fears that the speaker was too vulgar for respectable audiences. Once local journalists gave the green light to their readers, she could then advertise more controversial material—topics like marriage reform, prostitution, and sex education— but only on the second night.

Woodhull also anticipated her opposition by crafting a nonthreatening stage persona. Like other female lecturers during the 1870s, she took care to present herself on the stage as "ladylike," a self-presentation that intentionally confounded audience expectations. One small town paper commented, for example, that "most remarkable was the seeming disappointment of everybody that she appeared and acted for all the world like a woman—and a very pretty, lady-like woman at that." Many papers expressed similar surprise. Early in 1874, her failure to shock her audiences with crudeness or vulgarity was news in itself. This comment from the *Daily Times* of Leavenworth, Kansas, is typical: "Those who expected to be shocked were egregiously disappointed." Her reputation served her well, as the "unenviable newspaper notoriety" she enjoyed brought her an audience and then allowed her to use their negative expectations as part of her message. Another Leavenworth reporter had expected "a brawling bawd—newspaper accounts had led us to picture her as such—. . . [But] we found instead an accomplished and lady-like woman." The expectation of such prejudice became a powerful prop: her solitary appearance on stage in many cities, without introduction or male protection from hecklers, enlisted more sympathy than scorn and sometimes elicited a spontaneous burst of applause.[17] Woodhull walked a fine line between her reputation and her behavior, because she understood that there were limitations to her self-presentation if she wanted to be a commercial success. She had to be shocking enough to attract the curious, but tame enough not to offend the critical.

Under the guise of this ladylike manner, Woodhull mesmerized her listeners with her passionate delivery and blunt presentation of unvarnished ideas. In 1874, Woodhull impressed one reporter in St. Paul, Minnesota, because she spoke with "considerable fierceness, and with a degree of elocution that indicates no small amount of study and labor. As a speaker she irresistibly attracts attention, both on account of the matter and the manner, and one listens continually, wondering what will come next." The lecture itself, "Tried as by Fire; or the True and the False Socially," refined her earlier principles of social freedom in stark terms. Women sold into marriage for a home and a living endured unwanted sexual relations with their husbands, said Woodhull: such marital rapes could only produce degenerate offspring. Woodhull's passion on this subject drew notice. Anticipation of her unorthodox statements may explain why so many audiences found her stage presence "magnetic." She exhibited a fascinating combination of a fine voice and fiery passion. As a Kansas reporter put it, "when she paces the platform and stamps out her terrific sentences, the audience are electrified up to the highest pitch." One rural Massachusetts reporter called her stage manner "electrifying, sometimes astounding, now soaring to lofty oratorical heights, then gracefully descending to plain unvarnished facts, sending a thrill of conviction home to the minds of listeners." The audience expected nothing less, as evident in a comment overheard by a San Francisco reporter: "They do say as how she's lightnin' when she really do get warmed up."[18]

Skillful marketing tactics were necessary because in many towns Woodhull's lectures generated stiff opposition. Anticipating this, Woodhull and her friends used local newspapers to their advantage before she arrived. Her advertisements often generated resistance in local papers, perhaps deliberately, as much as eight to ten days before the lecture itself. In Council Bluffs, Iowa, for example, Woodhull or her agents scattered several provocative notices of the upcoming event throughout the columns of the *Nonpareil*, which appealed to the humor and daring of the local inhabitants. "The Woodhull pleased the bad boys and shocked the modest men, and oh how the women did scold!—at Kansas City," read one brief notice. "She has received, probably, more merciless criticism than any other person in America, but no one has denied her great eloquence, earnestness, and sincerity," read another advertisement. "Of course, everybody here will want to see and hear for themselves, and so we may look for an extraordinary jam at Dohany Hall on the 15th." One opponent, calling herself "A Mother," responded to these advertisements with alarm; she complained that the *Nonpareil* gave so much advance publicity to a woman who "cloaks her evil designs with a . . . respectable covering." According to this writer, Woodhull's "utter disregard of all the decencies of language is becoming a little disgusting, even to the multitude whose prurient curiosity leads them to listen to her." Such sentiments, far from dissuading a large crowd from attending, may have increased interest in the performance. In St. Paul, Woodhull countered demands in the local paper for a boycott with a vigorous letter of defense, then lectured on two successive nights to enormous crowds.[19] In such incidents, Woodhull adroitly turned the advance opposition into material, even before she mounted the stage.

Opposition to the lecture, including arrests and other attempts to silence Woodhull, increased her popularity, particularly in the midwest, and made her a sensational act in her own right. When she was arrested in Jackson, Michigan, for "corrupting" one audience member with her speech, for example, she sold more than three hundred printed copies of the speech and later spoke in the same town on the "social question" before an enormous audience. In Ann Arbor, Michigan, Woodhull gained a great deal of public sympathy when "the roughs of the University"—what one reporter described as "a lot of blackguards in good clothes"—heckled her into silence. "What consummate fools some of the opponents of Victoria Woodhull make themselves," the *Saturday Morning Journal* of Port Huron, Michigan, commented after this incident. Regardless of her views on the social question, the paper argued, "we do think that such conduct on the part of her opposers is outrageous." Similarly, in Bloomington, Indiana, when hall owner and U.S. Supreme Court Justice David Davis canceled Woodhull's lecture, the result was greater interest among Bloomington residents, to whom she subsequently delivered two very successful lectures. Censoring Woodhull only made her more interesting as a public spectacle.[20]

Local opposition to the spectacle was, in fact, an important part of the attraction to the Woodhull show, as she understood very well. Her arrest in Jackson could not have been better calculated to promote her message of openness. Even Horace Seaver, the free speech editor of the *Boston Investigator* who disapproved of Woodhull's critique of marriage and her negative tone, saw the publicity value of such episodes. Seaver wrote that she "has, of course, been well advertised, and will continue to prosper as long as a set of jackasses in different parts of the country make it a point to prosecute her." Woodhull even warned her audiences of the danger involved in trying to stop her message. One St. Paul, Minnesota, reporter quoted her as saying, "You may say that all this is vulgarity. If it is, it is not the less fact. You cannot put me down with vulgarity and blackguardism. If you want to put me down you must prove that I have not told the truth, otherwise *you will only fill my houses*."[21]

Controversy brought her full houses and thus financial success. This was true even before the 1873–74 season. In 1872, she delivered her free love lecture to northeast audiences ranging from 2,500 to 4,000. Her "Impending Revolution" lecture in March 1872, she claimed, had attracted an audience of 8,200, with an additional 10,000 denied admittance. Crowds flocked to her lectures in 1873 as well. In Detroit, for example, Woodhull secured an "immense" audience. "Hundreds were unable to gain admittance," reported one reviewer. "Every inch of sitting and standing room was occupied," said another. Overflowing houses were reported in such disparate places as in Grand Rapids, Michigan, St. Paul, Minnesota, and Salt Lake City, Utah.[22] Her celebrity, and thus her ability to attract an audience, outstripped those of far more respectable speakers. Compare her audience in St. Joseph, Missouri, for example, to that of the Honorable Thomas Finch, member of Congress from Nevada, who lectured just before and just after Woodhull: her audience of 500 outstripped his (50) by a factor of ten. Because she was "the last sensation" (latest sensation, in modern terms), one journalist rather cynically noted, even those who condemned her would come to hear her speak.[23] The surprisingly large houses were a tribute to her notoriety and her reputation as an exciting and novel speaker.

Her commercial power, evident in her ability to draw a crowd, allowed her to command a substantial lecturing fee. She earned from $100 to $300 per night (depending on the venue), which put her near the most celebrated "stars." By comparison, Queen of the Lyceum Anna Dickinson took in from $150 and $400 per night and boasted an annual income of $20,000 before she lost her audience in 1872. Political cartoonist Thomas Nast, a more respectable public man but nationally known for his innovative drawings, earned twice as much, pulling in $40,000 in seven months in 1873–74.[24] Woodhull could not at first surpass Nast, but she augmented her substantial lecturing income with the sale of printed lectures and other materials. Publicity photos of Woodhull and Claflin, showing them in the unconventional attire of social radicals, sold well all over the country (Figures 32–33). People attended and praised her lectures in spite of misgivings about her message. Woodhull was "the peer of any female lecturer on the rostrum, with more power and magnetism even than Anna Dickinson," according to one Nebraska paper.[25] By late 1873, Woodhull had adopted (and inflated) Dickinson's title and advertised herself the Queen of the American Rostrum.[26]

Woodhull was famous but still disreputable; her notoriety in this early phase of her lecturing career made it difficult for some to attend. "We know that many men and women were deterred from attending last evening lest she should say something which they would blush to hear," the *St. Joseph Herald* reported, a speculation entertained by reporters in many other towns.[27] The *Davenport Daily Democrat* reported, with approval, a "large, highly respectable and enthusiastic" audience as a sign of the town's open-mindedness. "We do not endorse Mrs. Woodhull's statements nor accept her theories, but we do say that she is a fearless earnest woman," said the Davenport reporter. "Let us have free speech on every subject and there is

Figures 32 and 33. Woodhull (left), and Claflin sold many pictures of themselves through *Woodhull & Claflin's Weekly* and to audiences at their lectures. Many versions have been recovered in archives, but these show both sisters sporting the costume of the "short haired woman." Their men's jackets and short hair testify to their radical politics. Emanie (Nahm) Sachs Arling Philips Collection. Manuscripts, Kentucky Building, Western Kentucky University, Bowling Green, Kentucky.

no doubt but the world will be better for it."[28] Gradually, the increasing respectability of her audiences became Woodhull's best advertisement, and ensured the lectures' commercial success. "The most refined people of the country have listened to Mrs. Woodhull's lectures," the *Port Huron Commercial* said in a review that Woodhull subsequently used as advertising in other towns. "We hope our people will not be found lacking in the spirit which prompts men and women to hear before they pass judgment."[29]

Her audiences were quite mixed. Few reporters commented on the racial breakdown of the audience, but there is some evidence that she drew a cross section of local citizenry to hear her speak. For example, a reporter in Council Bluffs, Iowa, noted with some surprise that "Jew and Gentile, believer and unbeliever, rich and poor, high and low, white and black—all were there." Listeners also represented a broad spectrum of social types, from professional men to prostitutes, according to one St. Paul reporter. "Ex-Governors and grave-looking Senators stalking in, mixed with a positive infusion of the demi-monde, and church dignitaries elbowed their way past the habitués of Eighth and Nash-street brothels."[30] These diverse crowds suggest that respectable white women feared to be found among what might be considered at the time a disreputable company.

Woodhull was well aware that men found it easier than women to attend her lectures in opposition to social critics.[31] Religious figures often explicitly warned women not to attend. For example, one Iowa minister called Woodhull a "hag of hell" and condemned all women from Des Moines who attended her lecture as "lost to all decency and purity."[32] Women, speculated one reporter, demonstrated "aversion" to Woodhull's doctrines, while men "exhibited an unaccountable desire to attend, for the purpose, as stated by many of them, of 'seeing what Mrs. Woodhull had to say, and how she looked.'"[33] When moral scruples kept audiences away, Woodhull incorporated this fact into her performance, and cleverly used it as material. She drew attention to the absence of women in an audience in Springfield, Illinois:

The question was often asked of women, "Are you going to hear Mrs. Woodhull tonight?" (The affectation of prim, half horror-stricken prudery with which this was brought out brought down the house). If this is not a fit place for women to come, it is not a fit place for men to come, [and] every wife should say to her husband, "wherever you go I will go."[34]

It was a clever device that used humor and sarcasm to shame her male listeners into rethinking notions of "proper" female behavior. Opposition to

Woodhull's lectures because she was not respectable dovetailed nicely with her radical sexual politics.

Woodhull's 1873–74 lecture tour, in this sense, accomplished its goal of taking her sexual revolution to the people. Her lectures that season drew an audience and affected many of her listeners, often in spite of a strong prejudice against the speaker. Papers that criticized her lectures as "revolting" or as "senseless drivel," nevertheless noted that her delivery was "entrancing" enough to stimulate enthusiastic and repeated rounds of applause. Most conceded that there was some merit in her lectures. As the *Decatur Republican* put it, "she told many plain truths in a forcible way." Excessive prudery on such subjects was foolish, a Nevada paper said: "Sensible people can always listen to square talk and honest argument with more or less profit, and no possible injury." Such examples suggest that controversy surrounding her performance, as much as her actual remarks, stimulated debate and forced audiences to reexamine cherished notions of gender and class.[35] "Has Social Crime a Gender?" wondered the *Iowa State Register* after Woodhull had gone:

We have had a Woodhull among us. If it were asked now, "How many persons in Des Moines condemned the woman for her life and her speech?" the answer would be, "Nine out of every ten." [In so doing,] . . . we have acted upon society's excuse, and spared the others because they were men. But we have good company in this. Some of our home preachers are with us. Some of them preached sermons of Woodhull's wickedness last Sunday, and it is said that all of them kept loyally within the current, popular idea that social crime is only a crime when it is in the feminine gender.[36]

Woodhull's critics enhanced her speaking power, by sparking local debates over social freedom and elite hypocrisy even after she left town.

The Trials of 1874–75

Early in 1874, Woodhull's status as an agent of sexual revolution received an unexpected boost when the libel suit filed by Luther Challis (in response to the allegations of his seduction of two young woman printed in the *Weekly*) finally came to trial.[37] It also reinforced a political trend in Woodhull's popularity. Democratic newspapers in the midwest were particularly taken with Woodhull's lecture, "Reformation or Revolution, Which? or, Behind the Political Scenes," which attacked the Grant administration, still under criticism from the Credit Mobilier scandal of the previous winter. Woodhull was "the object of slander; the accused of the ministry; the slandered object of a subsidized press," the *Ottumwa Democrat* said following her lecture there in January 1874: "she came among her audience with scarcely ten sympathizers and at the close of the speech she was the heroine, the idol of her worshipers."[38] On the eve of the trial that February, Woodhull reminded a lecture audience in St. Paul, Minnesota, that she was a victim of persecution by church and state, and promised that, if convicted, "she would speak louder than she could [on the lecture platform]."[39] The *Weekly* reinforced this perception of Woodhull as a free speech martyr. Its editorial page now featured this quotation from John Stuart Mill: "The diseases of society can, no more than corporeal maladies, be prevented or cured without being spoken about in plain language." Even nonpartisan papers reported that audiences appreciated her attacks on the church, the government and powerful businessmen.[40]

When the jury found the defendants "not guilty," the *Weekly* claimed it as a populist victory, particularly for sex radicals:

> The whole tendency of the conduct of the prosecution was to show that people holding such social theories as we hold, could not possibly be actuated by "good motives," or have "justifiable ends" in view, both of which are required by the Constitution of this State, in addition to the truth, in justification of an alleged libel. The jury, however, found all three of these requirements present in our case, and in spite of all efforts to the contrary, rendered a verdict accordingly.[41]

Sex radicals saw Woodhull's acquittal as a vindication of principled exposure. Juliet Severance, attending a Spiritualists meeting in Chicago, reported that, when the verdict was announced, the audience responded with resounding cheers and flocked to Severance (known to be a friend of Woodhull) "with streaming eyes to offer congratulations on *the triumph of free speech and a free press* and say God bless Victoria." Spiritualists meeting in Vineland, New Jersey, hearing by telegram of Woodhull's acquittal, likewise cheered and sent a check for $50 to aid in Woodhull's financial relief; in recognition of "the intrepid manner with which you have faced and beaten such fearful odds as were evidently pitted against you upon this occasion, as well as the fearless way in which you have this far carried the banner of social reformation." Moreover, Woodhull's supporters emphasized the danger to the principle of liberty itself. As one correspondent to the *Weekly* put it, "Let this case and that series of persecutions you have been subjected to, be a lesson to all Liberals, Spiritualists, Free-thinkers or whatever else; a warning that now, as ever, eternal vigilance is the price of liberty."[42] The trial became, for them, a case study in populist resistance to authority.

Woodhull's acquittal in the Challis case popularized a new merger of free love and free speech, but also furthered her celebrity for her resistance to the government, often in partisan terms. "The verdict carries a lesson with it," the Democratic *New York Star* wrote, "and individuals may as well learn first as last that Courts and juries are not instituted to serve private malice or further personal prosecution."[43] The court's hostility to Woodhull in the Challis case underscored the vulnerability of ordinary citizens to official prejudice. Judge Sutherland shocked the press in his denunciation of the jury after it had reached its decision, which he called "outrageous." "That judge," wrote the *Kansas City Daily Chronicle*, "if he had his just deserts, would be convicted of libel himself. It was a patent insult to the honor of the jurors as citizens of a free republic, to their oaths as jurors and peers of the parties to the cause." The Challis verdict increased Woodhull's popularity in the midwest, where political resistance to the power of the Republican Party was growing, despite the fact that her lectures were equally tough on officials in both parties. Even the jurors in the case, when interviewed, cited their disgust with the heavy-handed treatment of the sisters in their arrest and in the courtroom.[44]

The populist message was apparently effective, particularly for audiences who were able to hear Woodhull speak. "You have made converts many, you have made warm friends not a few in your Western trip," wrote a Chicago Spiritualist. "I know this for I have seen and conversed with many that have listened to your lectures." In 1874, Woodhull used her legal struggles as advertising, as in this Salt Lake City promotion:

Victoria C. Woodhull, who has gained such a wide notoriety through her connection with the Beecher-Tilton scandal, and the prosecutions growing out of the same, in which the United States courts were made the instruments to vindicate the reputation of Mr. Beecher, will lecture at the theatre this evening. Whatever her views may be she is undoubtedly a first-class sensation, and has given the Christian clergy and the politicians more trouble, and caused them more terror than all the other iconoclastic reformers combined.[45]

For libertarians and populists, her trial symbolized the dangers that entrenched power posed to the common man, and increased her popularity. "Mrs. Woodhull has been written and abused into almost a national prominence and notoriety," wrote one Nevada journalist that May, "until now wherever she goes everybody is desirous to see and hear her."[46]

Woodhull's notoriety increased dramatically late in the spring of 1874, when Theodore Tilton revived the Beecher scandal. The Plymouth church

had publicly dropped Tilton from its rolls the previous fall, but when critics charged that the church was attempting to hush up the scandal, Beecher's
allies responded with public attacks on Tilton's character. Tilton retaliated
by publishing a statement that included a letter of apology from Beecher,
dated January 1871, which expressed sorrow from the preacher for committing some unnamed wrong upon his friend. The press speculated, as Tilton
intended, that the letter constituted an apology for seducing Elizabeth
Tilton, his wife. The letter's publication gave a noticeable boost to Woodhull's west coast tour that month. Just prior to the publication of Tilton's
letter, Woodhull had opened her California tour with a poorly received lecture in San Francisco on June 1. At this event, an audience of "hundreds"
that included "persons who go into our best society" hissed her into silence
at several points, while her comments on sexual freedom allegedly prompted
the audience "to leave in groups."[47] Negative press reports preceded her,
forcing her to cancel advertised lectures in Salinas, Watsonville, Gilroy, Hollister, and San Diego, California.[48] After Tilton published Beecher's apology
letter, however, Woodhull gave two lectures in Sacramento to "large audiences," the second of which, titled "The Naked Truth," explicitly indicted the
government's intervention following her Beecher exposure in 1872. Back in
San Francisco at the conclusion of this California tour on July 3, 1874, she
gave two lectures to enthusiastic audiences.[49] So began a new and more successful phase of her lecturing career.

Woodhull's celebrity status soared over the next year, as the Beecher-
Tilton scandal remained headline news nationwide (via telegraph) until the
famous Beecher-Tilton trial ended in July 1875. In fall 1874, a Plymouth
Church Committee attempted to stem the scandal; it investigated the matter, and defended Beecher by denouncing the immoral character of "the
infamous women who have started this scandal," namely Woodhull and
Claflin. It was Beecher's goodness, committee member the Rev. Leonard
Bacon insisted, that led to his downfall. "I do not object to his being a friend
to publicans and sinners," he told the committee. "Our Lord was. But the
harlot who washed his feet with her tears and wiped them with her tresses
was a repentant harlot." Woodhull's lack of shame was apparently the root
of the matter; Bacon warned his fellow preachers to "be on your guard, lest
in your anxiety to do good to the low you should become liable to be
charged with their sins."[50] When the committee exonerated Beecher on all
charges, sex radicals renewed their attacks on the immorality of organized
religion, and praised social freedom as the only moral path. "In another

generation, everybody will be ashamed that they ever were anything else than free lovers," Stephen Pearl Andrews wrote. "If people behave well under constraint there is no virtue in that. In a high moral sense, people cannot do right unless they are free to do wrong. It is only in freedom that true virtue and morality can expand."[51]

Theodore Tilton was reluctant to let the situation rest with Beecher's whitewashing by the Plymouth Church Committee. Two days after the committee's exoneration of the pastor, he filed charges against Beecher for "alienating his wife's affections," setting off the most significant courtroom drama of the nineteenth century. For six months it filled the papers with daily revelations. The new publicity around the Beecher-Tilton scandal and ensuing trial coincided with the interruption of Woodhull's performances, as "nervous illness" and financial hardship forced her to cancel many lectures during the 1874–75 season.[52] Deprived of Woodhull's lecture income, the *Weekly* shrank from sixteen to eight pages and devoted itself to analyzing the trial as the great social question of the day. In May 1875, Woodhull herself appeared briefly in court, under subpoena to produce letters requested by Beecher's defense team (Figure 34). *The Days' Doings* used the opportunity to slip a small visual reference to Woodhull into its trial coverage.

Before the jury reached its verdict, the *Weekly* predicted a divided jury as the most socially useful outcome of the trial. A hung jury, the *Weekly* argued, "will leave the whole matter to be decided by the public in its own peculiar and generally just way." In addition, the *Weekly* insisted, the principles of social freedom that the case rested upon would be continually before the public, which could only further social reform. The paper anticipated that the Beecher scandal would be an ideal catalyst for free and public discussion of sexual freedom:

Never, until this whole question of the proper relations of the sexes is settled, will there cease to be a growing public demand for literature and journalism in which the principles involved, or the facts [elicited] are discussed. Of this those who consider themselves to be the conservators of morality may rest assured, and they will find, perhaps to their astonishment, that the public morality, instead of deteriorating under this tendency, will improve.[53]

In fact, the trial closed with a hung jury on July 2, 1875. The sexual and political implications of the Beecher-Tilton scandal resonated with a generation of Americans, fulfilling the *Weekly's* prediction.

"IT'S ALL A MUDDLE."

Microscopic view of a Brooklyn juror's brain, after hearing the evidence offered to prove Mr. Beecher innocent.

Figure 34. Woodhull never received significant coverage in *The Days' Doings* after the court appearances late in 1872. Her appearance in court during the Beecher-Tilton trial, however, generated this comic depiction in the paper. A long haired Theodore Tilton gazes longingly at the image of Beecher, as his young domestic Bessie Turner reveals his character with startling revelations on the witness stand. At the top, Tilton embraces Woodhull as he waves a flag that reads "Communism and Free Love." *The Days' Doings*, April 10, 1875.

Popularizing the Beecher-Tilton Scandal

The inconclusive verdict in the Beecher-Tilton trial breathed new life into Woodhull's lecturing machine in the 1875–76 season. As the underdog in the Beecher scandal, Woodhull gradually attracted a more mainstream following. "Mrs. Woodhull has been roundly abused," a Buffalo reporter noted soon after the verdict; "but the American people are the most generous people in the world, and the feeling is gaining that she has been misrepresented and has been made to suffer unnecessarily."[54] As she toured, Woodhull (or her associates) reinforced this theme in anonymous letters to the local press. One, signed "Fair Play," compared her past persecution to that of prominent abolitionists, like William Lloyd Garrison, Wendell Phillips and John Brown. "Who has convicted her of falsehood in the Beecher-Tilton case?—and yet, where is the religious paper in this land that has had the manliness to give her credit for her honesty and truth in this thing."[55] Some papers even adopted her self-proclaimed title of "Queen of the Rostrum." According to one Watertown, New York reporter, Woodhull's

brilliant perorations enforcing her most radical utterances, and uttered in the most highly dramatic and finely impassioned manner and rich-toned voice, fairly entrance the audience, and carry conviction whether they will or no. Her dramatic and tragic talent is irresistible. *She stands before her hearers as a veritable impersonation of the words she utters.*[56]

She had a gift for dramatizing the story; her personal experience with the hypocrisy she denounced may explain her ability to impress so many reviewers with her "spontaneity," despite a grueling series of nightly repetitions of the same performance. Her publication of the Beecher-Tilton scandal, this reporter believed, had given Woodhull's revolutionary ideas new significance. "As a strategic move to advance her peculiar ideas and secure the public ear, for which it was professedly done, this one stands before the world as a masterpiece." The Beecher-Tilton trial converted Woodhull's disreputable notoriety into popular celebrity. Woodhull was indeed, as advertised, "the most remarkable person of the age."

Her lecture of choice by autumn 1875, billed as "The Destiny of the Republic," combined old and new material in a way that showcased her skill in extemporaneous speech. The first part of this lecture, which she read from a manuscript, outlined the rise and fall of empires and the progress of human civilization from east to west. America, she argued, with its perpetual westward thrust, represented the pinnacle of this process but was doomed to decline without vigorous reform efforts. Americans were the strongest race by virtue of interbreeding: amalgamation would ultimately lead to the formation of "one people—one people with the characteristics, physically and mentally, of all the nations of the world." Here she typically rolled up her manuscript and proceeded to elaborate without notes for an hour or more. To achieve a perfected human race, she said, women must control their own bodies and, by extension, the future qualities of the species. Women should apply principles of scientific breeding to the awesome responsibility of motherhood, just as farmers selectively bred livestock to improve their herds. To do this, women would have to abandon their false modesty and frankly explain the facts of reproduction to their children. Rampant prostitution and sexual coercion brought children into the world destined to fill prisons and insane asylums, Woodhull believed. She no longer offered economic or political remedies to these problems, however. Instead, she advocated control over reproduction, practiced and taught by women. Audiences preferred this lecture to her work of biblical exegesis, called "The Garden of Eden," in which she claimed that the Bible's physical description of the Garden was in fact an elaborate metaphor for the female body. Instead, they applauded Woodhull's assertion, reminiscent of Lucinda Chandler's in 1871, that social purity was the best solution to society's problems. Unlike the republican mothers of the early 1800s, Woodhull's Darwinian motherhood emphasized biology rather than education as women's contribution to humanity. Such blunt talk from a woman about human sexuality, however, astonished many listeners.[57]

More remarkable to many observers was her growing control, with her family, over her lecturing business. The novelty of the traveling Woodhull show, which included warm-up performances by her sister and daughter, made it uniquely attractive after the verdict in 1875. Increasingly, Claflin took over the business management of the enterprise. The *Buffalo Courier* remarked that "as a business combination, the members of the family work well together" and were engaged in an apparently lucrative venture: "with such audiences as that of last evening, through an entire season, it must be evident to the most casual observer that 'advanced ideas,' when advertised boldly, are sometimes pecuniarily profitable." In cases where Woodhull's illness threatened to undermine the show, the more robust Claflin also took charge, granting interviews in her sister's place and using magnetic powers to keep her steady on the platform. Late in the tour, on the verge of heading into the south, Claflin fired their agent over a dispute about their payment (they had received only $100 out of house receipts exceeding $600) and took over the organization on her own, setting up a highly popular tour. Their expertise as a family show attracted a great deal of notice and furthered their celebrity.[58]

Excitement in smaller towns was particularly marked. In Parker City, Pennsylvania, for example, crowds gathered on Main Street to see Woodhull arrive by stage coach. But sophisticated urban audiences also flocked to hear her. As the *Cincinnati Enquirer* put it, "Victoria C. Woodhull, the best known woman in America, or we might modify by saying *the most generally known woman in America*, appeared upon the stage of a lecture hall, and for two hours talked to two thousand people upon some subjects that many men have lacked the courage to face publicly."[59] Her name alone filled opera houses, while her controversial subject matter kept the nation abuzz with revolutionary social ideas. "Several years ago she was hooted from the rostrum by a motley crew of bummers who attended her lectures," wrote a Kokomo, Indiana, reporter in early 1876, "and a respectable woman would no more have thought of listening to the Woodhull than she would have dared to visit Harry Hill's dance house in New York." Her celebrity must now assure her welcome, this reporter concluded: "It may be idle curiosity that brings [people] out to listen to her, but no matter what the attraction is, they go to hear the only woman in America who dares to express thoughts attacking the social evil sin, or who expresses thoughts so much in opposition to public opinion."[60]

The new enthusiasm also reflected Woodhull's growing skill at converting audience prejudice into sympathy. At the outset of her 1875–76 tour, audiences still feared the consequences of attending Woodhull's lecture, and hesitated to applaud her when she appeared on stage.[61] Religious leaders continued to discourage listeners from attending the lectures. In the wake of Beecher's humiliation in public court, however, Woodhull had learned to turn her audience's expectations to her own advantage. She delighted her audiences by targeting the hypocrisy of her critics. "It will be pleasant for [her absent detractors]," a St. Albans, Vermont, reporter wrote, "to know that an audience more than ordinarily intelligent and respectable applauded her to the echo when she told just why [critics] stayed away." As a reporter wrote in Greenville, Ohio, "Parsons that went to hear, prejudiced against her and expecting to have their ears tickled with low, base and vulgar slang and expressions, had a flea of a different stripe put in their ear, and left the hall fully impressed with the fact that a drunken, debauched, prostitute life is not the life to live, much less the life advocated by Mrs. Woodhull."[62] These accounts show a surprising tendency to endorse her version of the

Beecher-Tilton story, and also her toned-down sex radicalism, simply because she had survived to tell the tale.

Even Woodhull's critics felt some sympathy for the "strain of sadness" she exhibited on stage.[63] By 1875, her performance transcended her controversial message:

it must conceded that she is an extraordinary woman, and there is a peculiar fascination in her intense emotional nature, her utter devotion to an idea, her eager and passionate advocacy of her cause. Her eyes flash with enthusiasm. She trembles with excitement as she talks. Her care-worn face lights up in a wonderful manner, and her lips quiver with emotion. She is a strange, wonderful woman, and one cannot leave her presence after an hour's talk without a more kindly feeling for her.[64]

She manipulated prejudice to her own advantage, flattering members of the audience for their temerity in coming, cajoling their agreement with her ideas. "Many of her audience doubtless went to hear her to gratify a prurient curiosity, and these were disappointed," a Pittsburgh reporter commented; "for the lady uttered nothing calculated to raise a blush on the cheeks of a pure-minded woman." As an Indiana journalist put it, "The speaker was listened to with rapt attention, and now and then as she forced home some unpleasant truth, was encouraged by bursts of applause." Defying conservative prejudice, in fact, representatives of church and state attended and applauded her lectures in almost every town.[65]

The large number of sold-out shows suggests the growing popularity of the 1875–76 tour. For example, Chicago's McCormick Hall "was crowded to repletion" to hear Woodhull speak. As the *Chicago Times* reported, "the stairway leading to McCormick Hall was crowded with counter-currents of humanity—the one flowing up, delighted; the other pouring down, disgusted. The seats had all been taken at an early hour, and many hundreds were compelled to forego the privilege of listening to . . . Victoria C. Woodhull." That such crowds were unusual was a frequent comment in the press, and apparently impressed other radical lecturers: "The newspaper accounts of you and your labors in the field," said reformer Parker Pillsbury, "make me quite ashamed of my own little audiences and the interest my work awakens."[66] She was so popular that many towns appealed to her for a second or third performance. As one Washington reporter said, "it was the desire of nearly every one present that he or she should have the privilege, at an early day, of again sitting under the pleasing voice of Mrs. Woodhull to hear some more of her wholesome truths." Journalists in other towns voiced this sentiment as well."[67] In some cases, local citizens offered an immediate sum to bring Woodhull back, or circulated petitions begging her to stay one more night.[68] As one Woodhull enthusiast reported from Memphis after her lecture early in 1876, "Those who did not hear her are crazy to hear her."[69]

The most obvious sign of Woodhull's growing popularity and respectability was the growing presence of "the ladies" in the crowd, even though the audiences continued to be quite heterogeneous. Because many expected that "Mrs. Woodhull would say something 'smutty,'" women faced social criticism to attend at all. Commentators interpreted the presence of women in the audience as a sign of greater social acceptance of the speaker, as in Chicago, where "At least one-third of those present were ladies, and among their number were many who rank high in society." In general, few women attended the first night, with more women attending after the content of the lecture, the respectability of the audience, and the reception of the first lecture were confirmed in print. Woodhull often made a special plea to mothers and daughters at the end of her first lecture, or in interviews: her theme of maternal control of the species made a female audience all the more desirable. In Cincinnati, for example, she invited women and promised that "she will not say a word that any decent woman need blush at." These tactics were apparently effective. "One-fourth of the people in the house were ladies," the *Cincinnati Enquirer* noted, "and they were ladies of the best families too; ladies who were not too cowardly to come out to a public place and listen to a lecture which in their hearts they long since had a desire to hear. We venture to say that they went away well pleased with themselves at having had the 'grit' to go."[70] Attending Woodhull's lectures challenged audiences to defy the sexual double standard, and made her message the subject of debate on a personal, familial, level.

In fact, Woodhull used her growing popularity to argue that her "revolution" had been accomplished. Late in 1875, a promotion for the *Buffalo Express* reminded readers of the strange turn of events. The change could only be a reflection of the evolution in popular sentiments about her subject of social freedom:

Her present theme relates to a subject that has been tabooed too much for the good of the world; has been relegated to the physician's study or reserved for the after-marriage detection; if learned at all by the young in time to be of any value to them, has been done surreptitiously and made uselessly and wickedly a thing of shame and guilt.

Thoughtful people, said this endorsement, "will seek a remedy in freer discussion and better knowledge of the laws of life." By early 1876, Washington,

D.C., audiences received Woodhull's two lectures with enthusiasm. The *Sunday Gazette* published a promotion that Woodhull's improved reception signified a "revolution" in the "sentiments, feeling, and conduct of the people in this country." Thanks to Woodhull, the advertisement said, the "vexed social problem" could now be addressed publicly. As Woodhull put it more directly in the *Weekly*, "The change that public thought has undergone upon the social question amounts to nothing less than a revolution."[71]

The Beecher Scandal and Sectional Politics

The best evidence of the success of Woodhull's revolution, she felt, could be seen in her surprising popularity in the southwest and west in early 1876. Woodhull chose this tour for two reasons. A recent lung infection made the warmer climate attractive, but more important, she had received reports of growing southern enthusiasm for her paper.[72] To dispel southern prejudice against female performers, Woodhull changed her image. She adopted a more opulently "ladylike" costume, with rich fabrics and fashionable styling, and a new hairstyle, which had, by early 1876, grown to a more conventionally feminine length.[73] Woodhull's abandonment of visible nonconformity anticipated her southern critics. At the same time, it reflected the commercial impulse that accompanied her retreat from sexual radicalism.

Southern audiences, long hostile to lecturing in general, and to public appearances by women in particular, were unlikely candidates for Woodhull's sexual revolution. Reformer Helen Nash, who crossed paths with Woodhull in Galveston, Texas, reported to *Weekly* readers on the novelty of the southern tour. "Few of Mrs. Woodhull's friends and admirers would have thought it expedient for her to take herself and her 'peculiar views' into the south," Nash wrote: "it would be too much like bearding the lion in his den." But this was partly a misunderstanding of the southern people, and particularly southern women, Nash felt. Whereas Elizabeth Cady Stanton had lectured only to women in private settings in the 1860s, Woodhull brought her ideas before public, mixed audiences. As Nash saw it, "She knows that any sexual truth concerns both sexes alike, and as she has no idea of vulgarity in the matter, and apprehends no necessity for mawkishness, she speaks what she has to say to both sexes at once." Based on what Nash heard from women in the south, Woodhull's lectures were causing a startling, but not unwelcome, "upheaval" in social views.[74]

Woodhull's lecture for this southern tour, "The Human Body, The

Temple of God," represented a bold new step in which she abandoned her prepared texts and relied entirely on her capacity for extemporaneous speech. She billed the new work as a "Sermon"; her sole prop, appropriately, was a pocket-sized Bible. The lecture's content was familiar—the perfection of humanity through scientific breeding and sex education—but the form was new. She opened the lecture with a quotation from First Corinthians, "Know ye not that ye are the temple of God?" then dissected the hypocrisy of a society that equated women's ignorance with her virtue. She cited the false modesty of the YMCA that put fig leaves over nude statuary, or a woman who blushed to hold her naked infant son in her lap. She blamed community leaders for misrepresenting her own candid words on sexual hygiene. But mostly she criticized organized religion:

You have built your churches. You have worshipped God in your own way; you have liberally worshipped this holy book; it is lying upon every table throughout the land; wherever you find a family that can read, the bible is there; and yet with all this you are forced to hang your heads in shame and acknowledge that not one single body is worthy to be the temple of God. The temple built with hands is, indeed, filled to repletion Sunday after Sunday, but the temple built without hands—God's own temple—is so completely desecrated, so vile, so utterly unworthy to be called the temple of God that He can scarcely recognize it today.

Only mothers could properly teach children to respect their bodies, to reject sexual slavery in and out of marriage, and only if they dispensed with Victorian prudery. Some journalists found this frank treatment of such a delicate subject controversial, though they approved of the notion of sexual purity, especially for women. However, the new lecture reined in Woodhull's earlier radical demands for women's sexual rights: it was a far cry from her 1871 claim to the right to change lovers daily.[75]

At the same time, Woodhull's rhetorical skills and emotional delivery became increasingly powerful. Freed from her manuscript, she frequently enchanted her listeners. She began her lectures with a hesitant, quavering voice, possibly a calculated bid for sympathy, a strategy to win over the audience, but also an indication of the challenge of speaking without notes. An Atlanta paper described her voice as follows:

There was a tremor in the voice that betokened at first thought a dash of diffidence and timidity. As the lecture proceeded it seemed to be more like a tremor of tears in the [feelings] of a woman for a place in the hearts of the people, one who had suffered, one who had deep feelings of philanthropy and affection, and who did not wish to be cast out from the affections of her kind.[76]

Her tremulous opening, which many reviewers took as evidence of her sin-
cere commitment to the cause she espoused, enlisted the audience's sympathy. "Her strength as a speaker is in her earnestness," a St. Louis paper
reported. "Her audience at once became *en rapport* with her, for they felt
that they have before them a woman who is in 'dead earnest,' and that the
words which are falling from her lips are not the mere coinage of a mental
process, but they are thoughts coming straight from her heart, earnestly
uttered, because earnestly felt."[77] Her "fine voice, softer than Anna Dickinson's, [and] . . . more consistent," and her powers of elocution drew frequent
notice. "Mrs. Woodhull's elocution is almost faultless," a St. Louis journalist
wrote, "her voice at times ringing out full and clear as she promulgates
some grand idea, and again sinking into a whisper, every syllable distinct
and clear as if it were a thing hewn out of marble."[78] Though occasionally
contradicted by less laudatory reviews, such praises set her apart from other
opera house lecturers, who were often inaudible to listeners in the rear seats
of the hall.[79]

Southern audiences greeted these performances with surprising enthusiasm and were often reluctant to let her leave the hall. In New Orleans, "the
audience paid rapt attention throughout, and only at times would they
break out into applause, which, when they did, was unanimous and 'long
drawn out.'" A Memphis audience interrupted her lecture several times with
enthusiastic applause, "and at the close, when after what seemed vain efforts
on her part to leave, she finally bade adieu, the most deafening and pro-
longed shouts recalled her again and again to receive the warm and generous plaudits." According to the same paper, Woodhull "answered every call
until at last, breaking through hall form and ceremony, hundreds, both old
and young, stepped upon the stage and personally congratulated her upon
her success." In Texas, Dallas visitors crowded the hotel parlor all day to
meet the sisters, and a full house cheered her lecture in the evening. Similar
displays were repeated at Galveston and Houston. "If we had been told that
such a scene as was there witnessed could have been possible in a Southern
city," said a reporter for the *Houston Age*, "with Mrs. Woodhull as the central figure, we would have failed to realize it."[80]

As she toured the south, Woodhull plied her audiences with an
emotional delivery that invoked the region's traditional glorification of motherhood; it was apparently quite effective. "We rarely ever beheld an assem-
blage of any kind so completely under the influence of a speaker," reported
the *Houston Age*. Her repeated allusions to sanctified motherhood struck a
chord: as one Atlanta journalist put it, "No one could hear the appeal for

purity in connection with that holy name and tie without an obeisance of reverence, perhaps a memory of tears." She became more sentimental and personal in her performance, and southern audiences found this compelling. "Men and ladies were to be seen brushing tears from theirs eyes as the pathos of this strange woman went home to their hearts, linking them together in that chain of common sympathy whose weird spell no individual present could successfully resist if they would." Her status as the tragic victim of religious, social and state authority also resonated with white southern audiences in the process of memorializing the Confederate cause. They frequently paid tribute to Woodhull, as in New Orleans for example, with bouquets or baskets of flowers.[81]

Southern approval also reflected her growing celebrity status as a player in the Beecher-Tilton scandal, as the 1875–76 season progressed. As an Elmira, New York, newspaper put it before she ventured south, Woodhull had "probably been more talked and written about than any other woman living, save perhaps her namesake, the Queen of England." Over the fall and winter, reviewers and audiences began to reconsider her earlier reputation, and audiences became more immediately welcoming. By the time Woodhull and Claflin reached Texas, their celebrity status was complete. As a reporter for the *Galveston Daily News* saw it,

> The prominent position they have occupied in free-thought circles in this country, their intimate acquaintance with the circumstances of the greatest scandal of the age, the energy, pluck and perseverance with which they have pursued their course, in spite of what would be to others less gifted, insurmountable obstacles, entitle them to consideration.
>
> Oft, apparently, defeated, yet ever regaining their foothold; cast into jail for the expressions they made use of in explaining their views, yet beating the accusers before the courts of the country; their arrival in this city is an event to justify some special notice.[82]

Their very survival as public figures against formidable odds, it seemed, made them worthy of respect, despite their radical social views.

In addition, Woodhull represented to southern audiences a renegade northerner who had attacked the moral authoritarianism of the northeastern establishment. She rarely left the stage without alluding to her persecution as the instigator of the Beecher-Tilton scandal. Many southerners saw Woodhull as a symbol of the abuses of the federal state under Republican control. "[Woodhull and Claflin] have been traduced in the North, they have been imprisoned," one Austin, Texas, paper said; "they unearthed the whited sepulchre—Beecher—and our people owe them gratitude for that if for nothing else." Noting that Beecher had denounced slaveholders to English audiences before the war, the paper wrote indignantly that "Beecher was the envoy to England against our people [southern slaveholders] and was received as a saint," even as he (allegedly) seduced Tilton's wife. The imprisonment and financial hardship Woodhull had endured predisposed southern audiences to hear her with sympathy.[83]

The Beecher exposure was a potent illustration of the sexual double standard, but also merged with divisive sectional politics that made Reconstruction increasingly untenable. The Beecher scandal only added to the impression that the Republican Party was no longer acting honorably: even sporting illustrations found a way to link the scandal visually to the Grant administration (Figure 35). Woodhull's national success coincided with her declining radicalism; her commercial appeal was antithetical to radicalism because it pandered to popular sentiment instead of challenging it. The Woodhull machine, with its combination of canny opportunism, effective performance, and topical nature of material, was an important player in the

Figure 35. These twin images suggest the popular association of the Beecher scandal with the declining fortunes of the Republican Party. At left, Beecher preaches to an audience of men, who fear to let their women attend; at right, the artist uses bill-posting at the theater to link the economic scandals of the president with the sexual scandals of Beecher. *The Days' Doings*, February 13, 1875.

entertainment marketplace of Reconstruction, but it was increasingly non-threatening. Her economic success was indicative of the changing sexual politics of Reconstruction: the more "majestic" her stage presence, the more conservative her message became. She resumed the clothing, language, and hairstyles of conventional femininity and spoke to audiences about a mother's duty to educate her young in sexual matters for the future of the race. It may have been the price of commercial success, but it signaled the waning of her sexual revolution.

Sex radicals continued to promote and support Woodhull, even as she retreated from her earlier radicalism. "The Woodhull is winning golden opinions in every part of our country," enthused *The Spiritualist at Work* in May 1876. "The press speak well of her wherever she lectures."[84] By then, however, Woodhull's "revolution" had played itself out. She distanced herself from the Beecher exposure and claimed that Stephen Pearl Andrews had published the exposure issue without her knowledge or consent. (She made no reference to her own prior verbal exposure before the AAS.) This may have been an attempt to shield her daughter from unpleasant insinuations; it certainly revealed a growing concern for her family's respectability and reputation.[85] The *Weekly* folded that June, due to personal problems between Woodhull and Colonel Blood (who ran the paper while she lectured). Sex radicals turned to alternative newspapers like the free speech champion *The Word* and *Hull's Crucible* (now back in print) and became embroiled in legal controversies over freedom of the press instead of debating the morality of marriage and its alternatives. Woodhull herself became a celebrity of sexual freedom, but also an icon of populist resistance to federal government control, an inherent criticism to the political status quo. Like the exposures of Brigham Young's nineteenth wife, Woodhull's principled revelation of the Beecher-Tilton scandal became a political tool. A radical act in its own right, the Beecher exposure heralded the waning of the revolutionary days of Reconstruction and signaled the dawning of a new, more conservative era.

Conclusion
The Waning of the Woodhull Revolution

When *Woodhull & Claflin's Weekly* folded with the June 10, 1876 issue, Woodhull the lecturer disappeared from national (and historical) view. Only traces of her activities remain. The 1876 presidential election process was well underway, and Woodhull was, again, a candidate herself. As in the 1872 election, however, she failed to get herself on the ballot, and received no votes. Yet she did not sit idle. In October 1876, Woodhull divorced her second husband, Colonel Blood, on the grounds of adultery.[1] Without the *Weekly* to record them, her further activities are obscure, but there is evidence that she kept her promise to return to the rostrum for the 1876–1877 lecture season.[2] In August 1877, Woodhull and Claflin set sail for England amid rumors that (heir) William Henry Vanderbilt had bribed them to leave the country before the Vanderbilt probate case came to trial.[3] Once in England, Woodhull resumed her public speaking career, lecturing in several large cities.[4] It was at her lecture in London in December 1877, her celebration of pious motherhood entitled "The Human Body, Temple of God," that she first attracted her future husband, banker John Biddulph Martin. After years of negotiation to overcome his family's objections, she married him in 1883, living in his country estate until her death in 1927.

As Woodhull-Martin, she gradually abandoned the egalitarian principles that had driven her actions during Reconstruction. She paid a call on Frederick Douglass and his controversial new wife Helen Pitts Douglass (a white woman) in their Italian hotel in 1887.[5] But she also established a eugenics paper in the 1890s, called the *Humanitarian*, that promoted not amalgamation but instead racialized sexual reform and the scientific propagation of the species to perfect "the race," which now explicitly meant Anglo-Saxons. Like many other sex radicals, she was turning to science as a solution to social problems. Perhaps most indicative of her political shift from left to right in the half century from 1872 to 1927 is the panic of her daughter (Zula Maud Woodhull) and her niece (Carrie Miles), both in their sixties, upon learning of the publication of Emanie Sachs's muckraking biography,

"The Terrible Siren" (1928). Miles searched New York's second-hand book-stores to buy up and destroy stray copies of Sachs's damaging sources, especially the Treat pamphlet. But the cousins were particularly worried about the racial implications of Woodhull's controversial candidacy with Douglass, a long forgotten memory in the Woodhull-Martin family tradition.[6] When Zula Maud Woodhull died in 1941, at the height of Britain's war against Nazi Germany, she left the considerable Woodhull-Martin fortune to the Royal Institution of Great Britain "to be applied to research work in eugenics."[7]

With a few exceptions, Woodhull cut ties with the radical reformers of the 1870s and inaugurated a new phase of her life. Although she kept in touch with Elizabeth Cady Stanton and Isabella Beecher Hooker and returned periodically to run for president, Woodhull retained no connection to the organized suffrage movement in the United States.[8] When suffrage activity resumed in the early 1890s, the press and political opponents again unearthed "the Woodhull" as a symbolic agent of disorder. When the AWSA and NWSA combined in 1892 to form the new National American Woman Suffrage Association, it was Woodhull's name hecklers used to disparage the women attending the meeting (though she was not attending). That same year, in South Carolina, one paper sarcastically urged the women to invite Woodhull and other "Yankee female viragoes" down to plead their cause.[9] Twenty years after the Beecher exposure, and safely tucked away in her remote English estate, Woodhull remained a burden for American suffragists. Woodhull's legacy for international socialism was equally problematic. While Marx and the First International dismissed Woodhull and the claims of her section as inherently bourgeois, her legacy was the two-thirds rule, which effectively barred women's issues from the organization.[10]

Sex radicals were probably the most disappointed when Woodhull departed from America in 1877. "The friends of Mrs. Woodhull, in these parts, wonder what has become of her," one correspondent to Moses Hull's *Crucible* wrote in 1877. "what sort of work she is doing, if any—why she left the field so suddenly." Rumors of her divorce and her new religious views spread like wildfire. "Has she joined the Catholic church, as reported?" this writer wondered. Hull, who had been so active in the Woodhull/Douglass nomination at the Equal Rights Party Convention in 1872, had faced at least as much public vituperation as Woodhull for disclosing his open marriage in 1874. His response to this letter revealed some bitterness toward her. He reported that Woodhull had obtained a divorce from Blood on the grounds of (his) adultery in order to marry a "foreign gentleman" who had since deserted her. Hull also confirmed the rumor of Woodhull's Catholicism.

The source of his bitterness, however, was her betrayal of the cause. Newspapers stated that "Victoria Woodhull having failed as a lecturer in Europe is going on the stage." Hull concluded from these reports that "at this time she is a 'backslider' from the cause of reform."[11]

Woodhull relinquished many of her radical views once she left America. Her position in the world had changed; she worked hard to prove her respectability. Her endless redefinitions of "the Woodhull" later in life testify to the symbol's lasting and yet unseemly connotations, and she waged a many-fronted war to improve her reputation. With Martin's financial backing, she pursued individuals and organizations, including the British Museum, for their role in keeping alive some of the negative commentary of the 1870s. Prompted by Martin, Henry James issued a palpably false statement that the character of Nancy Headway in his novella "The Siege of London" bore no resemblance to Woodhull. Woodhull then published several carefully selected digests of news clippings that emphasized her magnetic power as a speaker, her respectable audiences, and their approval of her performance. These reports emphasized her celebrity over the ideas that had made her notorious. Woodhull complemented this partial and biased view of the past by inventing new genealogies that traced her line back to Alexander Hamilton.[12]

Her greatest victory over her tarnished reputation, appropriately, came in the realm of visual culture. Woodhull clinched her claims to respectability with a visual makeover of the immodest sporting illustrations from the 1870s. The new pictures retooled her image in important ways, and made her seem more genteel, and less controversial. One (Figure 36) remade the "fast woman" iconography of the brokerage opening by adding ruffles to lengthen the skirts. A second (Figure 37) revised their arrest, covering the ankle, removing the hard, mannish physiognomies of the original image, and replacing them with more genteel faces and hats. An image showing the sisters, with Woodhull's daughter and counsel, in jail (Figure 38), removed the bottles and glasses from the background, but also softened their faces and gestures. Their triumph came in the courtroom image (Figures 39), which not only gave the two women distinguished, mature heads of gentlewomen, but also changed the story line; instead of their indictment, the happy picture purported to show their "acquittal." These visual makeovers of Woodhull and Claflin reveal the power of nineteenth-century illustrations to create a sensation quite specific to the historical moment. The images shocked contemporaries, but a few decades later were proof of bygone fame. For over a century, only the revised images appeared in the Woodhull literature, proving that even posthumously Woodhull was a shrewd player in American cultural politics. These images effectively blurred the earlier, sensational associations, and the notoriety implicit in Woodhull's "public womanhood."[13]

Woodhull and the Decline of the Left

In the early 1870s, Woodhull's notoriety in sporting and commercial newspapers helped splinter the radical movements of Reconstruction. Negative, highly sexualized stereotyping of Woodhull discouraged even the radical reformers who favored women's suffrage, international socialism, and civil rights, let alone more moderate reformers. Her symbolic dominance in

Figure 36. Woodhull revised her symbolic legacy in a series of illustrated pamphlets published from England after her marriage to the respectable John Biddulph Martin. This image discreetly covers the tell-tale ankles with an additional ruffle of skirt. Otherwise the image is identical to the one appearing in *The Days' Doings* in 1870 (Figure 2). M. F. Darwin, *One Moral Standard for All: Extracts form the Lives of Victoria Claflin Woodhull, Now Mrs. John Biddulph Martin, and Tennessee Claflin, Now Lady Cook* (1900). Labadie Collection, University of Michigan.

radical political movements during the period divided their constituencies and forced them to narrow their claims. Woodhull's visibility in press accounts of the suffrage movement alienated moderate respectable women, who then sought new strategies to win over the antisuffrage elite. Media coverage of the American IWA that placed Woodhull and Claflin at the center of every image and therefore every debate over the organization's legitimacy, prompted Friedrich Sorge and Karl Marx to limit the agenda of international socialism to the interests of male workers. In embracing Frederick Douglass as her running mate in the 1872 presidential campaign, Woodhull exacerbated fears of race mixing implied in the civil rights demands of Radical Republicans. Even some sex radicals abandoned the movement when Woodhull took charge. It would be easy to conclude that leftist politics in general suffered from Woodhull's symbolic leadership. But her real legacy is far more complicated.

Figure 37. This image, otherwise identical to the arrest drawing from *The Days' Doings* in 1872 (Figure 26), gives the sisters the modest, ladylike heads, faces, and attire of the respectable woman. It also lengthens the skirt by one ruffle, covering the telltale ankle. M. F. Darwin, *One Moral Standard for All: Extracts form the Lives of Victoria Claflin Woodhull, Now Mrs. John Biddulph Martin, and Tennessee Claflin, Now Lady Cook* (1900). Labadie Collection, University of Michigan.

As a sign of the times, folk devil, or myth,[14] Woodhull demonstrated the power of gender and sexuality to define political struggle, even when such definitions are not explicit. As a negative symbol of radicalism, she became the justification for the moral authoritarianism set in motion by Comstock. As a signifier in the illustrated sporting press of Reconstruction's left wing political agenda, Woodhull represented the "dangers" of such agitation to family and polity. Divisions among left-leaning political causes can be partly explained as weariness with the ideals and practical reality of

VICTORIA CLAFLIN WOODHULL AND TENNESSEE CLAFLIN IN COUNSEL WITH THEIR LAW-
YER IN LUDLOW STREET JAIL, 1873.

Figure 38. This image softens the early depiction of their sojourn in the "Tombs" in 1872 (Figure 27). Aside from the gentler physiognomies and postures of the sisters in this later image, all signs of their infamy, including the bottle and glasses of the earlier picture, have been erased. M. F. Darwin, *One Moral Standard for All: Extracts form the Lives of Victoria Claflin Woodhull, Now Mrs. John Biddulph Martin, and Tennessee Claflin, Now Lady Cook* (1900). Labadie Collection, University of Michigan.

THE ACQUITTAL OF VICTORIA CLAFLIN WOODHULL AND TENNESSEE CLAFLIN, 1873.

Figure 39. This image vindicates Woodhull and Claflin from the scandal surrounding the Beecher exposure; the original comes from their indictment before a federal judge in 1872 (Figure 29). To further the impression of wronged gentility, the heads and collars have been altered to make them look more respectable and ladylike, and Claflin's expression (seated, at left) bestows upon the reader a look of martyred weariness. M. F. Darwin, *One Moral Standard for All: Extracts form the Lives of Victoria Claflin Woodhull, Now Mrs. John Biddulph Martin, and Tennessee Claflin, Now Lady Cook* (1900). Labadie Collection, University of Michigan.

Reconstruction. But concerted and well-established opposition also used Woodhull to overwhelm radical movements during these years. In this way, negative representations of Woodhull contributed to the decline of the period's radical social movements.

The sexual politics Woodhull represented had deep resonance in the religious climate of Victorian America. Sexuality became an easy subject of ridicule or contempt, but was also a distraction from universal rights agitation for activists themselves. As a private issue, Woodhull's sexual politics demanded personal rather than public regulation. They invoked moral rhetoric and deemphasized state intervention to achieve political goals. Federal intervention, in fact, effectively silenced her most radical views. As the three overlapping movements drew apart, a politics of difference took the place of the universal humanism that had formerly tied them together. Reformers' demands for action from the federal state lost credibility. The cycle of politics turned to the individualistic, free market liberalism that characterized the Gilded Age.

Woodhull's notoriety provides an overly pat explanation for the failure of left wing political movements to retain control of the universal rights discourse during Reconstruction. Rather, bringing all of these facets of Woodhull's life and impact together forces a reexamination of the underlying causes for the decline of the left. What happened to woman suffrage, international socialism, and civil rights transcends the impact of any one individual. What really happened to the sex radicalism of the period, in its swing from defiance to a commercially viable maternalism, is a far larger process than Woodhull the person can adequately explain. Woodhull the phenomenon, however, represented broader social and cultural trends.

Woodhull claimed in 1876 that her sexual revolution was complete, because people were talking about issues that had previously been ignored or prohibited. There is some evidence to support this view. Despite the waning of universal rights agitation in the 1870s, material keys to sexual equality, such as employment, education, and divorce, became more available to women during this period. Many of the controversial issues raised by Woodhull and other sexual politicians in the 1870s foreshadowed those raised in similar periods of crisis in the twentieth century. As in the Progressive Era and the Sixties, discourse about sexual openness accompanied labor agitation and claims for civil rights without race and gender bias.[15] Woodhull's politicization of the personal provides an early example of the intertwining of political and sexual radicalism that resonates in twentieth-century periods of sexual revolution. Her prominence raises new questions. Why do periods of labor, civil rights, and women's rights activism occur concurrently? How do they interact and compete with one another? What is the role of extremism in furthering and containing radical reform?

Woodhull was conscious of the importance of extreme views in making change possible. In 1872, a Boston publisher invited her to write the Introduction to a new edition of Goethe's *Elective Affinities*. In it, Woodhull acknowledged her role in spreading the "ideas of social freedom and of inevitable law governing the action of human affection," modestly using this to explain the association of her name with the "greatest Genius of Germany." Like herself, Goethe had

shocked the age he lived in, both by his writings and by his life, even in Germany, where the puritanical element has always had less sway than it has had among us; but now, if the book runs any risk of a failure to command the public interest, it will be . . . for the opposite reason, that *it may be thought not radical and outspoken enough.* [Therefore,] . . . it presents vividly the opportunity to compare two or three successive generations in respect to the growth of opinion upon a most important subject, and the comparison prepares the mind for the still more radical change which the next few years will inevitably produce.[16]

Did she write this introduction? Does it matter? Regardless of the author, it suggests the significance of the Woodhull phenomenon. The use of her name to boost sales of the Goethe reprint demonstrates her commercial power. The fact that the volume's translator chose to remain anonymous underscores Woodhull's courage in associating herself publicly with sexual radicalism. Most important, the implication that her own words and actions would seem tame to future generations highlights the underlying premise of extremism, that it will normalize ideas and behavior currently beyond the pale.

"Woodhullism" gave a name to the threat posed to the status quo by the left during Reconstruction. But Woodhull, the sexual politician, also brought the agenda of sex radicals to national attention. She embodied their boldest claims, and, in her own person, took them to remote towns across the nation. Through Woodhull, Americans in the 1870's witnessed, digested, and debated the sexual double standard. This debate took on national importance in the drama of Woodhull's arrest by Anthony Comstock. Her ability to evade the 1872 postal code prompted Comstock to enlist the support of cultural conservatives seeking moral legislation based on biblical Christianity, to push for broader latitude in prosecution of obscenity law.[17]

The amended legislation included newspapers under its jurisdiction and targeted for censorship any sexual information, including information about reproduction, birth control, and abortion. Sex radicals after Woodhull faced fierce legal opposition to publicly waged campaigns for sexual openness. Many of Woodhull's associates and staunchest defenders after the Beecher exposure of 1872, such as Moses Hull, Ezra Heywood, Lois Waisbrooker, and Benjamin Tucker, confronted Comstock themselves in the subsequent decades. Because of Comstock, notions of sexual openness became implicitly tied to notions of free speech, and led to tensions between proponents of sexual emancipation for women and defenders of pornography. Freedom from federal control, rather than federal protection for women's rights, then, became the new mantra for sex radicals.

Popular feeling, unlike public speech, is difficult to assess. Woodhull's lecturing success in 1875–76 suggests that audiences became more interested in her sexual politics after 1872. The same negative stereotyping that frightened political activists drew extreme sex radicals to Woodhull's defense, who championed her agenda of sexual openness and pushed it to its extreme form. Woodhull was in many ways an agent of radicalism, "choosing the margin," as bell hooks says in another context, as "a space of radical openness."[18] Woodhull posed such a threat to established order that initially only radicals rallied to her support, either to declare their allegiance to the principles she embodied or to demonstrate resistance to moral authoritarianism. However, conservatives gradually lost their power to control popular reception of Woodhull. Her popularity in the latter years of Reconstruction suggests a degree of popular resistance to state authority and Comstockery. People apparently chose to hear and judge Woodhull's forbidden obscenity for themselves, not despite, but because of Comstock's role in the Beecher coverup. Yet it was a passive kind of resistance that required only voyeuristic consumption rather than active participation.

Woodhull's sexual politics became muted as she became a national celebrity. As a sexual populist, she opened the doors for a widening discourse about sexual freedom on a national scale; as a celebrity, she acquiesced to the conservative reaction against the federal government's role in social issues. Her new Darwinian motherhood offered private rather than public solutions to social problems. In their willingness to see and hear Woodhull, audiences resisted government censorship and rewarded free speech under duress. Sexual radicalism drew from the same rhetoric of individual rights that legitimized abolition (and civil rights), women's suffrage, and Yankee socialism. Each of these political movements, however, demanded federal intervention to protect rights to work or vote, to pass new legislation enabling suffrage, or to provide unemployment relief. Only anarchists and sex radicals, who tended to support Woodhull, advocated individual resistance to the federal state. Woodhull's extreme individualism, and the commercial success of her sexual politics, provided a popular transition to the free market libertarianism of the Gilded Age.

Notes

Introduction. Victoria Woodhull, Sexual Revolutionary

1. On making $700,000 on Black Friday, see the interview in the *New York Herald*, January 22, 1870; *New York Sun*, October 1, 1869. See also Mary Gabriel, *Notorious Victoria: The Life of Victoria Woodhull, Uncensored* (Chapel Hill, N.C.: Algonquin Books, 1998), 42–44; Barbara Goldsmith, *Other Powers: The Age of Suffrage, Spiritualism, and the Scandalous Victoria Woodhull* (New York: Knopf, 1998), 189; Lois Beachy Underhill, *The Woman Who Ran for President: The Many Lives of Victoria Woodhull* (Bridgehampton, N.Y.: Bridge Works Press, 1995), 57–60 (she discusses the 1869 suffrage convention in the Introduction).

2. William Worthington Fowler, *Twenty Years of Inside Life in Wall Street; or, Revelations of the Personal Experiences of a Speculator* (New York: Orange Judd, 1880), 456; and *Ten Years in Wall Street; or, Revelations of Inside Life and Experience on 'Change* (Hartford, Conn.: Worthington, Dustin, 1870), 458.

3. *New York Courier*, February 14, 1870, reprinted in Victoria Woodhull, *The Human Body, the Temple of God; or The Philosophy of Sociology* (London, 1890); *The Days' Doings*, February 26, 1870, 194. Even for men, Wall Street had negative connotations. See Wayne Westbrook, *Wall Street in the American Novel* (New York: New York University Press, 1980), 32; James McCabe (Edward Winslow Martin), *Secrets of the Great City* (Philadelphia: Jones Brothers, 1868), 148.

4. See interview with the *Pittsburgh Evening Leader*, c. 1873, quoted in Gabriel, *Notorious Victoria*, 41. See, e.g., *New York World*, February 8, 1870; *New York Sun*, February 7, 1870; *New York Herald*, February 6, 13, 1870. Excerpts from these papers appear in Gabriel, *Notorious Victoria*.

5. Miss Virginia Penny, *How Women Can Make Money, Married or Single, In all Branches of the Arts and Sciences, Professions, Trades, Agricultural and Mechanical Pursuits* (1870; reprint New York: Arno and New York Times, 1971), 8–9. Susan B. Anthony quoted in *The Revolution*, March 10, 24, 1870, 159, 188. The pro-suffrage *San Francisco Pioneer* noted the opening in its February 12 and March 12, 1870 issues. James K. Medbery, *Men and Mysteries of Wall Street* (Boston: Fields, Osgood, 1870), for example, assumed that Wall Street was a male domain.

6. *The Days' Doings*, February 26, 1870.

7. The most reliable treatments of their early lives appear in Underhill, *The Woman Who Ran for President*, 11–39, and Gabriel, *Notorious Victoria*, 7–11. Colonel Blood's memories of Woodhull during this period are found in a sworn affidavit before Judge George M. Van Hoessen, July 26, 1876, New York Court of Common

Pleas. Typed facsimile in Emianie (Nahm) Sachs Arling Philips Collection, Manuscripts, Department of Library Special Collections, Kentucy Building, Western Kentucky University, Bowling Green, Kentucky (hereafter WKU).

8. Emianie Sachs, *"The Terrible Siren": Victoria Woodhull (1838–1927)* (New York: Harper & Bros., 1928); Johanna Johnston, *Mrs. Satan: The Incredible Saga of Victoria Woodhull* (New York: Putnam, 1967); M. M. Marberry, *Vicki: A Biography of Victoria C. Woodhull* (New York: Funk and Wagnalls, 1967); Underhill, *The Woman Who Ran for President*; Goldsmith, *Other Powers*; Gabriel, *Notorious Victoria*. Fictional biographies include James Brough, *The Vixens: A Biography of Victoria and Tennessee Claflin* (New York: Simon and Schuster, 1980); Beril Becker, *Whirlwind in Petticoats* (Garden City, N.Y.: Doubleday, 1947). Documentaries include *To Judge by Her Heart: Victoria Woodhull* (Suzanne Condray, 1995); *America's Victoria: Remembering Victoria Woodhull* (New York: Women Make Movies, 1995). Plays include Howard Richardson and E. G. Kasakoff, *A Thread in Scarlet* (1976); Geralyn Horton, *Spirit and Flesh: The Life of Victoria Woodhull* (1976); Keith Herrmann, *Onward Victoria* (1981). Chapters in volumes about American cranks include Gerald W. Johnson, *The Lunatic Fringe* (1957; reprint Westport, Conn.: Greenwood Press, 1973); Ishbel Ross, *Charmers and Cranks: Twelve Famous American Women Who Defied the Conventions* (New York: Harper and Row, 1965); Stewart Holbrook, *Dreamers of the American Dream* (Garden City, N.Y.: Doubleday, 1957); Irving Wallace, *The Nympho and Other Maniacs* (New York: Simon and Schuster, 1971). For international interpretations, see Françoise Basch, *Rebelles américaines au XIXe siècle: Mariage, amor libre et politique* (Paris: Klincksieck, 1990); Nicole Blondeau, *Victoria la scandaleuse: La vie extraordinaire de Victoria Woodhull, 1838–1927* (Paris: Éditions Menges, 1979).

9. Question from audience member to Barbara Goldsmith, Lecture, February 3, 1998. Temple Israel, New York City.

10. Benjamin Tucker to Emanie Sachs, n.d. (1927), reprinted in Sachs, *"The Terrible Siren"*, 258–60; Henry Woodhouse to Emanie Sachs, 1927, WKU.

11. A notable example of this is the diary of Susan B. Anthony. Two weeks of entries were torn out, by Anthony or by her biographer Ida Husted Harper, for the period during which the NWSA formally rejected Woodhull as a leader. See Goldsmith, *Other Powers*, 319–20. No comment by Frederick Douglass, nominated as Woodhull's running mate by the Equal Rights Party in 1872, appears in his extant letters. Frederick Douglass Papers, Library of Congress.

12. Theodore Tilton, *Victoria C. Woodhull, A Biographical Sketch: Mr. Tilton's Account of Mrs. Woodhull, Golden Age Tracts*, 3 (New York: McDivitt, Campbell, 1871). On the many revisions of her life story, see Candyce Homnick Stapen, "The Novel Form and Woodhull & Claflin's Weekly, 1870–76: A Little Magazine Edited by Women and Published for Suffragists, Socialists, Free Lovers, and Other Radicals" (Ph.D. thesis, University of Maryland, College Park, 1979).

13. G. S. Darewin, *Synopsis of the Lives of Victoria C. Woodhull, Now Mrs. John Biddulph Martin, and Tennessee Claflin, Now Lady Cook: The First Two Lady Bankers and Reformers of America* (London, 1891); M. F. Darwin, *One Moral Standard for All: Extracts from the Lives of Victoria Claflin Woodhull, Now Mrs. John Biddulph Martin, and Tennessee Claflin, Now Lady Cook* (New York: Caulon Press, 1915);

Roslyn D'Onston, *Brief Sketches in the Life of Victoria Woodhull (Now Mrs. John Biddulph Martin* (London, 1893); Madeleine Legge, *Two Noble Women, Nobly Planned* (London: Phelps Brothers, 1893).

14. Carrie Chapman Catt to Emanie Sachs, July 21, 1927; Harriet Stanton Blatch to Emanie Sachs, July 5, 1927; Ida Husted Harper to Emanie Sachs, July 10, 1927, all in Correspondence, WKU.

15. Joseph Greer to Emanie Sachs, September 28, 1927; Grace Ellery Channing-Stetson to Emanie Sachs, June 29, 1927, Correspondence, WKU.

16. Zula Maud Woodhull died in January 1941; legal wrangling over the proposed biography continued for more than a decade. See (C. K. Odgen), Memorandum, June 1, 1951; J. Kingsley Curtis, Esq. to C. K. Odgen, July 6, 1953. Victoria Woodhull Martin Collection, Special Collections/Morris Library, Southern Illinois University, Carbondale.

17. Marberry, *Vicki*; Johnson, *The Lunatic Fringe*; Ross, *Charmers and Cranks*; Holbrook, *Dreamers of the American Dream*; Wallace, *The Nympho and Other Maniacs*. Only one from this period acknowledged the possibility of Woodhull's principles. See Johnston, *Mrs. Satan*.

18. Eleanor Flexner, *Century of Struggle: The Woman's Rights Movement in the United States* (Cambridge, Mass.: Belknap Press of Harvard University Press, 1959); Madeleine Bettina Stern, *We the Women: Career Firsts of Nineteenth-Century America* (New York: Schulte, 1963). For the two collections of lectures, see Stern, *The Victoria Woodhull Reader* (Weston, Mass.: M & S Press, 1974); Arlene Kisner, *Woodhull & Claflin's Weekly: The Lives and Writings of Notorious Victoria Woodhull and Her Sister Tennessee Claflin* (Washington, N.J.: Time Change Press, 1972).

19. Ellen Carol DuBois, "Taking the Law into Our Own Hands: *Bradwell, Minor*, and Suffrage Militance in the 1870s," in Nancy A. Hewitt and Suzanne Lebsock, eds., *Visible Women: New Essays on American Activism* (Urbana: University of Illinois Press, 1993). A critical interpretation of Woodhull's impact on the suffrage movement appears in Andrea Moore Kerr, "White Women's Rights, Black Men's Wrongs: Free Love, Blackmail, and the Formation of the American Woman Suffrage Association," in Marjorie Spruill Wheeler, ed., *One Woman One Vote: Rediscovering the Woman Suffrage Movement* (Troutdale, Ore.: NewSage Press, 1995).

20. Mari Jo Buhle, *Women and American Socialism, 1870–1920* (Urbana: University of Illinois Press, 1981); Buhle, *Women and the American Left: A Guide to Sources* (Boston: G.K. Hall, 1983); Timothy Messer-Kruse, *The Yankee International: Marxism and the American Reform Tradition* (Chapel Hill: University of North Carolina Press, 1998). Most earlier scholars of the First International played down Woodhull's significance to the organization. Philip S. Foner, while he cautions against overly critical readings of Woodhull, praised the skill of Friedrich Sorge in successfully expelling her section. Foner, *History of the Labor Movement in the United States*, vol. 1, *From Colonial Times to the Founding of the American Federation of Labor* (New York: International Publishers, 1947).

21. For a detailed analysis of the three new biographies, see Helen Lefkowitz Horowitz, "A Victoria Woodhull for the 1990s," *Reviews in American History* 27 (1999): 87–97.

22. Richard Wightman Fox, *Trials of Intimacy: Love and Loss in the Beecher-Tilton Scandal* (Chicago: University of Chicago Press, 1999); Altina Laura Waller, *Reverend Beecher and Mrs. Tilton: Sex and Class in Victorian America* (Amherst: University of Massachusetts Press, 1982).

23. Helen Lefkovitz Horowitz, *Rereading Sex: Battles over Sexual Knowledge and Suppression in Nineteenth-Century America* (New York: Knopf, 2002); also Horowitz, "Victoria Woodhull, Anthony Comstock, and the Conflict over Sex in the United States in the 1870s," *Journal of American History* (September 2000): 403–34; Andrea Tone, *Devices and Desires: A History of Contraceptives in America* (New York: Hill and Wang, 2001).

24. See Joanne Passet, *Sex Radicals and the Quest for Women's Equality* (Urbana: University of Illinois Press, 2003).

25. On the rise of celebrities as mass mediated public individuals, see David L. Andrews and Steven J. Jackson, eds., *Sports Stars: The Cultural Politics of Sporting Celebrity* (London: Routledge, 2001), 3. See also Peter Buckley, "To the Opera House: Culture and Society in New York City, 1820–1860" (Ph.D. thesis, State University of New York, Stony Brook, 1984). On the impact of the graphic revolution, see Daniel J. Boorstin, *The Image: A Guide to Pseudo-Events in America* (New York, Harper and Row, 1964), 57. On the changing nature of celebrity caricatures, see Wendy Wick Reaves, *Celebrity Caricature in America* (New Haven, Conn.: National Portrait Gallery, Smithsonian Institution, in association with Yale University Press, 1998). On the growing demand for individual celebrity, see Leo Braudy, *The Frenzy of Renown: Fame and Its History* (New York: Oxford University Press, 1986), 498. See also Neal Gabler, *Life the Movie: How Entertainment Conquered Reality* (New York: Knopf, 1998). On the democratic implications of celebrityhood, see P. David Marshall, *Celebrity and Power: Fame in Contemporary Culture* (Minneapolis: University of Minnesota Press, 1997).

26. One of the best analyses of illustrated popular media in the nineteenth century is Judith R. Walkowitz, *City of Dreadful Delight: Narratives of Sexual Danger in Late-Victorian London* (Chicago: University of Chicago Press, 1992). See also Amy Srebnick, *The Mysterious Death of Mary Rogers: Sex and Culture in Nineteenth-Century New York* (New York: Oxford University Press, 1995); Patricia Cline Cohen, *The Murder of Helen Jewett: The Life and Death of a Prostitute in Nineteenth-Century New York* (New York: Knopf, 1998); Howard Chudacoff, *The Age of the Bachelor: Creating an American Subculture* (Princeton, N.J.: Princeton University Press, 1999); Lisa Duggan, *Sapphic Slashers: Sex, Violence, and American Modernity* (Durham, N.C.: Duke University Press, 2000).

27. No other individual or event received the amount of textual and illustrated coverage the sisters received in *The Days' Doings*. By my count, they appeared in twelve issues of the weekly tabloid between 1870 and the end of 1872. Three of these issues featured one or both sisters on the cover. By contrast, alleged murderess Laura D. Fair appeared three times, twice on the cover.

28. On the iconography of misogyny, see Bram Dijkstra, *Idols of Perversity: Fantasies of Feminine Evil in Fin-de-Siècle Culture* (New York: Oxford University Press, 1986). See also Gay L. Gullickson, *Unruly Women of Paris: Images of the Commune* (Ithaca, N.Y.: Cornell University Press, 1996); Adrienne Munich, *Andromeda's*

Chains: Gender and Interpretation in Victorian Literature and Art (New York: Columbia University Press, 1989); Ellen Wiley Todd, *The "New Woman" Revised: Painting and Gender Politics on Fourteenth Street* (Berkeley: University of California Press, 1993).

29. On the disorderly woman in the nineteenth century, see Carroll Smith-Rosenberg, "The New Woman as Androgyne: Social Disorder and Gender Crisis, 1870–1936," in Smith-Rosenberg, *Disorderly Conduct: Visions of Gender in Victorian America* (New York: Oxford University Press, 1985), 245. See also Lyn Pykett, *The "Improper" Feminine: The Woman's Sensation Novel and the New Woman Writing* (London: Routledge, 1992); Carol Vance, "Pleasure and Danger: Toward a Politics of Sexuality," in Vance, ed., *Pleasure and Danger: Exploring Female Sexuality* (Boston: Routledge, 1984).

30. Joshua Brown, *Beyond the Lines: Pictorial Reporting, Everyday Life, and the Crisis of Gilded Age America* (Berkeley: University of California Press, 2002).

31. The obsession was fueled in part by the traveling sideshow feature of the Siamese twins and in part by the streetwalkers' practice of traveling in pairs. On twins in popular culture, see Marc Shell, "Siamese Twins and Changlings," in his *Children of the Earth: Literature, Politics and Nationhood* (New York: Oxford University Press, 1993), 5–11. See also Susan Gillman, *Dark Twins: Imposture and Identity in Mark Twain's America* (Chicago: University of Chicago Press, 1989), 7, 209n127.

32. On religious and social objections to prominent female activists in the nineteenth century, see Karlyn Kohrs Campbell, ed., *Man Cannot Speak for Her*, vol. 2, *Key Texts of the Early Feminists* (Westport, Conn.; Greenwood Press, 1989), ix–xxviii; Kathleen Hall Jamieson, *Beyond the Double Bind: Women and Leadership* (New York: Oxford University Press, 1995), 85–86; Jean Fagin Yellin, *Women and Sisters: The Antislavery Feminists in American Culture* (New Haven, Conn.: Yale University Press, 1989), 65; Lori Ginzberg, "'The Hearts of Your Readers Will Shudder': Fanny Wright, Infidelity, and American Freethought," *American Quarterly* 46, 2 (June 1994): 195–226; Carolyn De Swarte Gifford, "Frances Willard and the Woman's Christian Temperance Union's Conversion to Woman Suffrage," in Wheeler, ed., *One Woman One Vote*. I discuss the sexualization of the "public woman" in more detail in "Sex in Politics: Victoria Woodhull as Public Woman," *Journal of Women's History* 12, 1 (June 2000): 89–110.

33. *New York Standard*, January 16, 1871.

34. Laura Cuppy Smith, "How One Woman Entered the Ranks of Social Reform; or, a Mother's Story," *WCW*, March 1, 1873, 3–5.

35. On "public womanhood," see Nancy Fraser, *Unruly Practices: Power, Discourse, and Gender in Contemporary Social Theory* (Minneapolis: University of Minnesota Press, 1989); Leonore Davidoff and Catherine Hall, *Family Fortunes: Men and Women of the English Middle Class, 1780–1850* (Chicago: University of Chicago Press, 1987); Glenda Matthews, *The Rise of Public Woman: Women's Power and Women's Place in the United States, 1630–1970* (New York: Oxford University Press, 1992); Mary Ryan, *Women in Public: Between Banners and Ballots, 1825–1880* (Baltimore: Johns Hopkins University Press, 1990). On the moral power of separate spheres, see Nancy Cott, *The Bonds of Womanhood: "Woman's Sphere" in New England, 1780–1835* (New Haven, Conn.: Yale University Press, 1977). On women's segregation from the public

sphere, see Jean Bethke Elshtain, *Public Man, Private Woman: Women in Social and Political Thought* (Princeton, N.J.: Princeton University Press, 1981). For the class implications of separate spheres and public access for women, see Walkowitz, *City of Dreadful Delight* and Christine Stansell, *City of Women: Sex and Class in New York, 1789–1860* (New York: Knopf, 1986). See also Gerda Lerner, "The Lady and the Mill Girl," in Lerner, *The Majority Finds Its Past: Placing Women in History* (New York: Oxford University Press, 1979).

36. Before leaving for England, Woodhull typically refused to confirm or deny these rumors, though she did sue one man, Joseph Treat, for libel for publishing such assertions. I discuss the question whether Woodhull engaged in prostitution in Chapter 4.

37. Incident cited in Sachs, *"The Terrible Siren"*, 63 On women dining in restaurants, see Timothy Gilfoyle, *City of Eros: New York City, Prostitution, and the Commercialization of Sex, 1820–1920* (New York: Norton, 1992), 122, 248.

38. Natalie Zemon Davis, "Women on Top," in her *Society and Culture in Early Modern France: Eight Essays* (Stanford, Calif.: Stanford University Press, 1975); Mary Russo, "Female Grotesques: Carnival and Theory," in Teresa De Lauretis, ed., *Feminist Studies, Critical Studies* (Bloomington: Indiana University Press, 1986); Temma Kaplan, *Crazy for Democracy: Women in Grassroots Movements* (New York: Routledge, 1997). On the "folk devil," see Stan Cohen, *Folk Devils and Moral Panics: The Creation of the Mods and Rockers* (London: MacGibbon and Kee, 1972), 43, 175, 190–93. See also Neil Hertz, "Medusa's Head: Male Hysteria Under Political Pressure," *Representations* 4 (Fall 1983): 27–54.

39. Elizabeth Cady Stanton quoted in *Newark Sunday Call*, January 2, 1876, reprinted in Goldsmith, *Other Powers*, 427.

Chapter 1. Principles of Social Freedom

1. Victoria Woodhull to *New York Herald*, March 29, 1870, printed April 2, 1870. Stephen Pearl Andrews's biographer, Madeleine Stern, asserts that Andrews and Colonel James Blood composed this letter. Stern, *The Pantarch: A Biography of Stephen Pearl Andrews* (Austin: University of Texas Press, 1968), 116–17.

2. Stephen Pearl Andrews, ed., *Love, Marriage, and Divorce and the Sovereignty of the Individual: A Discussion by Henry James, Horace Greeley, and Stephen Pearl Andrews* (New York: Stringer and Townsend, 1853). For a detailed examination of the sex radicals, see Joanne Ellen Passet, *Sex Radicals and the Quest for Women's Equality* (Urbana: University of Illinois Press, 2003). On Andrews's sex radicalism, see John Spurlock, *Free Love: Marriage and Middle-Class Radicalism in America, 1825–1860* (New York: New York University Press, 1988), 121–23, 138–46, 153. See also Roger Wunderlich, *Low Living and High Thinking at Modern Times* (Syracuse, N.Y.: Syracuse University Press, 1992). On the evolution of this sexual framework that put sex "at the core of being," see Horowitz, *Rereading Sex*, chaps. 14, 15, quote p. 9.

3. Ezra Heywood's 1870 book *Uncivil Liberty: An Essay to Show the Injustice and Impolicy of Ruling Woman Without Her Consent* (Princeton, Mass.: Cooperative

Publishing Company, 1870), for example, argued that woman suffrage led inevitably to the abolition of marriage. Martin Henry Blatt, *Free Love and Anarchism: The Biography of Ezra Heywood* (Urbana: University of Illinois Press, 1989), 100. Free love novelist Lois Waisbrooker achieved fame in 1894 when she was convicted of obscenity charges for her book *A Sex Revolution* (1879; reprint Philadelphia: New Society, 1985). Francis Barry founded Berlin Heights, a free love community near Cleveland, after 1854, merging Spiritualism and Free Love. Along with Modern Times, Berlin Heights represented "a small, but vigorous, counterculture within American society." Spurlock, *Free Love*, 157, 163. Moses Hull's paper, *The Crucible*, was a sex radical press like the *Weekly* (periodically suspended during these years).

4. See Ann Braude, *Radical Spirits: Spiritualism and Women's Rights in Nineteenth-Century America* (Bloomington: Indiana University Press, 2001); Alex Owen, *The Darkened Room: Women, Power and Spiritualism in Late Nineteenth Century England* (Philadelphia: University of Pennsylvania Pres, 1989); Barbara Taylor, *Eve and the New Jerusalem: Socialism and Feminism in the Nineteenth Century* (New York: Pantheon, 1983). Diana Basham, *The Trial of Woman: Feminism and the Occult Sciences in Victorian Literature and Society* (Basingstoke: Macmillan, 1992), 135.

5. Braude, *Radical Spirits*, 128–30; quote, 129. See also Basham, *The Trial of Woman*, 119; Howard Kerr, *Mediums, Spirit Rappers and Roaring Radicals: Spiritualism in American Literature, 1850–1900* (Urbana: University of Illinois Press, 1972), 11, 141. On the presence of sex radicals at Woodhull's lectures, see *New York Times, New York Herald*, August 12, 1871, *New York Star*, March 30, 1872. Like other sex radicals, Woodhull wore a reform costume, a variant on men's clothing, on some occasions. See *New York Sun*, n.d., *WCW*, October 8, 1870, cited also in Underhill, *The Woman Who Ran for President*, 127. Claflin occasionally went without a corset, another indication of allegiance to dress reformers who condemned the garment. See Sachs, *"The Terrible Siren"*, 82.

6. First two quotes from "The Social Evil," *WCW*, July 23, 1870, 11. Quotes three and four from "Woman's Ability to Earn Money," *WCW*, September 17, 1870, 11, emphasis in original. By contrast, the New York Woman's Club thought that "the chief and radical remedy for the social evil, lies in the political enfranchisement and thence personal emancipation of women." New York Women's Club resolution quoted in *New York Times*, October 30, 1871.

7. See "The Social Evil," *WCW*, August 20, 1870, 9; "Licensed Prostitution," *WCW*, August 20, 1870, 9.

8. On the doctrine of "no secrets," see William Leach, *True Love and Perfect Union: The Feminist Reform of Sex and Society* (New York: Basic Books, 1980), 38–63. On the competing discourses of sexual openness and social purity, see William O'Neill, *Everyone Was Brave: A History of Feminism in America* (Chicago: Quadrangle Books, 1971), 23–30.

9. See J. West Nevins, "Love," *WCW*, December 24, 1870, 3; Nancy Cott, "Passionlessness: An Interpretation of Victorian Sexual Ideology, 1790–1850," *Signs: A Journal of Women in Culture and Society* 4 (1978): 219–36.

10. Missouri suffragists Virginia and Francis Minor introduced the "New Departure" in 1869; many women on a local level subsequently acted on the theory and voted. By taking the argument to Congress, Woodhull gave the new departure

to a national forum. See Ellen Carol DuBois, "Taking the Law into Our Own Hands: *Bradwell, Minor,* and Suffrage Militance in the 1870s," in Nancy A. Hewitt and Suzanne Lebsock, eds., *Visible Women: New Essays on American Activism* (Urbana: University of Illinois Press, 1993), 21–29. In fact, it would take half a century to pass a separate amendment to enable women's vote on a national level: while some states passed suffrage legislation in the intervening years, it was not until 1920 that the Nineteenth Amendment, granting federal protection for female voters, was ratified. I discuss the race and gender politics over the Fifteenth Amendment more fully in Chapter 2.

11. Elizabeth Cady Stanton to Mrs. (Josephine) Griffing, December 1, 1870. Elizabeth Cady Stanton, Susan B. Anthony Papers, Library of Congress; Elizabeth Cady Stanton to Martha Coffin Pelham Wright, December 31, 1870; Garrison Family Papers, Sophia Smith Collection, Smith College, Northampton, Mass. More than once, NWSA leaders appealed to Woodhull for financial aid in spreading the new departure theory. See Susan B. Anthony to Victoria C. Woodhull, February 24, 1871, Victoria Woodhull Martin Collection, Special Collections/Morris Library, Southern Illinois University, Carbondale. On the political connections that made Woodhull's Memorial possible, see Underhill, *The Woman Who Ran for President,* chap. 10. Anthony, who rode the train back to New York with Woodhull just after the Memorial, wrote of her that "she is very charming—utterly forgetful of difference of sex in her approach to *men*." Susan B. Anthony, *Diary,* January 14, 1871, emphasis in original. Susan B. Anthony Papers, Library of Congress.

12. Quote from Stanton to Milo S. Townsend, April 5, 1871, cited in Gabriel, *Notorious Victoria,* 91; Isabella Beecher Hooker to Susan B. Anthony, March 11 (and 14), 1871, reprinted in Jeanne Boydston, Mary Kelley, and Anne Margolis, eds., *The Limits of Sisterhood: The Beecher Sisters on Women's Rights and Women's Sphere* (Chapel Hill: University of North Carolina Press, 1988), 205–9.

13. *True Woman,* March 1871 (first issue).

14. The first and most sensational coverage of the case appeared in *New York Star,* May 5, 6, 7, 1871. See also *New York Independent,* n.d., reprinted in *WCW* June 3, 1871; *New York Standard,* May 17, 1871; *Cleveland Leader,* n.d., reprinted in *WCW,* May 27, 1871; *New York Evening Post,* May 16, 1871. On divorce law, see Mary Somerville Jones, "An Historical Geography of the Changing Divorce Law in the United States" (Ph.D. thesis, University of North Carolina, Chapel Hill, 1978).

15. Harriet Beecher Stowe, *My Wife & I: or, Harry Henderson's History* (New York: J.B. Ford, 1871), 269. The episode concerning Woodhull's scandal appeared in *Christian Union,* May 31, June 7, 1871. The Rev. Phebe Hanaford to Isabella Beecher Hooker, September 12, August 9, 1871, reprinted in Boydston et al., *The Limits of Sisterhood,* 295. The debate over sex in politics was widespread during the early 1870s. See Cynthia Russett, *Sexual Science: The Victorian Construction of Womanhood* (Cambridge, Mass.: Harvard University Press, 1989) and Louise Newman, ed., *Men's Ideas, Women's Realities: Popular Science, 1870–1915* (New York: Pergamon, 1985), for discussions of biological arguments. For an analysis of the religious arguments about sex and gender, see Elizabeth Lemons, "Sex in Context: Toward a Contextual Feminist Theology of Heterosexual Relations in the Contemporary United States Through an Analysis of Victoria Woodhull's Nineteenth-Century Free-Love Discourse" (Ph.D.

thesis, Harvard University School of Divinity, 1997). For samples of the debate, see *The Nation,* May 25, 1871; *Pall Mall Gazette,* n.d.; *Harper's Weekly,* n.d., reprinted in *WCW,* June 10, 1871; *New York Tribune,* May 9–13, 1871; *New York Herald,* May 13, 1871.

16. See Ellen Carol DuBois, "Outgrowing the Compact of the Fathers: Equal Rights, Woman Suffrage, and the United States' Constitution, 1820–1878," in DuBois, *Woman Suffrage and Women's Rights* (New York: New York University Press, 1998).

17. Two other organizations, the National Labor Union (NLU) and the Knights of Labor, were developing a class-based consciousness, but in the early 1870s neither organization had much influence. The most comprehensive treatment of the IWA in America can be found in Timothy Messer-Kruse, *Yankee International: Marxism and the American Reform Tradition* (Chapel Hill: University of North Carolina Press, 1998). See also Kenneth Lapides, ed., *Marx and Engels on the Trade Unions* (New York: Praeger, 1987), 192n71. On Sorge, see Foner, *History of the Labor Movement,* 1: 413–15.

18. Woodhull and Claflin were active promoters of the IWA from the summer of 1871. Woodhull spoke at a convention for the New England Labor Reform League in May of 1871, and gave her speech "The Principles of Finance," supporting the Greenback movement, in early August. See for example "A Woman on Woman," *New York Star,* June 5, 1871; *New York Times,* August 4, 1871. They published articles such as "The Commune," "The International Society," the "Address of the General Council of the International Workingmen's Association," and an interview with Karl Marx (reprinted from *New York World*) in *WCW,* June 24, July 15, July 22, August 12, 1871. On their involvement with the organization, see Messer-Kruse, *Yankee International,* 158–63.

19. Sorge, *Report to General Council* for September, October 1, 1871, IWA Papers/North American Federal Council Records. Section Twelve's plea for leadership of the American IWA was read at the October 17, 1871 meeting of the General Council. *The General Council of the First International, Minutes* (Moscow: Progress Publishers, n.d.; hereafter *GCM*), 4: 305. Marx wrote that "Section 12 (New York) has submitted proposals to the General Council that it be constituted the leader in America. [Johann] Eccarius will have sent the decisions against these pretensions and for the present Committee to Section 12." Marx to Sorge, November 6, 1871, *Karl Marx and Friedrich Engels: Letters to Americans, 1848–1895* (Moscow: International Publishing Company, 1953), 85.

20. Braude, *Radical Spirits,* 167–75. See also Passet, *Sex Radicals,* 100–101.

21. AAS Convention proceedings and Woodhull's election reported in *BL,* September 30, 1871; Woodhull, "Children—Their Rights and Privileges," *BL,* October 28, 1871. For samples of the ensuing controversy, see "Victoria C. Woodhull," *BL,* October 28, 1871, 4; "Meeting of the Trustees of the American Association of Spiritualists," *BL,* November 11, 1871, 1. Her first and most vocal critic was Hudson Tuttle; see his "A Protest," *RPJ,* December 16, 1871, 2 and "American Association of Spiritualists and the New Disgrace," *RPJ,* February 17, 1872. Even a year later, correspondent Mary Phelps referred to Woodhull's election as "a swindle." Letter, *RPJ,* November 30, 1872. For details of how Woodhull got elected, see Hannah Brown, "The National Convention and Mrs. Woodhull," *BL,* March 9, 1872. Charles Holt denied Tuttle's suggestion of voting impropriety in "The New Disgrace," *BL* March 30, 1872.

22. Text of lecture showbill reprinted in Gabriel, *Notorious Victoria*, 146–47. Text of the "Principles of Social Freedom" speech appears in *The Victoria Woodhull Reader*, ed. Madeleine Stern (Weston, Mass: M & S Press, 1974). For typical press coverage, see *New York Herald*, November 21, 1871; *The Day's Doings*, December 3, 1871.

23. Descriptions of the audience appear in *New York Herald*, November 21, 1871, 10, *New York Star*, November 21, 1871.

24. Quotes from Victoria Woodhull, "'And The Truth Shall Make You Free,' A Speech on the Principles of Social Freedom," 26, 20, emphases in original. Facsimile of pamphlet reprinted in Stern, ed., *Victoria Woodhull Reader*. The lecture was probably the work of Stephen Pearl Andrews, with the assistance of Colonel James Blood and possibly Woodhull herself.

25. Woodhull, "'And the Truth Shall Make You Free,'" 33, 12, 34.

26. Woodhull, "'And the Truth Shall Make You Free,'" 35.

27. Woodhull, "'And the Truth Shall Make You Free,'" 23–24.

28. Tilton believed she said the words extemporaneously. See Sachs, *"The Terrible Siren"*, 137–38.

29. Incident described *New York Herald*, November 21, 1871.

30. *WCW*, December 9, 1871; Mary Bowles to *WCW*, December 16, 1871. Emanie Sachs claims that Tennie C. Claflin wrote this letter. Sachs, *"The Terrible Siren"*, 142. Barbara Goldsmith suggests that the letter may have come from well-known New York madam Annie Wood. Goldsmith, *Other Powers*, 339. It is possible that the *Weekly*'s managing editor, Colonel Blood, was in fact the author of both letters.

31. Friedrich Bolte, quoted in *New York World*, November 27, 1871, cited in Messer-Kruse, *Yankee International*, 152; for a nuanced discussion of the legacy of the two-thirds rule, see 173–74.

32. Typical commercial press coverage can be found in *New York Herald*, December 4, 1871, IWA Papers/Clippings; see also *New York Times*, December 15, 1871; *New York World* editorial, December 18, 1871; *New York World*, December 15, 1871. Labor-friendly presses, by contrast, placed the sisters in a carriage at the back of the march. See *New York Star*, December 13, 14, 16, 17, 18, 1871. The *New York Standard*, whose compositors formed the new "printers" section just prior to the parade in order to join the march, commended the efforts of Section Twelve, among others, in the December 12, and December 18, 1871 issues. Section Two's *Le Socialiste* endorsed the funeral parade in December 9, 1871 issue (in response to killings by Thiers and Versailles assembly, November 28, 1871); additional coverage of the controversy leading up to the march and the event itself appears in *Le Socialiste*, December 16, December 23, 1871. See also Philip Mark Katz, "Americanizing the Paris Commune, 1861–1877" (Ph.D. thesis, Princeton University, 1994), 350–52; Mark A. Lause, "American Radicals and Organized Marxism: The Initial Experience, 1869–1874," *Labor History* 33 (1992): 55–80. As Lause argues, "Sorge's 'Marxists' had not only opposed it but were lost in the crowd of thousands who had responded to the call by the supposedly alienating advocates of free love and spiritualism" (67n24).

33. *New York Herald*, February 21, 1872; *WCW*, March 2, 1872; *New York Sun*, February 21, 1872. Woodhull's own estimate was higher: she later claimed an audience of 8,200, with 10,000 more denied admittance outside. Woodhull, "Moral Cowardice and Modern Hypocrisy," *WCW*, December 28, 1872, 5.

34. *New York Times*, February 22, 1872.

35. After some confusion over the date, the meeting was finally held on March 14, thanks to "the circulation of a vast number of handbills," thereby bringing together a "large concourse of people." The meeting was originally scheduled for March 7, but almost nobody showed up; Theodore Banks announced at the time that the meeting was rescheduled for March 12. Organizers included Ira Davis, John Elliott, and Theodore Banks. See *New York Times*, March 8, 1872; *New York Herald*, March 15, 1872.

36. Other speakers included C. O. Ward, Ira B. Davies, and George Madox, all members of the Yankee International, many of Section Twelve; *New York Herald*, March 19, 1872; see also *New York Star*, March 19, 1872.

37. "Resolutions on the Split in the United States' Federation Passed by the General Council of the IWA in its Sittings of 5th and 12th March, 1872," *GCM*, 5: 120–25, 410–13.

38. "A Lady of Hartford" and "A Citizen of Hartford," letters to *Hartford Courant*, November 11, 14, 1871. Although anonymously written, Sachs credits these two letters (as did Woodhull herself) to Catharine Beecher. Sachs, *"The Terrible Siren"*, 124–25.

39. *New Northwest*, December 1, 1871.

40. Martha Coffin Wright to Elizabeth Cady Stanton, March 3, 1872. Garrison Family Papers, Sophia Smith Collection, Smith College, Northampton, Mass.

41. Stanton quote from Elizabeth Cady Stanton, *Golden Age*, December 1871, cited in Alma Lutz, *Created Equal: A Biography of Elizabeth Cady Stanton, 1815–1902* (New York: John Day, 1940), 215. Stanton, for example, appealed to her for help with publicizing the NWSA January 1872 convention. Elizabeth Cady Stanton to Victoria C. Woodhull, December 29, 1871, New York Public Library, Miscellaneous Papers. Anthony's comments to the NWSA convention reported in *WCW*, January 27, 1872. Addie Ballou later recalled her nomination of Woodhull in Addie Ballou to Mrs. Woodhull Martin, September 23, 1908, Victoria Woodhull Martin Collection, Special Collections/Morris Library, Southern Illinois University, Carbondale. On Anthony's response, see Underhill, *The Woman Who Ran for President*, 188–93.

42. Stanton was involved in the convention planning from early 1872 and had dreamed of forming a third party for years before that. See Elizabeth Cady Stanton to Isabella Beecher Hooker, February 2, 1872, Stowe-Day Memorial Collection, Hartford, Connecticut. She drafted a party platform and probably was responsible for the call that appeared in the *Weekly* in March 1872. This platform has been reprinted in DuBois, *Elizabeth Cady Stanton, Susan B. Anthony Reader*, 166–69.

43. Local officials obstructed Anthony's lectures in some cases, and this combined with heavy snows caused her to lament that "the Cash fates are all against me." *Diary*, September 23, 1871; November 30, 1871; December 2, 1871; December 20, 1871 (quote). Susan B. Anthony Papers, Library of Congress. There are indications of opposition to Woodhull's presence in the NWSA. In early 1872, Iowa suffragists asked Stanton and Anthony to keep out of the state during the legislative session, when a suffrage bill was under debate, because of the NWSA's association with Woodhull. Louise Noun, *Strong Minded Women: The Emergence of the Woman-Suffrage Movement in Iowa* (Ames: Iowa State University Press, 1969), 203. That

March, the Rev. O. B. Frothingham turned down an invitation to speak at the NWSA's May 1872 convention. O. B. Frothingham to Matilda Joslyn Gage, March 25, 1872. Matilda Joslyn Gage Papers, Schlesinger Library. Like Catharine Beecher, Anthony espoused the principle of "Victorianism," a rationale for women's moral superiority based on her sexual purity. See Kathryn Kish Sklar, *Catharine Beecher: A Study in American Domesticity* (New Haven, Conn.: Yale University Press, 1972), 211.

44. Quote from Hudson Tuttle, "American Association of Spiritualists—A New Disgrace?" *RPJ*, February 17, 1872. On the opposition of moderate Spiritualists, see J. K. Bailey, "A New Departure," *BL*, November 25, 1871; Emma Hardinge-Britten (formerly Emma Hardinge), "Spiritualism and Mrs. Victoria C. Woodhull," *BL*, February 3, 1872, 2. At least one AAS board member resigned because she "could not endorse the address of Mrs. Woodhull." "Mrs. Susan C. Waters," *RPJ*, March 16, 1872.

45. Juliet Severance to the Editor, "Our Disgrace," *RPJ*, March 2, 1872. Severance, later called the "Woodhull of Wisconsin," was an alternative physician and Spiritualist and, according to Joanne Passet, an "uncompromising reformer, [who] thrived on challenging orthodox views." Passet, *Sex Radicals*, 126.

46. Editorial "The New Departure," *BL*, February 17, 1872, 8; E. S. Wheeler, "Shall Victoria C. Woodhull be Impeached," *BL*, February 17, 1872; Laura Cuppy Smith, "The Social Problem Reviewed," *BL*, March 23, 1872.

47. Lois Waisbrooker, "Things as I See Them," *BL*, May 11, 1872. Waisbrooker, like her friend Juliet Severance, was a Spiritualist who "dedicated herself to exposing the negative consequences of the moral double standard." Passet, *Sex Radicals*, 115. For the *Banner of Light* coverage of the controversy, see "Free Speaking from a Woman," "Mrs. Woodhull at Steinway Hall, *BL*, December 9, 16, 1871; the entire lecture appears in *BL*, January 20, 1872. Additional responses from readers appear in "How Estimate Mrs. Woodhull?" *BL*, February 10, 1872; "'X' and Mrs. Victoria C. Woodhull," *BL* March 23, 1872.

48. Woodhull, "Impersonal Reform," *BL*, February 17, 1872.

49. Charles Holt to Hudson Tuttle, "The New Disgrace," reprinted in *RPJ*, March 16, 1872.

50. E. S. Wheeler, "The Woman Market," *WCW*, November 25, 1871, 5; Mary A. Leland, "The Spirit That Will Not Down," *WCW*, December 30, 1871, 10.

51. Response (attributed to Woodhull) to letter from Sada Bailey, "A Kindly Criticism," *WCW*, March 9, 1872, 5; Frances Rose McKinley, lecture, "Free Love: Its Science, Philosophy, and Poetry," *WCW*, March 23, 1872, 12; Sarah C. Somerby letter, *WCW*, January 13, 1872, 5–6; Henry Child remarks, "Official Report of the Third Annual Meeting of the New Jersey State Society of Spiritualists," *RPJ*, December 23, 1871, 2.

52. L. B. Chandler, "A Definition of Freedom," *WCW*, December 23, 1871, 5. Over the next two decades, Chandler refined her concerns about sex radicalism and concluded that varietism, "like marriage, represented a code of behavior constructed by men to suit their sexual desires." Passet, *Sex Radicals*, 164.

53. Mary E. Earley, "A Straw," *WCW*, March 2, 1872, 5; Bailey, "A Kindly Criticism," and response *WCW*, March 9, 1872, 5; Mrs. M.L. Sherman, "Progression," *WCW*, March 23, 1872, 5.

54. Anthony was particularly outraged, in early spring 1872, to see her own name used to endorse Woodhull's "Grand Combination Convention"; when she

arrived in New York in early May for the NWSA convention, she worked hard to persuade Stanton and Hooker to forgo the radicals' convention the next day. Goldsmith, *Other Powers*, 316–18.

Chapter 2. "A Shameless Prostitute and a Negro"

1. "Official Report of the Equal Rights Convention, Held in New York City on the 9th, 10th, and 11th of May 1872," *WCW*, May 25, 1872, 6–7.

2. Like other sexual radicals, Woodhull turned to scientific breeding and eugenics work toward the end of the century. See, for example, Stephanie Athey, "Contested Bodies: The Writing of Whiteness and Gender in American Literature" (Ph.D. thesis, University of Minnesota, 1993), 157–61.

3. Greeley quoted in Eric Foner, *Reconstruction: America's Unfinished Revolution, 1863–1877* (New York: Harper and Row, 1988), 503, 509–11. Greeley died within weeks of the election.

4. Michael Perman, *The Road to Redemption: Southern Politics, 1869–1879* (Chapel Hill: University of North Carolina Press, 1984), 77–78, 106, 108, 136–37, 170; George Frederickson, *The Inner Civil War: Northern Intellectuals and the Crisis of the Union* (New York: Harper and Row, 1965), 193; 198. Foner, *Reconstruction*, 503, 509–11.

5. Foner, *Reconstruction*, 545–59.

6. On the political implications of lynching and other forms of terror against formerly enslaved people, see Laura Edwards, *Gendered Strife and Confusion: The Political Culture of Reconstruction* (Urbana: University of Illinois Press, 1997), 198–210; Grace Hale, *Making Whiteness: The Culture of Segregation in the South, 1890–1940* (New York: Pantheon, 1998), chap. 5. See also Sandra Gunning, *Race, Rape, and Lynching: The Red Record of American Literature, 1880–1912* (New York: Oxford University Press, 1996); Patricia Morton, *Disfigured Images: The Historical Assault on Afro-American Women* (New York: Greenwood Press, 1991); Jacqueline Dowd Hall, *Revolt Against Chivalry: Jessie Daniel Ames and the Women's Campaign Against Lynching* (New York: Columbia University Press, 1993). See also Annecka Marshall, "From Sexual Denigration to Self-Respect: Resisting Images of Black Female Sexuality," in Delia Jarrett-Macauley, ed., *Reconstructing Womanhood, Reconstructing Feminism: Writings on Black Women* (London: Routledge, 1996).

7. On the mythology of the vengeful black rapist, see, for example, Gail Bederman, *Manliness and Civilization: A Cultural History of Gender and Race in the United States, 1880–1917* (Chicago: University of Chicago Press, 1995); Hale, *Making Whiteness*; Robyn Wiegman, *American Anatomies: Theorizing Race and Gender* (Durham, N.C.: Duke University Press, 1995).

8. Jean Fagin Yellin, *Women and Sisters: The Antislavery Feminists in American Culture* (New Haven, Conn.: Yale University Press, 1989), 45–50; Thomas Brown, "The Miscegenation of Richard Mentor Johnson as an Issue in the National Election Campaign of 1835–36," *Civil War History* 39 (1993): 5–30.

9. On the origins of miscegenation hysteria, see David Goodman Croly, *Miscegenation* (New York: H. Dexter, Hamilton, 1864; reprint Upper Saddle River, N.J.:

Literature House, 1970); Forrest Wood, *Black Scare: The Racist Response to Emancipation and Reconstruction* (Berkeley: University of California Press, 1968), 54, 129–30, 143–46; James Kinney, *Amalgamation! Race, Sex, and Rhetoric in the Nineteenth-Century American Novel* (Westport, Conn.: Greenwood Press, 1985). On miscegenation fear as a justification for social inequality for blacks, see Charles E. Wynes, "Social Acceptance and Unacceptance," in Joel Williamson, ed., *The Origins of Segregation* (Boston: D.C. Heath, 1968), 20, 29. See also Joel Williamson, "The Separation of Races," in Williamson, ed., *The Origins of Segregation*, 11, 13, 40.

10. Neil McMillen, *Dark Journey: Black Mississippians in the Age of Jim Crow* (Urbana: University of Illinois Press, 1989), 14–16. In fact, black women were vulnerable to what Catherine Clinton calls a kind of "sexual terrorism" in the postwar south; see Clinton, "Bloody Terrain: Freedwomen, Sexuality and Violence During Reconstruction," in Clinton, ed., *Half-Sisters of History: Southern Women and the American Past* (Durham, N.C.: Duke University Press, 1994), 149. On northern responses to racial "mingling," see David H. Fowler, *Northern Attitudes Towards Interracial Marriage: Legislation and Public Opinion in the Middle Atlantic and the States of the Old Northwest, 1780–1930* (New York: Garland, 1987), 238–40. On lynching and rape, see also Glenda Elizabeth Gilmore, *Gender and Jim Crow: Women and the Politics of White Supremacy in North Carolina, 1896–1920* (Chapel Hill: University of North Caroline Press, 1996), 67–71, and Chapter 4.

11. On rape mythology and lynching, see Stewart Tolway and E. M. Beck, *Festival of Violence: An Analysis of Southern Lynchings, 1882–1930* (Urbana: University of Illinois Press, 1974), 244; W. Fitzhugh Brundage, *Lynching in the New South: Georgia and Virginia, 1880–1930* (Urbana: University of Illinois Press, 1993), 48; Ida B. Wells-Barnett, *On Lynchings: Southern Horrors, A Red Record, Mob Rule in New Orleans* (New York: Arno Press, 1969). See also *Selected Works of Ida B. Wells-Barnett*, ed. Trudier Harris (New York: Oxford University Press, 1991); Edwards, *Gendered Strife and Confusion*, 199; Jeffrey Crow, "An Apartheid for the South: Clarence Poe's Crusade for Rural Segregation"; Jeffrey Crow, Paul Escott, and Charles Flynn, Jr., eds., *Race, Class, and Politics in Southern History: Essays in Honor of Robert F. Durden* (Baton Rouge: Louisiana State University Press, 1989), 240. The myth of the black rapist remains powerful even at the dawn of the twenty-first century. See bell hooks, *Yearning: Race, Gender, and Cultural Politics* (Boston: South End Press, 1990), 58, 61; Eva Saks, "Representing Miscegenation Laws," *Raritan* 8 (Fall 1988): 44.

12. On the split over the Fifteenth Amendment, see Andrea Moore Kerr, "White Women's Rights, Black Men's Wrongs," in Wheeler, ed., *One Woman, One Vote*, 66, 68, 76–77; see also Ellen Carol DuBois, *Feminism and Suffrage: The Emergence of an Independent Women's Rights Movement in America, 1848–1869* (Ithaca, N.Y.: Cornell University Press, 1978) and *The Elizabeth Cady Stanton, Susan B. Anthony Reader*; Paula Giddings, *When and Where I Enter: The Impact of Black Women on Race and Sex in America* (New York: W. Morrow, 1984), 64–69. See also Rosalyn Terborg-Penn, "African American Women and the Woman Suffrage Movement," in Wheeler, ed., *One Woman, One Vote*, 139–41; Nancy Caraway, *Segregated Sisterhood: Racism and the Politics of American Feminism* (Knoxville: University of Tennessee Press, 1991); Aptheker, *"Woman's Legacy"*; Shirley Yee, ed., *Black Women*

Abolitionists: A Study in Activism, 1828–1860 (Knoxville: University of Tennessee Press, 1992).

13. Stanton speech in DuBois, ed., *Elizabeth Cady Stanton, Susan B. Anthony Reader,* 123.

14. *New York Herald,* May 12, 1872.

15. *Rochester Democrat and Chronicle,* May 14, 1872.

16. William Preston Vaughn, *Schools for All: The Blacks and Public Education in the South, 1865–1877* (Lexington: University Press of Kentucky, 1974), 78–94, 127–28; James D. Anderson, *The Education of Blacks in the South, 1860–1935* (Chapel Hill: University of North Carolina Press, 1988), 80–81.

17. *New National Era,* May 2, 16, 1872 (emphasis added).

18. Decades later, W. E. B. Du Bois argued that the "propaganda of race hatred made [mixed schooling] eventually impossible, and the separate school system so increased the cost of public education in the South" that it became untenable. For Conservatives, interracial marriage and mixed schooling became indistinguishable issues. W. E. B. Du Bois, *Black Reconstruction in America: An Essay Toward a History of the Part Which Black Folk Played in the Attempt to Reconstruct Democracy in America, 1860–1880* (1935; reprint New York: Russell and Russell, 1966), 657–63; Foner, *Reconstruction,* 321. See also Vaughn, *Schools for All,* 76–77. Identical concerns about mixed schooling and miscegenation resurfaced during the 1950s amid the controversy over *Brown v. Board of Education.* See Renee Romano, "Sex at the Schoolhouse Door: Fears of 'Amalgamation' in the Southern Response to Brown v. Board of Education," paper presented at the 111th Annual Meeting of the American Historical Association, New York, 1997.

19. I discuss the social and cultural implications of this speech in Chapter 1.

20. "Queries and Responses," *RPJ,* April 13, 1872. I discuss the Beecher and Jones exposures in Chapter 3.

21. The *Banner of Light* expressed some excitement when Woodhull advertised the convention. Woodhull's nomination was by no means certain: one New York correspondent even reported prior to the convention that Henry Ward Beecher was the candidate of choice for the convention. If he accepted, this writer believed, he would "stand a fair chance for election next November." "Henry Ward Beecher for President," *BL,* May 4, 1872. The *Banner* also aired opposing views, however: debate between Woodhull and Spiritualist critic Alonzo Newton over social freedom filled the front pages of the *Banner* for five consecutive issues in spring 1872. See *BL,* March 2, March 30, April 13, May 4, May 25, 1872. Colonel Blood's good friend Henry J. Woodhouse later asserted that Blood had written this series of letters over Woodhull's name. See Woodhouse letter to biographer Emanie Sachs, March 12, 1928, WKU.

22. *BL,* editorial, March 30, 1872; Middlebrook, "Who Shall Represent Us? *BL,* March 30, 1872 (emphasis in original).

23. Tuttle, "Call for a Convention—Shall Spiritualism Assume a Political Aspect," *BL,* February 17, 1872.

24. See "The Organization Question," *BL,* April 27, 1872, 4; Waters, "Truth a Lie," *RPJ,* March 16, 1872. On the "no-organizationism" bent in the early phase of the movement, see Braude, *Radical Spirits.*

25. D. A. Eddy, "The New Departure," *RPJ*, March 23, 1872 (emphasis in original); Kent, "Is Mrs. Woodhull Understood?" *BL*, May 4, 1872. For additional critiques of Woodhull's definition of "social freedom," see C. Moore, "Freedom for Tigers," *RPJ*, April 27, 1872; Judge Edmund C. Holbrook, "True Issues and Their Methods," *RPJ*, May 18, 1872.

26. Woodhull's speech to the New York Labor Reformers reaffirmed her commitment to international socialism. See "The Widow Woodhull Furious," *New York Standard*, May 7, 1872. See also *New York World*, May 7, 1872.

27. Anthony's feelings are explained very clearly in Goldsmith, *Other Powers*, 318–20. See also DuBois, *Elizabeth Cady Stanton-Susan B. Anthony Reader*, 104–6.

28. Giles, an old school friend of Ezra Heywood, reported that Woodhull was surprised by the nomination and modestly hung back before taking the stage again. A. E. Giles, "Glimpses in New York," *BL*, June 1, 1872; "Woodhull and Douglass," *New York Sun*, May 11, 1872, 1. Full proceedings of the convention appeared in *WCW*, May 25, 1872 (the nomination is described on 6–7). The convention received wide if disparaging coverage. See, for example, *New York World*, May 11, 12, 1872; *New York Tribune*, May 11, 1872; *The Days' Doings*, June 1, 1872.

29. *New York Tribune*, May 11, 1872; *The Days' Doings*, June 1, 1872. Spotted Tail was the leader of the Brulé Sioux tribe who had recently negotiated a treaty with the U.S. government.

30. 'The Close of the Convention," *WCW*, June 1, 1872, 14.

31. "People's Convention in New York City," *BL*, May 25, 1872; Citizen Coleman Report to Section 26, in Philadelphia; Coleman report, May 13, 20, 1872; IWA Papers/Papers of Section 26. This is probably George D. Coleman, Philadelphia, listed in the Equal Rights Party Proceedings. Section 26, according to Messer-Kruse, was composed largely of former abolitionists and Spiritualists. *Yankee International*, 115–16. See also "The Convention," *WCW* editorial, May 25, 1872, 8.

32. *New York World*, May 11, 1872; *The Days' Doings*, June 1, 1872. See also *New York Herald*, May 12, 1872.

33. *New York Herald*, May 12, 1872; *New York World*, May 12, 1872.

34. *Rochester Democrat and Chronicle*, May 13, 14, 1872; *Pomeroy's Democrat*, May 25, 1872.

35. *New York Evening Telegram*, May 13, 1872; *Philadelphia Inquirer*, May 14, 1872; *Charleston Daily Courier*, May 13, 1872. See also *Atlanta Constitution*, May 11, 1872. The *New Orleans Bee* (*L'Abeille de Nouvelle Orléans*) ignored the nomination in its May 14, 1872, edition, but mocked Woodhull's acceptance letter in its June 6 edition. The *New York Herald* likewise mocked her letter on June 5, 1872. See also *Charleston Daily Courier*, June 11, 1872.

36. *New York Herald*, May 12, 1872; *Pomeroy's Democrat*, May 18, 25, 1872.

37. *Philadelphia Inquirer*, May 14, 1872; *New York Evening Telegram*, May 13, 1872; *Eugene Guard* reprinted in *New Northwest*, May 31, 1872; *New York Evening Telegram*, May 11, 1872 (emphasis added).

38. The Equal Rights Party ratified the nomination on June 5, 1872. See, for example, *New York Tribune*, June 7, 1872.

39. *The Days' Doings*, June 15, 1872. See also *New York Herald*, June 7, 1872; *Rochester Democrat and Chronicle*, June 3, 1872.

40. *Pomeroy's Democrat*, May 18, 1872.

41. Tuttle, "The Steinway Hall Convention," *RPJ*, May 25, 1872; Slocum, "To Daniel P. Wilder," WCW, June 8, 1872, 4.

42. Letter, *WCW*, May 25, 1872, 14 (emphasis in original).

43. Because of the notoriety now attending both Woodhull and Claflin, the Equal Rights Party was denied access to the Grand Opera House for the meeting, forcing the party to use the Cooper Institute instead. ERP members protested, first posting placards denouncing the move, and then parading with banners in front of the Opera House, purportedly to notify people of the change. *WCW*, June 8, 1872. National papers interpreted these conflicts as a sign of the foolishness of the sisters. For example, the *Charleston Daily Courier* reported the inability of Woodhull and later Claflin to engage the Grand Opera House for meetings: "again have this brazen pair made themselves the laughing stock of the community." *Charleston Daily Courier*, June 11, 1872. Campaign song cited in Johanna Johnston, *Mrs. Satan*, 149–50. "Mrs. Grundy" was shorthand for conventional snobs; journalist Austine Snead wrote a regular society column for the *New York World* under that name. See Summers, *The Press Gang*, 127.

44. The Associated Press dispatch succinctly dismissed the event as "a boisterous meeting of the equal rights party at Apollo Hall last night to ratify the nomination of Mrs. Woodhull and Fred. Douglass." See *Atlanta Constitution*, June 8, 1872; *New Orleans Republican*, June 8, 1872.

45. Carter quoted in *New York Tribune*, June 7, 1872; Bailey, "The Victoria Farce," *RPJ*, June 29, 1872. Braude's *Radical Spirits*, for example, accepts this interpretation of Woodhull's motives, but it does not explain why she didn't seek simpler methods of self-aggrandizement, such as the theater.

46. *WCW*, June 8, 1872, May 25, 1872.

47. *New York Times*, June 16, 1872; *New York Evening Telegram*, May 15, 1872; *The Days' Doings*, June 8, 1872.

48. *New York Herald*, June 14, 1872. See also *New York Sun*, n.d., clipped in *Rochester Democrat and Chronicle*, June 17, 1872. Timothy Messer-Kruse describes the formation of this regiment under a newly passed New York law allowing black militias to form. See *Yankee International*, 196–207.

49. *Rochester Democrat and Chronicle*, May 31, June 1, 1872; *New York Times*, June 16, 1872 (emphasis in original); *New York Evening Telegram*, June 14, 1872.

50. From *New National Era*, quoted in *Rochester Democrat and Chronicle*, May 17, 1872.

51. *New National Era*, October 1872. Greeley and Woodhull were connected through Theodore Tilton, a reform editor who had, for reasons disputed by historians, published a biography of Victoria Woodhull the previous November. He was Greeley's campaign manager throughout the campaign. He is also the Tilton whose wife, as Woodhull would allege that November, had had an affair with the popular minister of Plymouth Church, Henry Ward Beecher (see Chapter 3); *Southern Workman* (Hampton, Virginia), June, 1872; *Weekly Louisianian* (New Orleans), May 11, 18, 1872; *The Elevator* (San Francisco), May 4, 18, June 1, 15 1872.

52. Johnson to Garrison, May 12, 1872, *Anti-Slavery Letters of William Lloyd Garrison and Others*, Boston Public Library, reprinted in Philip Foner, *Life and Writings of Frederick Douglass* (New York: International Publishers, 1965), 4: 533n60.

53. Douglass had recently acted as an envoy to Santo Domingo (now Dominican Republic), which Grant was in favor of annexing to the United States. Charles Sumner, who opposed the annexation, supported Greeley in the 1872 campaign. Sumner insisted that Grant had slighted Douglass by not inviting him to dine at the White House with the president and the other commissioners upon their return to the United States. Douglass, however, suspected the Democrats of using Sumner and the Liberal Republicans to divide the black voters. As Winthrop Jordan notes, since the revolution in Haiti, Santo Domingo symbolized to most white Americans the "contagion of liberty." See "Letters on the Proposed Annexation of Santo Domingo," in John David Smith, *Racial Determinism and the Fear of Miscegenation, pre-1900* (New York: Garland, 1993). Winthrop D. Jordan, *The White Man's Burden: Historical Origins of Racism in the United States* (New York: Oxford University Press, 1974), 146–49.

54. *Semi-Weekly Louisianian* (New Orleans), May 11, 1872.

55. *New National Era*, May 23, 1872.

56. Robert L. Factor, *The Black Response to America: Men, Ideals, and Organization, from Frederick Douglass to the NAACP* (Reading, Mass.: Addison-Wesley, 1970), 64.

57. Foner, *Reconstruction*, 550, 552.

58. See Foner, *Reconstruction*, 553–54. See also Roger A. Fischer, *The Segregation Struggle in Louisiana, 1872–77* (Urbana: University of Illinois Press, 1974), 73–74; F. James Davis, *Who Is Black? One Nation's Definition* (University Park: Pennsylvania State University Press, 1991), 52.

59. *New York World*, June 24, 1872 (emphasis in original). See also Douglass, *Frederick Douglass: Selections from His Writings*, 302.

60. "A Colored Professor 'Cussin de Free Lub," in *The "All Among the Hay" Songster: Full of the Jolliest Lot of Songs and Ballads that Have Ever Been Printed* (New York: R.M. DeWitt, 1872). Minstrel shows and blackface as a genre "consistently ridiculed and condemned" women's rights activists. See Robert Toll, *Blacking Up: The Minstrel Show in Nineteenth Century America* (New York: Oxford University Press, 1974), 163. On the minstrel show as a political force of containment, see Eric Lott, *Love and Theft: Blackface Minstrelsy and the American Working Class* (New York: Oxford University Press, 1993), 234.

61. Douglass was so bitter about the fire, which he attributed to the KKK, that he left Rochester, his home of twenty-five years, and moved to Washington. Rochester papers rejected Douglass's accusation that racism was the motive, calling it an accident. *Rochester Democrat and Chronicle*, June 1, 3, 6, 1872; *Rochester Union and Advertiser*, June 3, 17 1872. It is possible that the fire was prompted by a small notice of the Spencer Grays' offer to Tennie C. Claflin that appeared in the *Rochester Democrat and Chronicle*, June 1, 1872. Some biographers suggest that anger at Claflin's connection to an African American militia unit led to the sisters' eviction. See Sachs, *"The Terrible Siren"*, 167.

62. Strikers were attempting, with the aid of IWA sections, to "compel the enforcement" of New York's Eight Hour Law (enacted in 1870). See the speech of Victoria C. Woodhull from the ERP ratification, reprinted in *The Victoria Woodhull Reader*. Few labor historians discuss these massive strikes, which in some cases

succeeded in shutting down industry for weeks and led to a blackout in the city of Philadelphia. See Ward Regan, "Transforming Consciousness: The Eight Hour Strike of 1872," unpublished paper in author's possession.

63. Even French Section Two, for example, long supportive of Section Twelve's grievances against the IWA General Council, abandoned the dissidents after the Convention: others threatened to do the same. *Le Socialiste*, May 18, 1872; also reported in *New York World*, dated May 13, 1872, *New York Herald*, May 20, 1872, IWA Papers. The flight of the French sections gave the IWA leverage to oust Woodhull and Section Twelve. Scathing news reports of the Apollo Hall Convention led Marx to persuade the General Council to give control of the American International to Friedrich Sorge and Section One. The "Apollo Hall Scandal," as Marx called it, had made the IWA the "Laughing-stock of New York and United States." Marx quoted in "American Split," *GCM*, 5: 323–32. See also Minutes, May 28, 1872 *GCM*, 5: 209–10; Marx to Sorge, May 29, 1872, in *Karl Marx, Frederick Engels: Collected Works* (New York: International Publishers, 1975), 388; Sorge/Bolte to Section 26, June 18, 1872, IWA Papers/Records of Section 26. Sorge used as evidence an undated clipping from an unnamed paper containing text of letter from the General Council, dated May 29, 1872, which outlined the May 28 resolutions. See also Bolte to Section 26, June (19), 1872, IWA Papers/Records of Section 26; *New York World*, July 7, 1872, IWA Papers. On the expulsion of Section Twelve at the IWA Hague Convention that fall, see Messer-Kruse, *Yankee International*, 177–83.

64. I discuss Woodhull's controversial impact on the suffrage movement in greater detail in "Sex in Politics: Victoria Woodhull as Public Woman," *Journal of Women's History* 12, 1 (Spring 2000): 89–110. Stanton and Hooker initially disagreed with Anthony. "Apollo Hall was a success," Hooker wrote to Stanton, "and through it the suffrage army moves in three [newspaper] columns instead of two." Isabella Beecher Hooker to Elizabeth Cady Stanton, May 12, 1872. Stowe-Day Memorial Collection, Hartford, Connecticut.

65. *WCW*, November 2, 1872. I discuss the "New Departure" in Chapter 1.

66. See, for example, Davis, *Who Is Black?*, 52–53.

Chapter 3. The Politics of Exposure

1. See Braude, *Radical Spirits*, 167–75. Proceedings of the American Association of Spiritualists Convention reprinted in "The Ninth National Convention of Spiritualists," *BL*, September 21, 1872. Henry T. Child of Philadelphia was reelected secretary for the organization at the same time. *BL*, September 28, 1872.

2. On the Beecher-Tilton scandal, as it was called, see Richard Wightman Fox, *Trials of Intimacy: Love and Loss in the Beecher-Tilton Scandal* (Chicago: University of Chicago Press, 1989); Altina Laura Waller, *Reverend Beecher and Mrs. Tilton: Sex and Class in Victorian America* (Amherst: University of Massachusetts Press, 1992). See also Robert Shaplen, *Free Love and Heavenly Sinners: The Story of the Great Henry Ward Beecher Scandal* (Lawrence: Regents Press of Kansas, 1977).

3. Details of her verbal exposure of Challis went unrecorded; all quotes come

from the printed version, attributed to Claflin. *WCW*, November 2, 1872. For a discussion of the French ball, see Gilfoyle, *City of Eros.*

4. Few newspapers published these verbal exposures, and consequently Jones's exposure (left out of Woodhull's published account) was a surprise to this historian. See *Boston Herald*, September 11, 1872. Her explanation for the Jones exposure appears in "Jones' Eulogies," *WCW*, September 13, 1873.

5. Henry T. Child, "Reputation," *WCW*, February 17, 1872.

6. "Sex scandal is a Victorian phenomenon," William Cohen argues. "The scandalousness of an act hinges upon the degree of secrecy requisite to its commission." William Cohen, *Sex Scandal: the Private Parts of Victorian Fiction* (Durham, N.C.: Duke University Press, 1996), 1, 5. On the use of sensational sex narratives as a political tool in abolitionist literature, see Arthur Young Lloyd, *The Slavery Controversy, 1831–1860* (Chapel Hill: University of North Carolina Press, 1939); Lewis Perry, *Radical Abolitionism: Anarchy and the Government of God in Antislavery Thought* (Ithaca, N.Y.: Cornell University Press, 1973), 291. On Beecher's mock auctions, see Milton Rugoff, *The Beechers: An American Family in the Nineteenth Century* (New York: Harper and Row, 1981), 374–75. On the reform impulse of early sanitarians, see Nancy Tomes, *The Gospel of Germs: Men, Women, and the Microbe in American Life* (Cambridge: Oxford University Press, 1998), 58. On muckrakers and exposure, see Rochelle Gurstein, *Repeal of Reticence: A History of America's Cultural and Legal Struggles over Free Speech, Obscenity, Sexual Liberation, and Modern Art* (New York: Hill and Wang, 1996), 63. Quote from Fox, *Trials of Intimacy*, 294. On "reverend rakes," see Horowitz, "Victoria Woodhull, Anthony Comstock, and the Conflict over Sex in the United States in the 1870s," *Journal of American History* (September 2000): 403–34.

7. Proponents of reticence worried that urban life and new journalism would corrupt and debauch. See Peter T. Cominos, "Late-Victorian Sexual Respectability and the Social System," *International Review of Social History* 8 (1963): 18–48, quote 37, 48. On Anthony Comstock, see Heywood Broun and Margaret Leech, *Anthony Comstock, Roundsman of the Lord* (New York: A & C Boni, 1927), 127. The best account of Comstock's obscenity crusade appears in Horowitz, *Rereading Sex.* See also Nicola Beisel, *Imperiled Innocents: Anthony Comstock and Family Reproduction in Victorian America* (Princeton, N.J.: Princeton University Press, 1997); Anna Bates, *Weeder in the Garden of the Lord: Anthony Comstock's Life and Career* (New York: University Press of America, 1995).

8. Historian Richard Wightman Fox refers to Beecher's liberal views of religion and marriage as his "therapeutic brand of Christianity." Fox, "Intimacy on Trial: Cultural Meanings of the Beecher-Tilton Affair," in Fox and T. Jackson Lear, eds., *The Power of Culture: Critical Essays in American History* (Chicago: University of Chicago Press, 1993), 120.

9. Henry Ward Beecher, *Sermons by Henry Ward Beecher* (New York: 1869), cited in Clifford E. Clark, Jr., *Henry Ward Beecher: Spokesman for a Middle-Class America* (Urbana: University of Illinois Press, 1978), 84.

10. Henry Ward Beecher, "Progress of Society by Educating the Individual," 1849, Yale MSS, cited in Clark, *Henry Ward Beecher*, 84 (emphasis in original). Conservatives

did make the comparison between Beecherism and free love at the time; see Beisel, *Imperiled Innocents*, 83.

11. On the twenty-fifth anniversary celebrations of Plymouth Church, see *New York Herald*, October 8, 1872; *Harper's Weekly*, October 26, 1872.

12. For articles on the transgressions of clergymen in the *Religio-Philosophical Journal*, see "Elopement of a Methodist Clergyman," January 22, 1870; "Shameful Inconsistency of a Minister," November 26, 1870; "Another Clerical Free Lover," September 30, 1871; "Another Black Sheep," May 4, 1872; and "Young Girl Ruined by a Clergyman in Northern Ohio," March 8, 1873. On "reverend rakes" in popular literature, see Helen Lefkovitz Horowitz, "Victoria Woodhull, Anthony Comstock, and the Conflict over Sex in the United States in the 1870s," *Journal of American History* (September 2000): 403–34. See also David S. Reynolds, *Beneath the American Renaissance: The Subversive Imagination in the Age of Emerson and Melville* (New York: Knopf, 1988).

13. See "Veiled Profanity," *RPJ*, October 16, 1869; "Henry Ward Beecher's Views on Spiritualism," *RPJ*, July 23, 1870; "Beecher Wants to Be a Spiritualist," *RPJ*, October 22, 1870; see also *RPJ*, December 9 and 30, 1871; *BL*, December 16, 1871; *BL*, "Happiness," January 7, 1871.

14. In 1869, Beecher had presided at the sensational deathbed marriage of Abby Sage McFarland to her lover Albert Richardson, who was shot by McFarland's ex-husband. Noting Beecher's involvement in this sensational case, conservative and radical Spiritualists alike complained about the hypocrisy that protected Beecher from the free love accusations that plagued Spiritualists. Editorial, *RPJ*, January 22, 1870; see also "The McFarland-Richardson Case," *RPJ*, June 4, 1870.

15. "An Open Letter to Henry Ward Beecher," *BL*, November 11, 1871; "Plymouth Church and Its Pastor," *WCW*, January 6, 1872. Quote from "Mr. Beecher's Dilemma," *BL*, December 23, 1871.

16. *New York World*, *New York Herald*, May 22, 1871; "More Editorial Honesty," *WCW*, June 3, 1871. On Tilton's motivations for publishing Woodhull's biography, see "The Great Social Earthquake," *WCW*, August 8, 1874.

17. Victoria Woodhull, letter to Henry Ward Beecher, n.d., reprinted in *Theodore Tilton v. Henry Ward Beecher. Action for crim. con. Tried in the City Court of Brooklyn. Verbatim Report in Three Volumes* (New York, 1875), 829;Victoria Woodhull, "And the Truth Shall Make You Free; or, The Principles of Social Freedom" (Woodhull, Claflin & Co., 1871) (emphasis in original). For a discussion of Tilton's motives, see Goldsmith, *Other Powers*, 298–99.

18. "The American Association of Spiritualists," *RPJ*, September 28, 1872; "Woodhull-Claflin," *RPJ* November 16, 1872.

19. "The Beecher-Tilton Scandal Case," *WCW*, November 2, 1872. Woodhull probably omitted any mention of Jones's adultery in this printed account to avoid alienating Spiritualist allies.

20. "The Beecher-Tilton Scandal Case," *WCW*, November 2, 1872.

21. See Jesse F. Battan, " 'The Word Made Flesh': Language, Authority, and Sexual Desire in Late Nineteenth-Century America." *Journal of the History of Sexuality* 3, 2 (1992): 223–44; "The Beecher-Tilton Scandal Case."

22. "The Beecher-Tilton Scandal Case," 9.

23. "The Beecher-Tilton Scandal Case," 13.

24. "The Beecher-Tilton Scandal Case," 11.

25. Victoria Woodhull, "The Religion of Humanity," text of speech given in Boston, September 11, 1872, reprinted in full in *WCW*, November 2, 1872, 3–7.

26. Laura Cuppy Smith to Victoria Woodhull, September 16, 1872; reprinted in *WCW*, November 2, 1872.

27. Woodhull, "To the Public," *WCW*, November 2, 1872, 9 (emphasis added).

28. "The Beecher-Tilton Scandal Case," 10.

29. Victoria Woodhull, "To the Public," *WCW* November 2, 1872, 9 (emphasis added).

30. The article appeared in the *Genius of Universal Emancipation*, November 20, 1829, reprinted in *William Lloyd Garrison: The Story of His Life Told by His Children*, vol. 1, *1805–1835* (New York: Century, 1885), 165. Garrison was coeditor with Quaker abolitionist Benjamin Lundy. The two editors parted ways as a result of Garrison's action, and he subsequently began publication of the *Liberator* in 1831.

31. "The Beecher-Tilton Scandal Case," 10.

32. The best treatment of Comstock and obscenity law in this period appears in Horowitz's *Rereading Sex*, 376, 379–83. See also Gaines Foster, *Moral Reconstruction: Christian Lobbyists and the Federal Legislation of Morality, 1865–1920* (Chapel Hill: University of North Carolina Press, 2002), 48–52.

33. General Davis quoted in *New York Tribune*, November 4, 1872 (emphasis added). Commissioner Osborne and Woodhull's (unnamed) counsel quoted in *New York Herald*, November 3, 1872. On the history of "obscene libel" prosecutions, see Horowitz, *Rereading Sex*, 176–79.

34. Comstock's diary entry quoted in Broun and Leech, *Anthony Comstock*. Leslie's indictment is reported in the *New York Times*, January 29, 1873. According to Comstock's official record book, "Counsel for Leslie induced Comstock to visit Leslie at his office, where Leslie gave instructions to all his men, not to receive any advertisements of doubtful characters, [and] his artists not to put in any picture of lewd character." Records of the New York Society for the Suppression of Vice, vol. I, 1873, entry 51, page 16, n.d. Manuscripts Division, Library of Congress.

35. See, for example, the Associated Press quoted in *Chicago Times*, November 5, 1872; *New York Herald*, November 3, 1872. *WCW*, December 28, 1872.

36. *Frank Leslie's Illustrated Newspaper*, December 7, 1872. Emphasis in original. Leslie's vocal defense of Woodhull may explain why Comstock went after *The Days' Doings*.

37. Woodhull quoted in *Chicago Times*, November 5, 1872.

38. Ezra Heywood, editorial, *The Word*, December 1872, 2. Woodhull letter to the *New York Herald*, n.d., published in the *Boston Investigator*, December 18, 1872, 5. Victoria C. Woodhull to Susan B. Anthony, January 2, 1873. Alma Lutz Collection, Huntington Library.

39. Train eventually avoided prosecution on an insanity plea, a ploy that cost him his fortune and left him a broken man. On Train's legal plight, see "Hark from the Tombs," *WCW*, April 12, 1873.

40. Laura Cuppy Smith, "Victoria C. Woodhull and the Spiritualists," letter dated December 4, 1872, published in the *Boston Investigator*, December 11, 1872, 2.

Seaver made no reference to the case unless prompted by correspondents, and his brief editorial responses to these letters reveal that he was strongly inclined to view the Beecher exposure as slander (if false) or poor taste (if true).

41. Woodhull claimed that at the time of suspension of *WCW* in June 1872, the paper cost $300 per issue above receipts from subscription and individual purchases. Woodhull, editorial, *WCW*, November 2, 1872, 8.

42. Woodhull editorial, *WCW*, December 28, 1872, 8.

43. Woodhull, "Moral Cowardice and Modern Hypocrisy," reprinted in *WCW*, December 28, 1872, 6

44. "Woodhull & Claflin's Weekly," *BL*, January 11, 1873.

45. A panel thief was a combination of a prostitute and confidence woman who brought male clients to her room and seduced them as a compatriot cleaned out the man's wallet from behind a panel. Governor Claflin quoted in Broun and Leech, *Anthony Comstock*, 114.

46. Woodhull, "Moral Cowardice," *WCW*, December 28, 1872, 9. "Woodhull—Mrs. E. A. Merriwether's Account," *WCW*, December 28, 1872, 12. A correspondent to the *Boston Investigator* estimated her bail at $200,000; Woodhull's own estimate was slightly higher, roughly a quarter of a million dollars. See M.A., "The Woodhull-Claflin Case," *Boston Investigator*, January 29, 1873; Woodhull, "Moral Courage," December 28, 1872, 13–14.

47. "Mrs. Woodhull's Address," *WCW*, January 25, 1873, 4. This speech was later published as "The Naked Truth, or the Situation Revisited," reprinted in Stern, ed., *The Victoria Woodhull Reader*.

48. "Mrs. Woodhull's Address," 5.

49. Woodhull, "Moral Cowardice," December 28, 1872, 6 (emphasis added).

50. M.A., "The Woodhull-Claflin Case," January 29, 1873.

51. Woodhull, "The Effort Against Free Speech," *WCW*, February 8, 1873, 9.

52. Editorial, *Boston Investigator*, January 15, 1873, 6; editor, "Free Speech in Boston," *Boston Investigator*, January 22, 1873, 4. Seaver was so uncomfortable with the exposure that he suppressed Beecher's name, where possible, "in accordance with our long-established rule of never charging any man with guilt until it is legally and fairly proved upon him." Editorial comment following a correspondent's report of Francis Train's trial, dated March 6, 1873. M.A., "The Constitution Tinkers," *Boston Investigator*, March 12, 1873. On the damages paid by the Boston Music Hall, see *Boston Investigator*, January 15, 1873.

53. Benjamin Tucker, letter to Emanie Sachs, n.d., reprinted in Sachs, *"The Terrible Siren"*, 244–45.

54. F. H. Marsh, "Mrs. Woodhull and Geo. F. Train," *Boston Investigator*, May 7, 1873, 2; editor, "Henry Ward Beecher," *Boston Investigator*, June 25, 1873, 4; F. H. Marsh, "The Case of Train, Woodhull, &c., Again," *Boston Investigator*, September 10, 1873, 2.

55. Quote from "Woohull-Chaflin," *RPJ*, November 16, 1872. See also *RPJ*, "A Call for a Mass Meeting," October 19, 1872; "Proposed Mass Meeting," November 30, 1872; "The Proposed Mass Meeting," January 11, 1873; "The Mass Meeting," February 9, 1873.

56. Frances Rose MacKinley to Woodhull and Claflin, November 25, 1872, reprinted in *WCW*, December 28, 1872.

57. Laura Cuppy Smith reported that Henry Child was one of very few Spiritualists to support Woodhull while she was in jail. See Laura Cuppy Smith, "Victoria C. Woodhull and the Spiritualists," letter dated December 4, 1872, published in *Boston Investigator*, December 11, 1872, 2. Child resigned his post as AAS secretary, perhaps to protest the Association's refusal to back Woodhull. See his letter to editor, dated December 23, 1872; published in *RPJ*, January 11, 1873.

58. Angela Heywood, a radical lecturer, was even more outspoken and explicit in her public statements on sexuality than Woodhull herself. Angela Heywood, *The Word*, December 1872, 3.

59. Wm. K. Cowing to editor, *The Word*, February 1873, 3.

60. Leo Miller to Amy Post, January 23, 1873. Amy Post Papers, University of Rochester Library. Inspired by Woodhull's crusade against hypocrisy, Miller would publicly flout the institution of marriage three years later by living openly with his lover Mattie Strickland. On the Miller-Strickland controversy, see letter from Leo Miller to editors, *WCW*, December 25, 1875; see also "Free Love," *WCW*, January 8, 1876; "Brave Mattie Strickland," *WCW*, January 15, 1876. See also Braude, *Radical Spirits*, 134.

61. Woodhull, "Moral Cowardice," *WCW*, December 28, 1872, 6. Emphasis in original.

62. Woodhull, "More Indictments," June 14, 1873, 6.

63. *Pomeroy's Democrat, Pittsburgh Leader* quoted in Johnston, *Mrs. Satan*, 191–93. The Challis libel suit eventually took place in March 1874 (see Chapter 4).

64. See Benjamin Butler, Letter to the Editor, *New York Star*, February 3, 1873. The source of the excerpt was the book of Deuteronomy.

65. Although it could not apply to Woodhull's exposure issue, dated in 1872, Comstock pushed through a new federal statute, known as the Comstock Law, which included newspapers, on March 3, 1873; he became the "Special Agent of the U.S. Postal Office" on March 6. See Bates, *Weeder in the Garden of the Lord*, 90; see also Horowitz, *Rereading Sex*, 381–84.

66. Joseph Treat, *Beecher, Tilton, Woodhull, the Creation of Society* (New York: Joseph Treat, 1874) (emphasis in original). Treat was part of Woodhull's radical network, had been a free lover, and was a former member of the Berlin Heights community in Ohio with Francis Barry. He had separated from his wife Mary Treat, a widely published and respected natural scientist who studied sexual differentiation among insects (and corresponded with Charles Darwin), when she converted to Methodism, so as to remain true to his sectarian science. Joseph Treat, *The Future of Vineland* (Vineland, N. J., n.d.), 4; Spurlock, *Free Love*, 215. See for example Mary Treat, "Controlling Sex in Butterflies," *American Naturalist* (March 1873).

67. On Brookes's death and autopsy, see Gabriel, *Notorious Victoria*, 212–13. On the veracity of Treat's accusations, little record remains. Treat was extremely poor, and later admitted that he had published the tract "for money—to make a living." Like Woodhull, he was arrested under the Comstock obscenity statute. Treat quoted in the Papers of the New York Society for the Suppression of Vice, Volume 5, August 7, 1875. Library of Congress. Anarchist Benjamin Tucker (not one to cover up Woodhull's faults) called Treat a "reckless slanderer" and denied that his claims had any bearing in reality. Benjamin Tucker, Letter to Emanie Sachs, n.d., (1927), reprinted in Sachs, *"The Terrible Siren"*, 262. Woodhull eventually sued Treat for libel, but Treat

died before the case came to court. See *WCW*, October 3, November 21, December 12, 1874. On the libel suit against Treat, and his death, see Underhill, *The Woman Who Ran for President*, 266. For responses from the free love community, see Heywood editorial, *The Word*, May 1874, 2; William Denton and Francis Barry to *The Word*, published in August 1874, 3.

68. John Jenkins, "Spiritual Camp Life at Silver Lake Grove, Plympton, Mass," *Boston Investigator*, September 10, 1873, 3. Editor Horace Seaver buried an apology for these "rather too personal comments" on page 6.

69. Minutes of the American Association of Spiritualists, reprinted in *WCW*, October 25, 1873.

70. Nathaniel Randall to *WCW*, July 31, 1873, reprinted in *WCW*, August 30, 1873.

71. J. W. Evarts, dated September 13, 1873, reprinted in *WCW*, November 29, 1873.

72. The Universal Association of Spiritualists folded in 1876: Woodhull, reelected over continued objections in 1874 and 1875, remained the new association's only president until she resigned in 1876. Braude, *Radical Spirits*, 167–75.

73. Augusta White refers to UAS members as martyrs in "Official Report of Primary Council No. 1 of Illinois," *WCW*, December 13, 1873; see also "The Chicago Convention," *BL*, September 27, 1873.

74. Elizabeth Cady Stanton to Isabella Beecher Hooker, November 3, 1873; also her letter to *Chicago Tribune*, August 24, 1874, reprinted in *WCW*, October 17, 1874; both cited in Underhill, *The Woman Who Ran for President*, 247–48. Paulina Wright Davis, Woodhull's second official source, dying of tuberculosis in Paris, would not publicly support Woodhull's allegations at the time, but privately reassured her friend of their essential truth. On Thomas Beecher and Isabella Beecher Hooker's positions, see Underhill, *The Woman Who Ran for President*, 245.

75. Beecher was coy on the subject. His first denial was when he agreed with a supporter that the story was "entirely" fraudulent (quoted in Sachs, *"The Terrible Siren"*, 188–89 and Underhill, *The Woman Who Ran for President*, 244); he later said by letter that all the rumors about him were "grossly untrue." *Brooklyn Eagle*, June 30, 1873, cited in Underhill, 247.

76. Comstock quoted in Broun and Leech, *Anthony Comstock*, 123.

77. Spurlock, *Free Love*, 208. Foster, *Moral Reconstruction*, 50.

78. Hal Sears, *The Sex Radicals: Free Love in High Victorian America* (Lawrence: Regents Press of Kansas, 1977), 71–73.

79. Beisel, *Imperiled Innocents*, 78.

80. Sears, *The Sex Radicals*, 23. On the trend in liberal thought toward defense of all speech, regardless of content, in the final third of the nineteenth century, see Rochelle Gurstein, *Repeal of Reticence*.

Chapter 4. *"Queen of the Rostrum"*

1. Her first lecture is covered in "The Body Is a Temple," and "Mrs. Woodhull Again," *Atlanta Constitution*, February 10, 1876. See also interview, "Victoria C. Woodhull," *Atlanta Constitution*, February 11, 1876. Editorially, the paper was not so

enthusiastic, stating that her "views and theories . . . must certainly shock the sense of right and propriety in every right minded person." *Atlanta Constitution*, February 12, 1876. Her second lecture was scheduled for February 13, 1876, but was not reviewed in the paper the next day, perhaps due to editorial suppression.

2. It is difficult to gauge her audience sizes accurately: her more successful lectures had a nightly audience of 3,000, and she delivered between 30 and 150 lectures per year after 1873. Woodhull claimed in a printed version of a speech published in 1874 to have delivered it to 250,000 people in the 1873–74 season alone, possibly an exaggeration. See Victoria C. Woodhull, *Tried as By Fire; or, the True and the False, Socially* (New York: Woodhull, Claflin & Co., 1874). However, her popularity in the 1875–76 season was even greater.

3. Most biographers downplay this phase of Woodhull's career; some discussion appears in Underhill, *The Woman Who Ran for President* and Gabriel, *Notorious Victoria*. Despite her popularity, Woodhull is also absent from histories of lecturing for this period. See Major James B. Pond, *Eccentricities of Genius: Memories of Famous Men and Women of the Platform and Stage* (New York: G.W. Dillingham, 1900), 37–39.

4. As one correspondent put it, "Let sexual science be an indispensable subject in every institution, both private and public, in the land." E. Wheeler, "The Marriage Question," *WCW*, December 27, 1873. See also "Sexual Ignorance," *WCW*, November 8, 1873; "Medical Literature," *WCW*, April 4, 1874. On Moses Hull's adultery, see his letter, October 25, 1873 and Elvira Hull's defense in a letter dated December 16, 1873, reprinted *WCW*, January 3, 1874. On the pernicious effects of the sexual double standard, see Benjamin Tucker's letter, dated June 21, 1873, reprinted *WCW*, August 30, 1873; Augusta White, letter to *WCW*, December 20, 1873; On individual regulation of sexual relations, see "Personal Sovereignty," *WCW*, November 29, 1873.

5. On moderate Spiritualist dismay over sex radicalism, see editorial "The *Banner of Light* and the Social Question," *BL*, October 3, 1874. Radicals, by contrast, argued that Woodhull's critiques of marriage were too tame. Francis Barry's Western Reserve Woman's Emancipation Society, founded after the Beecher exposure, condemned Woodhull and other sex radicals for their "moderate" positions on the marriage question at its 1874 convention; see Spurlock, *Free Love*, 217. *The Word* defended Moses Hull's public declaration of adultery on the grounds that "though [Hull] were Satan incarnate, he does not forfeit his right to speak, so long as he accords to others equal freedom." *The Word*, April 1875, 2. *Weekly* editor James Blood later claimed that 5,000 subscribers canceled their subscriptions following the revelations of Moses and Elvira Hull in late 1873. James H. Blood, "What Broke Down the Woodhull Paper," *American Socialist*, April 18, 1878.

6. On the art of lecturing, see Donald Scott, "The Public Lecture and the Creation of a Public in Mid-Nineteenth-Century America," *Journal of American History* 66 (March 1980): 796–97, 805, 806–8. See also Donald Scott, "Print and the Public Lecture System, 1840–60," in William Joyce et al., eds., *Printing and Society in Early America* (Worcester, Mass.: American Antiquarian Society, 1983) and Scott, "Knowledge and the Marketplace," in James Gilbert et al., eds., *The Mythmaking Frame of Mind: Social Imagination and American Culture* (Belmont, Calif.: Wadsworth, 1993).

7. On the rise of the celebrity or "star" lecture circuit, see Peter Cherches, "Star Course: Popular Lectures and the Marketing of Celebrity in Nineteenth Century America" (Ph.D. thesis, New York University, 1997). See also David Mead, *Yankee Eloquence in the Middle West: The Ohio Lyceum, 1850–1870* (East Lansing: Michigan State College Press, 1951), 231–38; Patricia Click, *The Spirit of the Times: Amusements in Nineteenth-Century Baltimore, Norfolk, and Richmond* (Charlottesville: University Press of Virginia, 1989). On the rise of commercial public culture, see David Nasaw, *Going Out: The Rise and Fall of Public Amusements* (New York: Basic Books, 1993); Peter Buckley, "To The Opera House: Culture and Society in New York City, 1820–1860" (Ph.D. thesis, State University of New York, Stony Brook, 1984). See also Lawrence Levine, *Highbrow/Lowbrow: The Emergence of Cultural Hierarchy in America* (Cambridge, Mass.: Harvard University Press, 1990), 244–45. On the Chautauqua Assembly, see Louise Stevenson, *The Victorian Homefront: American Thought and Culture, 1860–1880* (New York: Twayne Publishers, 1991), 157–58. Quote from J. C. Holland, "The Popular Lecture," *Atlantic Monthly* (March 1865): 364.

8. Abigail Solomon-Godeau, "The Other Side of Venus: The Visual Economy of Feminine Display," in Victoria de Grazia, ed., *The Sex of Things: Gender and Consumption in Historical Perspective* (Berkeley: University of California Press, 1996), 116, 117, 128, 141–42, 144. As Faye Dudden observes of the rise of the leg show by 1870, theater managers "were learning to sell a spectacle, an eroticized vision that offered suggestion and arousal rather than satisfaction." Faye Dudden, *Women in the American Theatre: Actresses and Audiences, 1790–1870* (New Haven, Conn.: Yale University Press, 1994), 155. See also Robert J. Greef, "Public Lectures in New York, 1851–1878: A Cultural Index of the Times" (Ph.D. thesis, University of Chicago, 1941), 120–26. On the boundaries of public life for nineteenth-century women, see Mary Kelley, *Private Woman, Public Stage: Literary Domesticity in Nineteenth-Century America* (New York: Oxford University Press, 1984).

9. Young earned $20,000 in the lecture circuit in 1873–74 before she turned to private life. Cherches, "Star Course," 183–92.

10. James Blood quoted in *WCW*, November 28, 1874.

11. See Goldsmith, *Other Powers*, 67, 104–5. See also Underhill, *The Woman Who Ran for President*, 22–39; Gabriel, *Notorious Victoria*, 12–25.

12. *Dubuque Daily Times*, n.d.; reprinted in *WCW*, February 21, 1874; *Salt Lake Daily Herald*, May 5, 1874.

13. To trace Woodhull's lecturing career during these years, I rely on clippings from newspapers throughout the country that were reprinted in the *Weekly*; I have confirmed the text of these clippings where possible, by checking against those newspapers that have been preserved in archives and newspaper projects. I have also tracked down reviews from newspapers not reprinted in the *Weekly* to provide more objective coverage. Woodhull's lectures often generated new subscribers to the *Weekly*, and occasionally free copies were distributed at the lecture. See *St. Joseph Herald*, January 10, 1874, reprinted in *WCW*, January 31, 1874, 11; *Leavenworth Daily Times*, January 31, 1874, 4.

14. "In the West," *WCW*, December 13, 1873, 10. Negative reviews typically criticized the speaker for her "disregard for the Christian religion" bordering on

"blasphemy," and a performance "inferior" to what the audience had been led to expect. See for example "Victoria C. Woodhull's Lecture," *Port Huron Times*, November 20, 1873, 8.

15. Episode described in Tucker letter, 1928, reprinted in Sachs, *"The Terrible Siren"*, 248–49.

16. Kate Field, "Leaves from a Lecturer's Notebook," in Field, *Hap-Hazard* (Boston: James Osgood, 1873), 48–49.

17. *Wolverine Clipper*, Cedar Springs, Michigan, December 3, 1873, 1; *Leavenworth Daily Times*, January 13, 1874, 4; *Leavenworth Freeman*, n.d., reprinted in *WCW*, March 7, 1874, 11. It was typical for a man to introduce women speakers, so Woodhull's choice here drew frequent comment. See, for example, *Salt Lake Daily Herald*, May 14, 1874; reprinted in *WCW*, June 6, 1874.

18. On her delivery of plain truths in a fearless manner, see, for example, *Council Bluffs Daily Nonpareil*, January 17, 1874; *Decatur Republican*, January 27, 1874, 3. *St. Paul Daily Pioneer*, February 12, 1874, 4; *Leavenworth Daily Times*, January 11, 1874, 4; *Lynn Record*, November 8, 1873, 2; *San Francisco Chronicle*, July 4, 1874.

19. Advertising appeared in the *Council Bluffs Daily Nonpareil*, January 8, 1874, 4; the letter from "A Mother," appeared on January 15, 1874; reviews of the two lectures appeared on January 16, 17, 1874. For the demand for boycott in St. Paul and Woodhull's response (under the pseudonym "Expediency"), see *St. Paul Daily Pioneer*, February 11, 12, 13, 1874.

20. Opposition in Jackson and Ann Arbor reported in "Free Speech at Ann Arbor," *Detroit Commercial Advertiser*, December 20, 1873; *Saturday Morning Journal*, Port Huron, Michigan, n.d.; both reprinted in *WCW*, January 10, 1874, 12; Bloomington incident reported in *WCW*, February 21, 1874, 10–11.

21. Horace Seaver, editorial, *Boston Investigator*, December 24, 1873, 6; Woodhull quoted in *St. Paul Daily Pioneer*, February 13, 1874, 4 (emphasis added).

22. On her lectures in the 1871–72 season, see *WCW*, March 2, 1872. On the enormous audience at "The Impending Revolution," see Woodhull, "Moral Cowardice and Modern Hypocrisy," December 28, 1872, 6. *Detroit Evening News*, November 17, 1873, 4; *Detroit Daily Union*, November 17, 1873, 4. See also *Grand Rapids Daily Democrat*, November 25, 1873; *Grand Rapids Eagle*, November 21, 1873; reprinted in *WCW*, December 13, 1873; *St. Paul Daily Pioneer*, February 12, 1874, 4; *Salt Lake City Daily Herald*, May 13, 1874.

23. *St. Joseph Daily Gazette*, January 7–10, 1874, January 18, 1874, February 27, 1874.

24. On her fees, see Underhill, *The Woman Who Ran for President*, 252. See also a letter to Mr. Wilson, n.d., cited in Gloria Steinem, *Moving Beyond Words* (New York: Simon and Schuster, 1994), 171, and Woodhull to J. S. Bliss, December 29, 1873. J. S. Bliss Correspondence, Department of Special Collections, Syracuse University Library. See also Hoeltje, "Notes on the History of Lecturing in Iowa," 115–16. On Dickinson's star power, see Girard Chester, *Embattled Maiden*, 164–68, 217. On Nast, see Cherches, "Star Course," 183–92. Theodore Tilton, trading on his celebrity as victim in the Beecher scandal, netted $30,000 during the 1875–76 circuit. New York *Tribune*, November 4, 1876, cited in Cherches, "Star Course," 137.

25. *Nebraska State Journal*, January 14, 1874.

26. She calls herself "Queen of the American Rostrum" on her showbill from Worcester (Figure 31). The first paper to pick up on the title and call Woodhull queen of the rostrum (to my knowledge) was the *Dubuque Telegraph,* February 3, 1874, reprinted in *WCW,* February 21, 1874. She frequently used the title in her own advertisements during her 1875–76 tour. See *Akron Daily Argus,* November 3, 1875, reprinted in *WCW,* November 20, 1875; *Atlanta Constitution,* February 5, 1876.

27. *St. Joseph Herald,* January 10, 1874; reprinted in *WCW,* January 31, 1874.

28. *Davenport Daily Democrat,* February 2, 1874, 4.

29. The respectability of the Port Huron audience, including its mayor, noted by the *Port Huron Commercial,* November 16, 1873, reprinted in *WCW,* December 13, 1873; see also *Port Huron Saturday Morning Journal,* November 22, 1873, reprinted in *WCW,* December 20, 1873, 7. A more critical report of this lecture appeared in the only extant paper available today from that city; see *Port Huron Times,* November 20, 1873, 8. Respectable audiences were noted with some surprise in *St. Joseph Herald,* January 10, 1874, reprinted in *WCW,* January 31, 1874, 11; *Council Bluffs Daily Nonpareil,* January 17, 1874; *Rock Island Daily Argus,* February 2, 1874, 4.

30. *Council Bluffs Daily Globe,* January 16, 1874, reprinted in *WCW,* February 7, 1874; *St. Paul Daily Press,* February 12, 1874, reprinted in *WCW,* March 7, 1874.

31. *St. Paul Daily Pioneer,* February 12, 1874, 4. On the moral scruples that kept women away, see, for example, *Davenport Daily Democrat,* February 2, 1874, 4.

32. "Has Social Crime a Gender?" *Iowa State Register,* February 1, 1874, 2.

33. *St. Paul Daily Press,* February 12, 1874, reprinted in *WCW* March 7, 1874, 10.

34. *Springfield State Journal,* January 25, 1874, reprinted in *WCW,* February 21, 1874.

35. *Decatur Republican,* January 27, 1874, 3; *Gold Hill Daily News,* May 20, 1874, 3. See also *Davenport Daily Democrat,* February 2, 1874, 4; *Dubuque Daily Times,* February 3, 1874, 1; *Detroit Evening News,* November 17, 1873, 4; *Cedar Springs Clipper,* December 3, 1873, 1.

36. "Has Social Crime a Gender?" *Iowa State Register,* February 1, 1874, 2.

37. She had already been acquitted on federal obscenity charges in the Challis case.

38. *Ottumwa Democrat,* January 22, 1874, 4; Woodhull, "Reformation or Revolution, Which? or Behind the Political Scenes," reprinted in Stern, ed., *The Victoria Woodhull Reader.*

39. *St. Paul Daily Pioneer,* February 13, 1874, 4.

40. See, for example, *Leavenworth Daily Times,* January 11, 1874, 4; *Gold Hill Daily News,* May 19, 1874, 3. Mill quotation appears on the editorial page; see *WCW,* October 25, 1873.

41. "Vindicated," *WCW,* March 28, 1874.

42. Juliet Severance to Victoria Woodhull, March 19, 1874, reprinted in *WCW,* March 21, 1874 (emphasis added); John Gage, letter dated February 15, 1874, published as "Vineland Leading the Advance," *WCW,* April 4, 1874; William Foster, Jr., to Victoria Woodhull, March 15, 1874, reprinted in *WCW,* April 18, 1874.

43. *New York Star,* n.d., reprinted in *WCW,* March 28, 1874.

44. *Kansas City Daily Chronicle,* March 17, 1874, reprinted in *WCW,* April 18,

1874. For jurors' explanation of the surprise verdict, see press clippings under the headline "The Spirit of the City Press," *WCW*, March 28, 1874.

45. *Salt Lake Daily Herald*, May 12, 1874.

46. *Gold Hill Daily News*, May 19, 1874, 3.

47. *San Francisco Chronicle*, June 2, 3, 1874; *San Francisco Daily Examiner*, June 2, 3, 1874; *Daily Alta California*, June 1, 2, 3, 1874.

48. Woodhull claimed that she canceled these lectures because the towns were too small to entertain a lecturer, but the hostility of the local newspapers must have been a contributing factor. See *Hollister Enterprise*, quoted in *Salinas City Index*, June 18, 1874; *Watsonville Pajaronian*, June 11, 1874; *Gilroy Advocate*, June 13, 1874.

49. *Sacramento Daily Record*, June 27, 29, 1874; *San Francisco Chronicle*, July 4, 1874; on the second lecture see *San Francisco Elevator*, June 27, 1874. Woodhull, "The Naked Truth; or, The Situation Reviewed," reprinted in Stern, *The Victoria Woodhull Reader*.

50. "Dr. Bacon's Speech," August 1874, reprinted in Charles F. Marshall, *The True History of the Brooklyn Scandal* (Philadelphia: National Publishing Company, 1874).

51. Stephen Pearl Andrews to *The Word*, November 1874, 4.

52. Less than two weeks before the trial began, Woodhull, lecturing in Chicago, became disoriented as she stood on the stage and had to be led off by her mother, Roxanna Claflin. Incident cited in Goldsmith, *Other Powers*, 411. She also suffered financially from her inability to lecture during the early months of 1875. In January, she petitioned Congress (unsuccessfully) for restitution for her persecution by Comstock, and in April she publicly begged her first patron, Cornelius Vanderbilt, for financial support. She claimed that she had lost over $500,000 in legal fees and confiscated property, and asked that $100,000 of that be restored to her. See "Our Petition," *WCW*, January 30, 1875, 5–6. Her appeal to Vanderbilt appeared in "An Open Letter," *WCW*, April 3, 1875, 4.

53. "The Brooklyn Business," *WCW*, May 29, 1875.

54. *Buffalo Courier*, December 12, 1875.

55. Fair Play, "Guilty or Not Guilty," *Pittsburgh Leader*, November 16, 1875, 4. Based on the appearance of letters from this pseudonym in other places, which sought to stimulate favorable debate about Woodhull, I deduce that she or one of her close associates (possibly Colonel Blood) was the author. For example, a letter from "Fair Play" to the *Boston Investigator* prompted freethinker Horace Seaver to discuss her recent lectures in that city. "Victoria C. Woodhull," *Boston Investigator*, October 25, 1876, 4.

56. Quote from "Victoria C. Woodhull," *Watertown Dispatch*, September 1, 1875 (emphasis added). For comparisons to Anna Dickinson, see *Erie Observer*, December 2, 1875, 3; "Victoria C. Woodhull," *Rock Island Daily Argus*, February 2, 1874, 4.

57. *Wheeling Evening Register*, November 17, 1875; see also *Binghamton Democrat*, September 16, 1875. She referred to the "Garden of Eden" lecture as "the chief work of her life," but delivered it on only a few occasions. See *Chicago Times*, October 17, 1875. On Woodhull's evolving female-centered Christianity in this and other lectures, see Lemons, "Sex in Context."

58. See *Buffalo Courier*, December 12, 1875; *Nashville Daily American*, February 6, 1876; *Chicago Inter-Ocean*, October 16, 1875.

59. On crowds awaiting Woodhull's arrival in town, see *Parker City Daily*, September 20, 1875, reprinted in *WCW*, October 9, 1875. Quote from *Cincinnati Enquirer*, November 7, 1875, 1 (emphasis added).

60. "Naughty Vic," *Kokomo Saturday Tribune*, January 29, 1876, 1.

61. Audience hesitation is evident, for example, in *Mount Vernon Democratic Banner*, November 19, 1875, and *Buffalo Sunday News*, December 12, 1875, reprinted in *WCW*, January 22, 1876.

62. *St. Albans Advertiser* (Vermont), August 31, 1875, reprinted in *WCW*, October 2, 1875; second quote from *Greenville Journal* (Ohio), November 25, 1875.

63. See, for example, *Binghamton Democrat*, September 16, 1875.

64. *Syracuse Courier*, n.d., reprinted in *WCW*, December 25, 1875.

65. First quote from *Pittsburgh Evening Leader*, November 15, 1875, 4; second quote from *Logansport Daily Star* (Indiana), October 22, 1875, 1. On the presence of clerical men and legislators, see *Parker City Daily*, September 20, 1875, reprinted in *WCW*, October 9, 1875; *Chicago Inter-Ocean*, 12; *Chicago Times*, October 17, 1875, 9; *Springfield Republican*, December 13, 1875, 5; *Atlanta Constitution*, February 10, 1876.

66. "Woodhull's Whims," *Chicago Times*, October 16, 1876, 5; Parker Pillsbury, letter to Woodhull, October 25, 1875, reprinted in *WCW*, November 13, 1875. Unusually large crowds were reported in *Parker City Daily*, September 20, 1875, reprinted in *WCW*, October 9, 1875; *Chicago Tribune*, October 16, 1875; *Chicago Times*, October 16, 1875, 5; October 17, 1875, 9; *Meadville Evening Republican*, November 27, 1875, 4; *Washington Chronicle*, January 11, 1876, 8; *Nashville Daily American*, February 8, 1876, 4; *Atlanta Constitution*, February 9, 1876; *New Orleans Republican*, February 18, 1876.

67. *Washington Daily Critic*, January 11, 1876, 1. See also *Mount Vernon Democratic Banner*, November 19, 1875; *Ashtabula News*, January 26, 1876; *Providence Evening Press*, April 17, 1876, 3.

68. An Erie, Pennsylvania, paper reported that "The sisters will return here in February, having been assured, so they say, two hundred dollars by 'some of our most prominent citizens.'" *Erie Observer*, December 2, 1875, 3. Local citizens sometimes begged Woodhull for a second lecture, but a tight schedule usually prevented her from complying. See for example, "The Social Problem," *Nashville Daily American*, February 8, 1876, 4; *Memphis Daily Avalanche*, February 8, 1876, 4. See also letters from Charles and M. P. Verlander (of Hemstead, Texas) to Tennie C. Claflin, dated March 12, 1876, reprinted in *WCW*, April 15, 1876.

69. E. A. Merriwether, letter to *WCW*, dated February 11, 1876, reprinted in *WCW*, April 8, 1876.

70. *Chicago Inter-Ocean*, October 16, 1875, 12. Woodhull's plea to women appears in an interview in *Cincinnati Enquirer*, November 6, 1875, 8. The presence of women was noted in *Cincinnati Enquirer*, November 7, 1875, 1. On the expectation of "smut," see "Mrs. Woodhull at the Opera House," *Oil City Daily Derrick*, September 18, 1875, 3. See also letter from Mrs. M. P. Verlander, Hemstead, Texas, March 12, 1876, reprinted in *WCW*, April 15, 1876. Other concerns kept women away, however. "My husband attended your lecture . . . and was very much elated," one Ottumwa, Iowa, woman wrote to the *Weekly*. "I regret that I could not have been a listener; but I am one of that class you depicted so forcibly—a mother—bound to a life of

seclusion, tied down to little, helpless babes." Unsigned, dated January 20, 1874, reprinted in *WCW*, February 21, 1874. On her continued wide appeal across class lines, see "Victoria Woodhull," *Memphis Daily Appeal*, February 8, 1876, 4.

71. *Buffalo Express*, reprinted in *Washington Chronicle*, January 10, 1876, 8; *Washington Sunday Gazette*, January 16, 1876, reprinted in *WCW*, February 5, 1876. Both quotations are so close to Woodhull's own advertising copy that I assume they were planted by Woodhull or one of her associates, and then sent on to subsequent papers as if the words of the local papers that printed them. It is only another example of the adroit business practices of Woodhull and her companions. Woodhull quote from "A Vision, No. II," *WCW*, May 6, 1876.

72. Woodhull claimed a southern following based on reports from friends, as well as a rapid increased circulation of the *Weekly* in the south. See her interview with the *Atlanta Constitution*, February 11, 1876.

73. She wore her plain black gown until she launched her southern tour in February 1876; see, for example, *Pittsburgh Evening Leader*, November 15, 1875, 4. On her more elaborate costume in the south, see "Victoria Woodhull," *Memphis Daily Appeal*, February 8, 1876, 4; *St. Louis Republican*, February 2, 1876, 5; "The Social Problem," *New Orleans Daily Picayune*, February 21, 1876, 4; *Galveston Daily News*, February 29. She continued to avoid jewelry, however, perhaps an indication of continued mourning for her father and sister, Utica Brooker. She had her hair cut to her shoulders in 1873–74 tours, and long but combed back late in 1875. See, for example, *Nebraska State Journal*, January 14, 1874; *Chicago Inter-Ocean*, October 16, 1875, 12. By the time she reached the south, she wore her hair in a classic "Grecian" knot. See "Victoria Woodhull," *Memphis Public Ledger*, February 7, 1876, 3; *Atlanta Constitution*, February 10, 1876; *Galveston Daily News*, February 29, 1876, 4.

74. Helen Nash, "The Work in the South," letter to the *Weekly*, reprinted in *WCW*, March 18, 1876, 1. On the resistance of southern audiences to lecturers, see Carl Bode, *The American Lyceum: Town Meeting of the Mind* (New York: Oxford University Press, 1956), 163–64. See also Cherches, "Star Course." Anna Dickinson's abortive southern tour in 1875, for example, met with little financial success; see Chester, *Embattled Maiden*, 163. On southern scorn for women lecturers and public speakers, see LeeAnn Whites, *The Civil War as a Crisis in Gender: Augusta, Georgia, 1860–1890* (Athens: University of Georgia Press, 1995).

75. No printed version of this lecture exists (and it was not included in the volume of collected works she published under the same title in 1890). The most extensive report of the lecture (and the quotation included here) appeared in *Memphis Daily Appeal*, February 8, 1876. On the simplicity of her "pleasing, and not at all stagy" manner, see *Newark Daily Journal*, January 4, 1876, 3. The lecture was advertised as a "sermon" in *New Orleans Daily Picayune*, February 20, 1876, 1, for example. For praise of the theme of motherhood, see *Kokomo Saturday Tribune*, January 29, 1876, 1; *Dallas Herald*, March 16, 1876, reprinted in *WCW*, April 8, 1876; *Houston Age*, March 2, 1876, reprinted in *WCW*, March 18, 1876. The *New Orleans Democrat* disapproved of educating young women out of their most attractive quality—their innocence—yet reported an enthusiastic audience response. *New Orleans Democrat*, February 22, 1876, 2. On her entrance onto the stage, and its set-up, see *Atlanta Constitution*, February 10, 1876; *Cincinnati Commercial*, November 7, 1875, 1; *Providence*

Evening Press, April 17, 1876, 3. On her use of a Bible, see "Mrs. Woodhull's Lecture," *Ashtabula News*, January 26, 1876; *Memphis Public Ledger*, February 7, 1876, 3; *Providence Evening Press*, April 17, 1876, 3. A statue of the Virgin Mary appears in *New York Herald*, May 6, 1876, 10.

76. *Atlanta Herald*, February 10, 1876, reprinted in *New Orleans Times*, February 20, 1876, 12. On her theatrical powers, see *Newark Journal*, January 4, 1876, 3. Not everyone applauded the new theatrical bent, however. Susan B. Anthony, for one, deplored Woodhull's transformation from "earnest simplicity to stage acting." SBA *Diary*, November 21, 1876, cited in DuBois, *The Elizabeth Cady Stanton, Susan B. Anthony Reader*, 106.

77. *St. Louis Globe-Democrat*, February 2, 1876, 5.

78. *Rock Island Daily Argus*, February 2, 1874, 4; *St. Louis Journal*, February 2, 1876, reprinted in *WCW*, February 26, 1876. On the femininity of her voice, see *Johnstown Democrat*, January 22, 1876.

79. As lyceum bureau guru James Redpath wrote of the Music Hall to a speaker "only the most practiced speakers, of powerful voices, can be heard in all parts of it." James Redpath to Henry Longfellow, August 25, 1873, reprinted in Marjorie Harrell Eubank, "The Redpath Lyceum Bureau from 1868 to 1901" (Ph.D. thesis, University of Michigan, 1968), 148–51. A more cosmopolitan paper found the idea of comparing Woodhull to Dickinson "absurd." See *Washington National Republican*, January 11, 1876, 4.

80. "The Social Problem," *New Orleans Daily Picayune*, February 21, 1876, 4; "Victoria Woodhull," *Memphis Daily Appeal*, February 8, 1876, 4; *Houston Age*, March 2, 1876, reprinted in *WCW*, March 18, 1876. See also *Galveston Daily News*, February 29, 1876, 4; *Atlanta Herald*, February 10, 1876, reprinted in *New Orleans Times*, February 20, 1876, 12; *New Orleans Weekly Republican*, February 21, 1876, reprinted in *WCW*, March 18, 1876; *L'Abeille de Nouvelle Orléans*, February 16, 1876; "Victoria Woodhull," *Memphis Daily Appeal*, February 8, 1876, 4; *Austin Daily Statesman*, March 10, 1876.

81. *Houston Age*, March 2, 1876, reprinted in *WCW*, March 18, 1876; *Atlanta Herald*, February 10, 1876, reprinted in *New Orleans Times*, February 20, 1876. "The Social Problem," *New Orleans Daily Picayune*, February 21, 1876, 4. Woodhull consciously played up her status as victim to appeal to audience sympathies. See *St. Louis Republican*, February 2, 1876, 5.

82. *Elmira Daily Advertiser*, September 14, 1875; *Galveston Weekly News*, February 28, 1876. A Springfield, Massachusetts, journalist noticed a big difference in the quality of and reception by her audience between the fall of 1873 and 1875, for example. See *Springfield Republican*, December 13, 1875, 5. See also *Watertown Morning Dispatch*, September 1, 1875; *Madison Daily Democrat*, October 15, 1875, 4.

83. *Daily State Gazette*, Austin Texas, n.d., reprinted in *WCW*, March 9, 1876.

84. *The Spiritualist at Work*, March 1, 1876.

85. Woodhull later blamed Andrews for publishing the Beecher exposure in her absence and without her consent. See her extensive comments reprinted in Sachs, *"The Terrible Siren"*, 304–5. On her desire to shield her daughter from comments and innuendo, see her interview with the *Washington Chronicle*, January 9, 1876, 8.

Conclusion. The Waning of the Woodhull Revolution

1. Adultery was the only legal grounds for divorce in New York in 1876.

2. Her decision in February 1876 to take the southern tour forced her to cancel a tour into the northwest that spring. At the time, she promised to honor her commitments at a later date. See "Lecture Engagements," *WCW*, February 5, 1876. She lectured in Boston in October 1876 and in Toronto in June 1877, for example; see Johnston, *Mrs. Satan*, 254–55.

3. Cornelius Vanderbilt died in January 1877. William Vanderbilt allegedly wanted to convince the sisters not to join his siblings in contesting the will. Goldsmith, *Other Powers*, 430–31. Woodhull and Claflin never confirmed that their departure had anything to do with the case, which came to trial in November 1877. However, they had presented a claim demanding $100,000 (roughly $1.5 million in today's dollars) for money they claimed he had held in trust for them (with interest). *New York Times*, May 13, 1877, 12. Their exact departure date is unknown.

4. She spoke in Nottingham and Liverpool in September, Manchester in October, and London in December 1877. Gabriel, *Notorious Victoria*, 246–47.

5. McFeely, *Frederick Douglass*, 332–33; Underhill, *The Woman Who Ran for President*, 290. This was their first meeting, though she had seen him speak at a suffrage convention in 1869. Douglass was surprised by his visitor, whom he did not immediately recognize. Douglass Diary, March 19, 1887, quoted in McFeely, *Frederick Douglass*, 331–32.

6. See the letters of Carrie [Miles] to Zula Maud Woodhull-Martin, December 1927–March 1928, Victoria Woodhull Martin Collection, Special Collections/Morris Library, Southern Illinois University, Carbondale.

7. The worth of Zula Maud Woodhull's estate was valued in excess of £300,000, roughly $15 million in today's dollars. "Wills and Bequests," *London Times*, January 7, 1941, 7.

8. A tiny Equal Rights Party nominated Woodhull in 1892. Belva Lockwood was that party's choice in the 1884 and 1888 elections. Underhill, *The Woman Who Ran for President*, 293; Messer-Kruse, *Yankee International*, 115.

9. Antoinette E. Taylor, "South Carolina and the Enfranchisement of Women: the Early Years." *South Carolina Historical Magazine* 77 (April 1976): 115–26, 117.

10. Florence Kelley, for example, struggled to maintain professional standing with Engels, because of her gender, regardless of her own solidly working-class credentials, and her skill as a translator of his work. Kathryn Kish Sklar, *Florence Kelley and the Nation's Work: The Rise of Women's Political Culture, 1830–1900* (New Haven, Conn.: Yale University Press, 1995), 131–36.

11. "Mrs. Woodhull," *Crucible*, December 15, 1877.

12. The best description of this phase of Woodhull's life appears in Underhill, *The Woman Who Ran for President*, 277–311.

13. With the exception of Underhill's *The Woman Who Ran for President*, only the revised images have appeared in biographies, for example. Underhill, whose diligence unearthed a new collection of Woodhull papers at the home of the Holland-Martin family in England, included one cover picture from *The Days' Doings* that Woodhull had preserved in a scrapbook.

14. See Stan Cohen, *Folk Devils and Moral Panics: the Creation of the Mods and Rockers* (London: MacGibbon and Kee, 1972), 43, 175, 190–93; Roland Barthes, "Myth Today" in *Mythologies*, trans. Annette Lavers (1957; New York: Hill and Wang, 1972), 114, 143.

15. Jeffrey Weeks, *Sex, Politics and Society: The Regulation of Sexuality Since 1800* (New York: Longman, 1981), 277, 283.

16. Victoria Woodhull, Introduction to Goethe's *Elective Affinities* (Boston: D.W. Niles, 1872), iii, vi–vii.

17. As Gaines Foster notes, the 1873 bill passed in such "hot haste"—without debate in Congress—that it had to be revised in 1876. See Foster, *Moral Reconstruction*, 53.

18. bell hooks, "Choosing the Margin as a Space of Radical Openness," in *Yearning*.

Bibliography

Newspapers

L'Abeille de Nouvelle Orléans (*New Orleans Bee*)
Akron Daily Argus (Ohio)
American Socialist
Ashtabula News (Ohio)
Atlanta Constitution
Atlanta Herald
Atlantic Monthly
Banner of Light (*BL*) (Boston)
Binghamton Democrat (New York)
Boston Herald
Boston Investigator
Brooklyn Eagle
Buffalo Sunday News
Buffalo Courier
Buffalo Express
Cedar Springs Wolverine Clipper (Michigan)
Charleston Daily Courier (Illinois)
Chicago Inter-Ocean
Chicago Times
Chicago Tribune
Cincinnati Commercial
Cincinnati Enquirer
Cleveland Leader
Council Bluffs Daily Nonpareil (Iowa)
The Crucible (aka *Hull's Crucible*; Boston)
Daily Alta California (San Francisco)
Daily State Gazette
Dallas Herald
Davenport Daily Democrat (Iowa)
The Days' Doings
Decatur Republican (Illinois)
Detroit Commercial Advertiser
Detroit Daily Union
Detroit Evening News
Dubuque Daily Times (Iowa)

Dubuque Telegraph
Elmira Daily Advertiser (New York)
Erie Observer (Pennsylvania)
Eugene Guard (Oregon)
Frank Leslie's Illustrated Newspaper
Galveston Daily News (Texas)
Galveston Weekly News
Gilroy Advocate (California)
Gold Hill Daily News (Nevada)
The Golden Age
Grand Rapids Eagle
Grand Rapids Daily Democrat
Greenville Journal (Ohio)
Harper's Weekly
Hartford Courant
Hollister Enterprise (California)
Houston Age
Illustrated Police News (Boston)
Iowa State Register
Johnstown Democrat
Kansas City Daily Chronicle
Kokomo Saturday Tribune (Indiana)
Leavenworth Daily Times (Kansas)
Leavenworth Freeman
Logansport Daily Star (Indiana)
London Times
Lynn Record (Massachusetts)
Madison Daily Democrat (Pennsylvania)
Meadville Evening Republican (Pennsylvania)
Memphis Daily Appeal
Memphis Daily Avalanche
Memphis Public Ledger
Mount Vernon Democratic Banner (Ohio)
Nashville Daily American
The Nation
National Police Gazette
Nebraska State Journal
New National Era
New Northwest
New Orleans Bee (L'Abeille de Nouvelle Orléans)
New Orleans Daily Picayune
New Orleans Democrat
New Orleans Republican
New Orleans Weekly Republican
New York Courier
New York Evening Post

New York Evening Telegram
New York Herald
New York Independent
New York Republican
New York Standard
New York Star
New York Sun
New York Times
New York Tribune
New York World
Newark Daily Journal
Oil City Daily Derrick (Pennsylvania)
Ottumwa Democrat (Iowa)
Pall Mall Gazette (England)
Parker City Daily (Indiana)
Philadelphia Inquirer
Pittsburgh Evening Leader
Pomeroy's Democrat
Port Huron Commercial (Michigan)
Port Huron Saturday Morning Journal
Port Huron Times
Providence Evening Press (Rhode Island)
Religio-Philosophical Journal (*RPJ*; Chicago)
The Revolution
Rochester Democrat and Chronicle (New York)
Rochester Union and Advertiser
Rock Island Daily Argus (Illinois)
Sacramento Daily Record
Salinas City Index (California)
Salt Lake Daily Herald (Utah)
San Francisco Chronicle
San Francisco Daily Examiner
San Francisco Elevator
San Francisco Pioneer
Saturday Tribune
Semi-Weekly Louisianian (New Orleans)
Le Socialiste
Southern Workman (Hampton, Virginia)
Spiritualist at Work
Springfield Republican (Massachusetts)
Springfield State Journal (Illinois)
St. Alban's Advertiser (Vermont)
St. Joseph Daily Gazette (Missouri)
St. Joseph Herald (Missouri)
St. Louis Globe-Democrat
St. Louis Journal

St. Louis Republican
St. Paul Daily Pioneer
Syracuse Courier (New York)
True Woman
Washington Chronicle
Washington Daily Critic
Washington National Republican
Watertown Morning Dispatch (New York)
Watsonville Pajaronian (California)
Weekly Louisianian (New Orleans)
Woodhull & Claflin's Weekly (*WCW*)
The Word

Manuscript Collections

Susan B. Anthony Papers. Library of Congress.
J. S. Bliss Correspondence. Department of Special Collections, Syracuse University Library.
Colonel James H. Blood Papers. New-York Historical Society
Frederick Douglass Papers. Library of Congress.
Matilda Joslyn Gage Papers. Schlesinger Library, Radcliffe College, Cambridge, Massachusetts.
Garrison Family Papers. Sophia Smith Collection, Smith College, Northampton, Massachusetts.
International Workingmen's Association Papers. State Historical Society of Wisconsin, Madison.
Alma Lutz Collection. Huntington Library, San Marino, California.
Miscellaneous Papers. New York Public Library.
New York Society for the Suppression of Vice Papers. Library of Congress.
Emanie Phillips (Nahm) Arling Sachs Phillips Collection. Department of Library Special Collections, Manuscripts, Western Kentucky University, Bowling Green, Kentucky (cited as WKU).
Amy Post Papers. University of Rochester Library, Rochester, New York.
Elizabeth Cady Stanton Papers. Library of Congress.
Stowe-Day Memorial Collection, Hartford, Connecticut
Victoria Woodhull Papers. Boston Public Library
Victoria Woodhull Martin Collection. Special Collections/Morris Library, Southern Illinois University, Carbondale.

Unpublished Papers and Dissertations

Athey, Stephanie. "Contested Bodies: The Writing of Whiteness and Gender in American Literature." Ph.D. thesis, University of Minnesota, 1993.

Buckley, Peter. "To the Opera House: Culture and Society in New York City, 1820–1860." Ph.D. thesis, State University of New York, Stony Brook, 1984.

Cherches, Peter. "Star Course: Popular Lectures and the Marketing of Celebrity in Nineteenth Century America." Ph.D. thesis, New York University, 1997.

Eubank, Marjorie Harrell. "The Redpath Lyceum Bureau from 1868 to 1901." Ph.D. thesis, University of Michigan, 1968.

Greef, Robert J. "Public Lectures in New York, 1851–1878: A Cultural Index of the Times." Ph.D. thesis, University of Chicago, 1941.

Jones, Mary Somerville. "An Historical Geography of the Changing Divorce Law in the United States." Ph.D. thesis, University of North Carolina, Chapel Hill, 1978.

Katz, Philip Mark. "Americanizing the Paris Commune, 1861–1877." Ph.D. thesis, Princeton University, 1994.

Lemons, Elizabeth. "Sex in Context: Toward a Contextual Feminist Theology of Heterosexual Relations in the Contemporary United States Through an Analysis of Victoria Woodhull's Nineteenth-Century Free-Love Discourse." Ph.D. thesis, Harvard University School of Divinity, 1997.

Regan, Ward. "Transforming Consciousness: The Eight Hour Strike of 1872." Unpublished paper in author's possession.

Romano, Renee. "Sex at the Schoolhouse Door: Fears of 'Amalgamation' in the Southern Response to *Brown v. Board of Education.*" Paper presented at the 111th Annual Meeting of the American Historical Association, New York, 1997.

Stapen, Candyce Homnick. "The Novel Form and *Woodhull & Claflin's Weekly*, 1870–76: A Little Magazine Edited by Women and Published for Suffragists, Socialists, Free Lovers, and Other Radicals." Ph.D. thesis, University of Maryland, College Park, 1979.

Published Books, Articles, Pamphlets

"All Among the Hay" Songster: Full of the Jolliest Lot of Songs and Ballads that Have Ever Been Printed. New York: DeWitt, 1872.

Anderson, James D. *The Education of Blacks in the South, 1860–1935.* Chapel Hill: University of North Carolina Press, 1988.

Andrews, David L. and Steven J. Jackson, eds. *Sports Stars: The Cultural Politics of Sporting Celebrity.* London: Routledge, 2001.

Andrews, Stephen Pearl, ed. *Love, Marriage, and Divorce and the Sovereignty of the Individual: A Discussion by Henry James, Horace Greeley, and Stephen Pearl Andrews.* New York: Stringer and Townsend, 1853.

Aptheker, Bettina. "Woman's Legacy," In Shirley Yee, *Black Women Abolitionists: A Study in Activism, 1828–1860.* Knoxville: University of Tennessee Press, 1992.

Barthes, Roland. "Myth Today." In *Mythologies.* Trans. Annette Lavers. 1957; New York: Hill and Wang, 1972.

Basch, Françoise. *Rebelles américaines au XIXe siècle: Mariage, amor libre et politique,* Paris: Klincksieck, 1990.

Basham, Diana. *The Trial of Woman: Feminism and the Occult Sciences in Victorian Literature and Society*. Basingstroke: Macmillan, 1992.

Bates, Anna. *Weeder in the Garden of the Lord: Anthony Comstock's Life and Career.* New York: University Press of America, 1995.

Battan, Jesse F. "'The Word Made Flesh': Language, Authority, and Sexual Desire in Late Nineteenth-Century America." *Journal of the History of Sexuality* 3, 2 (1992): 223–44.

Becker, Beril. *Whirlwind in Petticoats*. Garden City, N.Y.: Doubleday, 1947.

Bederman, Gail. *Manliness and Civilization: A Cultural History of Gender and Race in the United States, 1880–1917.* Chicago: University of Chicago Press, 1995.

Beisel, Nicola. *Imperiled Innocents: Anthony Comstock and Family Reproduction in Victorian America*. Princeton, N.J.: Princeton University Press, 1997.

Blatt, Martin Henry. *Free Love and Anarchism: The Biography of Ezra Heywood.* Urbana: University of Illinois Press, 1989.

Blondeau, Nicole. *Victoria la scandaleuse: La vie extraordinaire de Victoria Woodhull, 1838–1927*, Paris: Éditions Menges, 1979.

Bode, Carl. *The American Lyceum: Town Meeting of the Mind*. New York: Oxford University Press, 1956.

Boorstin, Daniel J. *The Image: A Guide to Pseudo-Events in America*. New York, Harper and Row, 1964.

Boydston, Jeanne, Mary Kelley, and Anne Margolis, eds. *The Limits of Sisterhood: The Beecher Sisters on Women's Rights and Woman's Sphere*. Chapel Hill: University of North Carolina Press, 1988.

Braude, Ann. *Radical Spirits: spiritualism and Women's Rights in Nineteenth-Century America*. Boston: Beacon Press, 1989.

Braudy, Leo. *The Frenzy of Renown: Fame and Its History*. New York: Oxford University Press, 1986.

Brough, James. *The Vixens: A Biography of Victoria and Tennessee Claflin*. New York: Simon and Schuster, 1980.

Broun, Heywood and Margaret Leech. *Anthony Comstock, Roundsman of the Lord.* New York: A. & C. Boni, 1927.

Brown, Joshua. *Beyond the Lines: Pictorial Reporting, Everyday Life, and the Crisis of Gilded Age America*. Berkeley: University of California Press, 2002.

Brown, Thomas. "The Miscegenation of Richard Mentor Johnson as an Issue in the National Election Campaign of 1835–36." *Civil War History* 39 (1993): 5–30.

Brundage, W. Fitzhugh. *Lynching in the New South: Georgia and Virginia, 1880–1930.* Urbana: University of Illinois Press, 1993.

Buhle, Mari Jo. *Women and American Socialism, 1870–1920*. Urbana: University of Illinois Press, 1981.

———. *Women and the American Left: A Guide to Sources*. Boston: G.K. Hall, 1983.

Campbell, Karlyn Kohrs, ed. *Man Cannot Speak for Her*. Vol. 2, *Key Texts of the Early Feminists*. Westport, Conn.: Greenwood Press, 1989.

Caraway, Nancy, *Segregated Sisterhood: Racism and the Politics of American Feminism*. Knoxville: University of Tennessee Press, 1991.

Chester, Giraud, *Embattled Maiden: The Life of Anna Dickinson*. New York: Putnam, 1951.

Chudacoff, Howard P. *The Age of the Bachelor: Creating an American Subculture.* Princeton, N.J.: Princeton University Press, 1999.

Clark, Clifford E., Jr. *Henry Ward Beecher: Spokesman for a Middle-Class America.* Urbana: University of Illinois Press, 1978.

Click, Patricia. *The Spirit of the Times: Amusements in Nineteenth-Century Baltimore, Norfolk and Richmond.* Charlottesville: University Press of Virginia, 1989.

Clinton, Catherine. "Bloody Terrain: Freedwomen, Sexuality and Violence During Reconstruction." In Clinton, ed., *Half-Sisters of History: Southern Women and the American Past.* Durham, N.C.: Duke University Press, 1994.

Cohen, Patricia Cline, *The Murder of Helen Jewett: The Life and Death of a Prostitute in Nineteenth-Century New York.* New York: Knopf, 1998.

Cohen, Stan. *Folk Devils and Moral Panics: The Creation of the Mods and Rockers.* London: MacGibbon and Kee, 1972.

Cohen, William, *Sex Scandal: The Private Parts of Victorian Fiction.* Durham, N.C.: Duke University Press, 1996.

Cominos, Peter T. "Late-Victorian Sexual Respectability and the Social System." *International Review of Social History* 8 (1963): 18–48.

Cott, Nancy, *The Bonds of Womanhood: "Woman's Sphere" in New England, 1780–1835.* New Haven, Conn.: Yale University Press, 1977.

———. "Passionlessness: An Interpretation of Victorian Sexual Ideology, 1790–1850." *Signs: A Journal of Women in Culture and Society* 4 (1978): 219–36.

Croly, David Goodman. *Miscegenation.* New York: H. Dexter, Hamilton, 1864; reprint Upper Saddle River, N.J.: Literature House, 1970.

Crow, Jeffrey. "An Apartheid for the South: Clarence Poe's Crusade for Rural Segregation." In Jeffrey Crow, Paul Escott, and Charles Flynn, Jr. eds., *Race, Class, and Politics in Southern History: Essays in Honor of Robert F. Durden.* Baton Rouge: Louisiana State University Press, 1989.

Darewin, G. S. *Synopsis of the Lives of Victoria C. Woodhull, Now Mrs. John Biddulph Martin, and Tennessee Claflin, Now Lady Cook: The First Two Lady Bankers and Reformers of America.* London, 1891.

Darwin, M. F. *One Moral Standard for All: Extracts form the Lives of Victoria Claflin Woodhull, Now Mrs. John Biddulph Martin, and Tennessee Claflin, Now Lady Cook.* New York: Caulon Press, 1910 (?).

Davidoff, Leonore and Catherine Hall. *Family Fortunes: Men and Women of the English Middle Class, 1780–1850.* Chicago: University of Chicago Press, 1987.

Davis, F. James. *Who Is Black? One Nation's Definition.* University Park: Pennsyvania State University Press, 1991.

Davis, Natalie Zemon. *Society and Culture in Early Modern France: Eight Essays.* Stanford, Calif.: Stanford University Press, 1975.

Dijkstra, Bram. *Idols of Perversity: Fantasies of Feminine Evil in Fin-de-Siècle Culture.* New York: Oxford University Press, 1986.

D'Onston, Roslyn. *Brief Sketches in the Life of Victoria Woodhull (Now Mrs. John Biddulph Martin.* London, 1893.

Douglass, Frederick. *Frederick Douglass: Selections from His Writings.* Ed. Philip S. Foner. 1945; New York: International Publishers, 1964.

Du Bois, W. E. B. *Black Reconstruction in America; An Essay Toward a History of the Part Which Black Folk Played in the Attempt to Reconstruct Democracy in America, 1860–1880.* 1935; New York: Russell and Russell, 1966.

DuBois, Ellen Carol, ed. *The Elizabeth Cady Stanton, Susan B. Anthony Reader: Correspondence, Writings, Speeches.* Boston: Northeastern University Press, 1992.

———. *Feminism and Suffrage: The Emergence of an Independent Women's Rights Movement in America, 1848–1869.* Ithaca, N.Y.: Cornell University Press, 1978.

———. "Outgrowing the Compact of the Fathers: Equal Rights, Woman Suffrage, and the United States' Constitution, 1820–1878." In DuBois, *Woman Suffrage and Women's Rights.* New York: New York University Press, 1998.

———. "Taking the Law into Our Own Hands: *Bradwell, Minor,* and Suffrage Militance in the 1870s." In Nancy Hewitt and Suzanne Lebsock, eds., *Visible Women: New Essays on American Activism.* Chicago: University of Illinois Press, 1993.

———. "Woman Suffrage and the Left: An International Socialist-Feminist Perspective." In DuBois, *Woman Suffrage and Women's Rights.* New York: New York University Press, 1998.

Dudden, Faye. *Women in the American Theatre: Actresses and Audiences, 1790–1870.* New Haven, Conn.: Yale University Press, 1994.

Duggan, Lisa. *Sapphic Slashers: Sex, Violence, and American Modernity.* Durham, N.C.: Duke University Press, 2000.

Edwards, Laura. *Gendered Strife and Confusion: The Political Culture of Reconstruction.* Urbana: University of Illinois Press, 1997.

Elshtain, Jean Bethke. *Public Man, Private Woman: Women in Social and Political Thought.* Princeton, N.J.: Princeton University Press, 1981.

Factor, Robert L. *The Black Response to America: Men, Ideals, and Organization, from Frederick Douglass to the NAACP.* Reading, Mass.: Addison-Wesley, 1970.

Field, Kate. "Leaves from a Lecturer's Notebook." In Field, *Hap-hazard.* Boston: James Osgood, 1873.

Fischer, Roger A. *The Segregation Struggle in Louisiana, 1872–77.* Urbana: University of Illinois Press, 1974.

Flexner, Eleanor. *Century of Struggle: The Woman's Rights Movement in the United States* Cambridge, Mass.: Belknap Press of Harvard University Press, 1959.

Foner, Eric. *Reconstruction: America's Unfinished Revolution, 1863–1877.* New York: Harper and Row, 1988.

Foner, Philip S. *History of the Labor Movement in the United States.* Vol. 1, *From Colonial Times to the Founding of the American Federation of Labor.* New York: International Publishers, 1947.

———. *Life and Writings of Frederick Douglass.* New York: International Publishers, 1965.

Foster, Gaines. *Moral Reconstruction: Christian Lobbyists and the Federal Legislation of Morality, 1865–1920.* Chapel Hill: University of North Carolina Press, 2002.

Fowler, David H. *Northern Attitudes Towards Interracial Marriage: Legislation and Public Opinion in the Middle Atlantic and the States of the Old Northwest, 1780–1930.* New York: Garland, 1987.

Fowler, William Worthington. *Ten Years in Wall Street; or, Revelations of Inside Life and Experience on Change.* Hartford, Conn.: Worthington, Dustin, 1870.

———. *Twenty Years of Inside Life in Wall Street; or, Revelations of the Personal Experiences of a Speculator.* New York: Orange Judd, 1880.

Fox, Richard Wightman. "Intimacy on Trial: Cultural Meanings of the Beecher-Tilton Affair." In Fox and T. J. Jackson Lears, eds., *The Power of Culture: Critical Essays in American History.* Chicago: University of Chicago Press, 1993.

———. *Trials of Intimacy: Love and Loss in the Beecher-Tilton Scandal.* Chicago: University of Chicago Press, 1999.

Fraser, Nancy. *Unruly Practices: Power, Discourse, and Gender in Contemporary Social Theory.* Minneapolis: University of Minnesota Press, 1989.

Frederickson, George. *The Inner Civil War: Northern Intellectuals and the Crisis of the Union.* New York: Harper and Row, 1965.

Frisken, Amanda. "Sex in Politics: Victoria Woodhull as Public Woman." *Journal of Women's History* 12, 1 (Spring 2000): 89–110.

Gabler, Neal. *Life the Movie: How Entertainment Conquered Reality.* New York: Knopf, 1998.

Gabriel, Mary. *Notorious Victoria: The Life of Victoria Woodhull, Uncensored.* Chapel Hill, N.C.: Algonquin Books of Chapel Hill, 1998.

The General Council of the First International, Minutes. Moscow: Progress Publishers, n.d.

Giddings, Paula. *When and Where I Enter: The Impact of Black Women on Race and Sex in America.* New York: W. Morrow, 1984.

Gifford, Carolyn De Swarte. "Frances Willard and the Woman's Christian Temperance Union's Conversion to Woman Suffrage." In Marjorie Spruill Wheeler, ed., *One Woman One Vote: Rediscovering the Woman Suffrage Movement.* Troutdale, Ore.: New Sage Press, 1995.

Gilfoyle, Timothy. *City of Eros: New York City, Prostitution, and the Commercialization of Sex, 1820–1920.* New York: Norton, 1992.

Gillman, Susan. *Dark Twins: Imposture and Identity in Mark Twain's America.* Chicago: University of Chicago Press, 1989.

Gilmore, Glenda Elizabeth. *Gender and Jim Crow: Women and the Politics of White Supremacy in North Carolina, 1896–1920.* Chapel Hill: University of North Carolina Press, 1996.

Ginzberg, Lori. "'The Hearts of Your Readers Will Shudder': Fanny Wright, Infidelity, and American Freethought." *American Quarterly* 46, 2 (June 1994).

Goldsmith, Barbara. *Other Powers: The Age of Suffrage, Spiritualism, and the Scandalous Victoria Woodhull.* New York: Knopf, 1998.

Gullickson, Gay. *Unruly Women of Paris: Images of the Commune.* Ithaca, N.Y.: Cornell University Press, 1996.

Gunning, Sandra. *Race, Rape, and Lynching: The Red Record of American Literature, 1880–1912.* New York: Oxford University Press, 1996.

Gurstein, Rochelle. *Repeal of Reticence: A History of America's Cultural and Legal Struggles over Free Speech, Obscenity, Sexual Liberation and Modern Art.* New York: Hill and Wang, 1996.

Hale, Grace. *Making Whiteness: The Culture of Segregation in the South.* New York: Pantheon, 1998.

Hall, Jacqueline Dowd. *Revolt Against Chivalry: Jessie Daniel Ames and the Women's Campaign Against Lynching.* New York: Columbia University Press, 1993.

Hertz, Neil. "Medusa's Head: Male Hysteria Under Political Pressure." *Representations* 4 (Fall 1983): 27–54.

Heywood, Ezra. *Uncivil Liberty: An Essay to Show the Injustice and Impolicy of Ruling Woman Without Her Consent.* Princeton, Mass.: Cooperative Publishing Company, 1870.

Hoeltje, Hubert H. . "Notes on the History of Lecturing in Iowa." *Iowa Journal of History* 25 (January 1927),

Holbrook, Stewart. *Dreamers of the American Dream.* Garden City, N.Y.: Doubleday, 1957.

Holland, J. C. "The Popular Lecture." *Atlantic Monthly* (March 1865): 364.

hooks, bell. *Yearning: Race, Gender and Cultural Politics.* Boston: South End Press, 1990.

Horowitz, Helen Lefkovitz. *Rereading Sex: Battles over Sexual Knowledge and Suppression in Nineteenth-Century America.* New York: Knopf, 2002.

———. "A Victoria Woodhull for the 1990s." *Reviews in American History* 27 (1999): 87–97.

———. "Victoria Woodhull, Anthony Comstock, and the Conflict over Sex in the United States in the 1870s." *Journal of American History* 87, 2 (September 2000): 403–34.

Jamieson, Kathleen Hall. *Beyond the Double Bind: Women and Leadership.* New York: Oxford University Press, 1995.

Johnson, Gerald W. *The Lunatic Fringe.* 1957; reprint, Westport, Conn.: Greenwood Press, 1973.

Johnston, Johanna. *Mrs. Satan: The Incredible Saga of Victoria Woodhull.* New York: Putnam, 1967.

Jordan, Winthrop D. *The White Man's Burden: Historical Origins of Racism in the United States.* New York, Oxford University Press, 1974.

Kaplan, Temma. *Crazy for Democracy: Women in Grassroots Movements.* New York: Routledge, 1997.

Kelley, Mary. *Private Woman, Public Stage: Literary Domesticity in Nineteenth-Century America.* New York: Oxford University Press, 1984.

Kerr, Andrea Moore. "White Women's Rights, Black Men's Wrongs: Free Love, Blackmail, and the Formation of the American Woman Suffrage Association." In Marjorie Spruill Wheeler, ed., *One Woman One Vote: Rediscovering the Woman Suffrage Movement.* Troutdale, Ore.: New Sage Press, 1995.

Kerr, Howard. *Mediums, and Spirit-Rappers, and Roaring Radicals: Spiritualism in American Literature, 1850–1900.* Urbana, University of Illinois Press, 1972.

Kinney, James. *Amalgamation! Race, Sex, and Rhetoric in the Nineteenth-Century American Novel.* Westport, Conn. : Greenwood Press, 1985.

Kisner, Arlene. *Woodhull & Claflin's Weekly: The Lives and Writings of Notorious Victoria Woodhull and Her Sister Tennessee Claflin.* Washington, N.J.: Time Change Press, 1972.

Lapides, Kenneth, ed. *Marx and Engels on the Trade Unions*. New York: Praeger, 1987.

Lause, Mark A. "The American Radicals and Organized Marxism: The Initial Experience, 1869–1874." *Labor History* 33 (1992): 55–80.

Leach, William. *True Love and Perfect Union: The Feminist Reform of Sex and Society*. New York: Basic Books, 1980.

Legge, Madeleine. *Two Noble Women, Nobly Planned*. London: Phelps Brothers, 1893.

Lerner, Gerda. "The Lady and the Mill Girl." In Lerner, *The Majority Finds Its Past: Placing Women in History*. New York: Oxford University Press, 1979.

Levine, Lawrence. *Highbrow/Lowbrow: The Emergence of Cultural Hierarchy in America*. Cambridge, Mass.: Harvard University Press, 1990.

Lloyd, Arthur Young. *The Slavery Controversy, 1831–1860*. Chapel Hill: University of North Carolina Press, 1939.

Lott, Eric. *Love and Theft: Blackface Minstrelsy and the American Working Class*. New York: Oxford University Press, 1993.

Lowell, James Russell. *Letters of James Russel Lowell*. Ed. Charles Elliot Norton. 2 vols. New York: Harper and Bros, 1894.

Lutz, Alma. *Created Equal: A Biography of Elizabeth Cady Stanton, 1815–1902*. New York: John Day, 1940.

Marberry, M. M. *Vicki: A Biography of Victoria C. Woodhull*. New York: Funk and Wagnalls, 1967.

Marshall, Annecka. "From Sexual Denigration to Self-Respect: Resisting Images of Black Female Sexuality." In Delia Jarrett-Macauley, ed., *Reconstructing Womanhood, Reconstructing Feminism: Writings on Black Women*. London Routledge, 1996.

Marshall, Charles F. *The True History of the Brooklyn Scandal*. Philadelphia: National Publishing Company, 1874.

Marshall, P. David. *Celebrity and Power: Fame in Contemporary Culture*. Minneapolis: University of Minnesota Press, 1997.

Marx, Karl and Frederick Engels. *Karl Marx and Freidrich Engels: Collected Works*. New York: International Publishers, 1975.

———. *Karl Marx and Friedrich Engels: Letters to Americans, 1848–1895*. Trans. Leonard E. Mins. Moscow: International Publishing, 1953.

Matthews, Glenda. *The Rise of Public Woman: Women's Power and Women's Place in the United States, 1630–1970*. New York: Oxford University Press, 1992.

McCabe, James (Edward Winslow Martin). *Secrets of the Great City*. Philadelphia: Jones Brothers, 1868.

McFeely, William S. *Frederick Douglass*. New York: Norton, 1991.

McMillen, Neil. *Dark Journey: Black Mississippians in the Age of Jim Crow*. Urbana: University of Illinois Press, 1989.

Mead, David, *Yankee Eloquence in the Middle West: The Ohio Lyceum, 1850–1870*. East Lansing: Michigan State College Press, 1951.

Medbery, James K. *Men and Mysteries of Wall Street*. Boston: Fields, Osgood, 1870.

Messer-Kruse, Timothy. *The Yankee International: Marxism and the American Reform Tradition*. Chapel Hill: University of North Carolina Press, 1998.

Morton, Patricia. *Disfigured Images: The Historical Assault on Afro-American Women*. New York: Greenwood Press, 1991.

Munich, Adrienne. *Andromeda's Chains: Gender and Interpretation in Victorian Literature and Art.* New York: Columbia University Press, 1989.

Nasaw, David. *Going Out: The Rise and Fall of Public Amusements.* New York: Basic Books, 1993.

Newman, Louise, ed. *Men's Ideas, Women's Realities: Popular Science, 1870–1915.* New York: Pergamon Press, 1985.

Noun, Louise. *Strong Minded Women: The Emergence of the Woman-Suffrage Movement in Iowa.* Ames: Iowa State University Press, 1969.

O'Neill, William L. *Everyone Was Brave: A History of Feminism in America.* Chicago: Quadrangle Books, 1971.

Owen, Alex. *The Darkened Room: Women, Power and Spiritualism in Late Nineteenth Century England.* Philadelphia: University of Pennsylvania Press, 1989.

Passet, Joanne Ellen. *Sex Radicals and the Quest for Women's Equality.* Urbana : University of Illinois Press, 2003.

Penny, Miss Virginia. *How Women Can Make Money, Married or Single, In all Branches of the Arts and Sciences, Professions, Trades, Agricultural and Mechanical Pursuits.* 1870; New York: Arno and the New York Times, 1971.

Perman, Michael. *The Road to Redemption: Southern Politics, 1869–1879.* Chapel Hill: University of North Carolina Press, 1984.

Perry, Lewis. *Radical Abolitionism: Anarchy and the Government of God in Antislavery Thought.* Ithaca, N.Y.: Cornell University Press, 1973.

Pond, Major James B. *Eccentricities of Genius: Memories of Famous Men and Women of the Platform and Stage.* New York: G.W. Dillingham, 1900.

Pykett, Lyn. *The "Improper" Feminine: The Woman's Sensation Novel and the New Woman Writing.* London: Routledge, 1992.

Reaves, Wendy Wick. *Celebrity Caricature in America.* New Haven, Conn.: National Portrait Gallery, Smithsonian Institution, in association with Yale University Press, 1998.

Reynolds, David S. *Beneath the American Renaissance: The Subversive Imagination in the Age of Emerson and Melville.* New York: Knopf, 1988.

Smith-Rosenberg, Caroll. "The New Woman as Androgyne: Social Disorder and Gender Crisis, 1870–1936." In Smith-Rosenberg, *Disorderly Conduct: Visions of Gender in Victorian America.* New York: Oxford University Press, 1985.

Ross, Ishbel. *Charmers and Cranks: Twelve Famous American Women Who Defied the Conventions.* New York: Harper and Row, 1965.

Rugoff, Milton. *The Beechers: An American Family in the Nineteenth Century.* New York: Harper and Row, 1981.

Russett, Cynthia. *Sexual Science: The Victorian Construction of Womanhood.* Cambridge, Mass.: Harvard University Press, 1989.

Russo, Mary. "Female Grotesques: Carnival and Theory." In Teresa De Lauretis, ed., *Feminist Studies, Critical Studies.* Bloomington: Indiana University Press, 1986.

Ryan, Mary. *Women in Public: Between Banners and Ballots, 1825–1880.* Baltimore: Johns Hopkins University Press, 1990.

Sachs, Emanie. *"The Terrible Siren": Victoria Woodhull, 1838–1927.* New York: Harper and Bros., 1928.

Saks, Eva. "Representing Miscegenation Laws." *Raritan* 8 (Fall 1988).

Scott, Donald. "Knowledge and the Marketplace." In James Gilbert et al., eds., *The Mythmaking Frame of Mind: Social Imagination and American Culture.* Belmont, Calif.: Wadsworth, 1993.

———. "Print and the Public Lecture System, 1840–60." In William Joyce et al., eds., *Printing and Society in Early America.* Worcester, Mass.: American Antiquarian Society, 1983.

———. "The Public Lecture and the Creation of a Public in Mid-Nineteenth-Century America." *Journal of American History* 66 (March 1980).

Sears, Hal. *The Sex Radicals: Free Love in High Victorian America.* Lawrence: Regents Press of Kansas, 1977.

Shaplen, Robert. *Free Love and Heavenly Sinners: The Story of the Great Henry Ward Beecher Scandal.* New York: Knopf, 1954.

Shell, Marc. "Siamese Twins and Changlings." In Shell, *Children of the Earth: Literature, Politics and Nationhood.* New York: Oxford University Press, 1993.

Sklar, Kathryn Kish. *Catharine Beecher: A Study in American Domesticity.* New Haven, Conn.: Yale University Press, 1973.

———. *Florence Kelley and the Nation's Work: The Rise of Women's Political Culture, 1830–1900.* New Haven, Conn.: Yale University Press, 1995.

Smith, John David, *Racial Determinism and the Fear of Miscegenation, pre-1900.* New York: Garland, 1993.

Solomon-Godeau, Abigail. "The Other Side of Venus: The Visual Economy of Feminine Display." In Victoria de Grazia, ed., *The Sex of Things: Gender and Consumption in Historical Perspective.* Berkeley: University of California Press, 1996.

Spurlock, John. *Free Love: Marriage and Middle-Class Radicalism in America, 1825–1860.* New York: New York University Press, 1988.

Srebnick, Amy. *The Mysterious Death of Mary Rogers: Sex and Culture in Nineteenth-Century New York.* New York: Oxford University Press, 1995.

Stansell, Christine. *City of Women: Sex and Class in New York, 1789–1860.* New York: Knopf, 1986.

Steinem, Gloria. *Moving Beyond Words.* New York: Simon and Schuster, 1994.

Stern, Madeleine Bettina. *The Pantarch: A Biography of Stephen Pearl Andrews.* Austin: University of Texas Press, 1968.

Stern, Madeleine Bettina. *We the Women: Career Firsts of Nineteenth-Century America.* New York: Schulte, 1963.

Stevenson, Louise. *The Victorian Homefront: American Thought and Culture, 1860–1880.* New York: Twayne, 1991.

Stowe, Harriet Beecher, *My Wife & I: or, Harry Henderson's History.* Serialized in *The Christian Union,* 1871. New York: J.B. Ford, 1871.

Summers, Mark. *The Press Gang: Newspapers and Politics, 1865–1878.* Chapel Hill: University of North Carolina Press, 1994.

Taylor, Antoinette E. "South Carolina and the Enfranchisement of Women: The Early Years." *South Carolina Historical Magazine* 77 (April 1976).

Taylor, Barbara. *Eve and the New Jeruselum: Socialism and Feminism in the Nineteenth Century.* New York: Pantheon, 1983.

Terborg-Penn, Rosalyn. "African American Women and the Woman Suffrage

Movement." In Marjorie Spruill Wheeler, ed., *One Woman One Vote: Rediscovering the Woman Suffrage Movement*. Troutdale, Ore.: New Sage Press, 1995.

Theodore Tilton v. Henry Ward Beecher. Action for crim. con. Tried in the City Court of Brooklyn. Verbatim Report in Three Volumes. New York: 1875.

Tilton, Theodore. *Victoria C. Woodhull, A Biographical Sketch: Mr. Tilton's Account of Mrs. Woodhull. Golden Age Tracts*, 3. New York: McDivitt, Campbell, 1871.

Todd, Ellen Wiley. *The "New Woman" Revised: Painting and Gender Politics on Fourteenth Street*. Berkeley: University of California Press, 1993.

Toll, Robert. *Blacking Up: The Minstrel Show in Nineteenth Century America*. New York: Oxford University Press, 1974.

Tolway, Stewart and E. M. Beck, *A Festival of Violence: An Analysis of Southern Lynchings, 1882–1930*. Urbana: University of Illinois Press, 1995.

Tomes, Nancy. *The Gospel of Germs: Men, Women, and the Microbe in American Life* Cambridge, Mass.: Harvard University Press, 1998.

Tone, Andrea. *Devices and Desires: A History of Contraceptives in America*. New York: Hill and Wang, 2001.

Treat, Joseph. *Beecher, Tilton, Woodhull: The Creation of Society*. New York: Joseph Treat, 1874.

———. *The Future of Vineland*. Vineland, N.J., 1870(?).

Treat, Mary. "Controlling Sex in Butterflies." *American Naturalist* 7, 3 (March 1873): 129–32.

Underhill, Lois Beachy. *The Woman Who Ran for President: The Many Lives of Victoria Woodhull*. Bridgehampton, N.Y.: Bridge Works Press, 1995.

Vance, Carol. "Pleasure and Danger: Toward a Politics of Sexuality." In Vance, ed., *Pleasure and Danger: Exploring Female Sexuality*. Boston: Routledge, 1984.

Vaughn, William Preston. *Schools for All: The Blacks and Public Education in the South, 1865–1877*. Lexington, University Press of Kentucky, 1974.

Walkowitz, Judith R. *City of Dreadful Delight: Narratives of Sexual Danger in Late-Victorian London*. Chicago: University of Chicago Press, 1992.

Wallace, Irving. *The Nympho and Other Maniacs*. New York: Simon and Schuster, 1971.

Waller, Altina Laura. *Reverend Beecher and Mrs. Tilton: Sex and Class in Victorian America*. Amherst: University of Massachusetts Press, 1982.

Weeks, Jeffrey. *Sex, Politics and Society: The Regulation of Sexuality Since 1800*. New York: Longman, 1981.

Wells-Barnett, Ida B. *On Lynchings: Southern Horrors, A Red Record, Mob Rule in New Orleans*. New York, Arno Press, 1969.

———. *Selected Works of Ida B. Wells-Barnett*. Ed. Trudier Harris. New York: Oxford University Press, 1991.

Westbrook, Wayne. *Wall Street in the American Novel*. New York: New York University Press, 1980.

Whites, LeeAnn. *The Civil War as a Crisis in Gender: Augusta, Georgia, 1860–1890*. Athens: University of Georgia Press, 1995.

Wiegman, Robyn. *American Anatomies: Theorizing Race and Gender*. Durham, N.C.: Duke University Press, 1995.

Williamson, Joel. "The Separation of Races." In Williamson, ed., *The Origins of Segregation*. Boston: D.C. Heath, 1968.

Wood, Forrest. *Black Scare: The Racist Response to Emancipation and Reconstruction.* Berkeley, University of California Press, 1968.

Woodhull, Victoria C. "Cartter and Carpenter Reviewed: A Speech Before the National Woman Suffrage Association, Lincoln Hall, Washington, D.C., January 10,1872." Reprinted in *Woodhull & Claflin's Weekly,* February 3, 1872.

———. "The Garden of Eden, or, The Paradise Lost and Found." Revised version reprinted in Woodhull and Claflin, *The Human Body, Temple of God.*

———. "The Human Body, Temple of God." Lecture reprinted in *Memphis Daily Appeal,* February 8, 1876.

———. Introduction to Goethe's *Elective Affinities.* Boston: D.W. Niles, 1872.

———. "The Naked Truth, or, The Situation Reviewed." Reprinted in Stern, *Victoria Woodhull Reader.*

———. "Reformation or Revolution, Which? Or, Behind the Political Scenes." Reprinted in Stern, *Victoria Woodhull Reader.*

———. "The Religion of Humanity." Lecture delivered to the AAS, September 1872. Reprinted in *WCW,* November 2, 1872.

———. "A Speech on the Impending Revolution: Delivered in Music Hall, Boston, Thursday, February 1, 1872 and the Academy of Music, February 20, 1872." Reprinted in Stern, *Victoria Woodhull Reader.*

———. "The Speech on the Principles of Finance." 1871. Reprinted in Stern, *Victoria Woodhull Reader.*

———. "Tried as By Fire, or, the True and the False, Socially." 1874. Reprinted in Stern, *Victoria Woodhull Reader.*

———. "And the Truth Shall Make You Free, or, The Principles of Social Freedom." 1871. Reprinted in Stern, *Victoria Woodhull Reader.*

———. *The Victoria Woodhull Reader.* Ed. Madeleine Stern. Weston, Mass.: M&S Press, 1974.

Woodhull, Victoria and Tennessee Claflin. *The Human Body, the Temple of God; or, The Philosophy of Sociology by Victoria Clafflin Woodhull (Mrs. John biddulph Martin) and Tennessee C. Claflin (Lady Cook), Together with Other Essays, Ets., Etc., Also Press Notices of Extemporaneous Lectures Delivered Throughout America and England from 1869 to 1882.* London, 1890.

Wunderlich, Roger. *Low Living and High Thinking at Modern Times.* Syracuse, N.Y.: Syracuse University Press, 1992.

Wynes, Charles E. "Social Acceptance and Unacceptance." In Joel Williamson, ed., *The Origins of Segregation.* Boston: D.C. Heath, 1968.

Yellin, Jean Fagin. *Women and Sisters: The Antislavery Feminists in American Culture.* New Haven, Conn.: Yale University Press, 1989.

Index

Acknowledgments

Countless people have lent their expertise, insights, and suggestions with a generosity and a spirit of free inquiry that made this project exciting and, at times, even joyous. It is impossible to acknowledge everyone whose ideas influenced my thinking; space allows me only to thank those whose contributions were particularly significant to the book's development. To the many others who helped me along the way, I am grateful.

This project began in 1991, when Judy Wishnia at Stony Brook first introduced me to Victoria Woodhull. I am indebted to the vibrant community of feminists and cultural historians at Stony Brook. Nancy Tomes was both a tough mentor and a sympathetic supporter from the outset, as well as a model of academic integrity and scholarship. Matthew Jacobson and Bill Taylor drew me into the realm of cultural history with their innovative perspectives on the past. Adrienne Munich, Iona Man-Cheong, and Eva Kittay introduced me to feminist analysis and an interdisciplinary approach to knowledge. Virginia Acevedo, Alejandra Osorio, Katy Stewart, and Alejandra Vassallo made our seminars lively sessions of feminist and historical debate.

My colleagues in the American Studies Department at Old Westbury have constantly encouraged and supported me; I am especially indebted to Ros Baxandall for her unstinting generosity of faith, time, and effort on my behalf. I am grateful to my students for reminding me that history needs to be relevant to contemporary readers; I particularly thank my students in my Protest & Change seminars in 2000–2002 for perpetually asking new questions in their debates over the role of activism in America's past.

Librarians and archivists all over the country helped me track down elusive newspapers and images from the 1870s. I owe special thanks to Patricia Hodges at Western Kentucky University for her untiring assistance with the Emanie Sachs collection. Without the help over several years of Donna Sammis, at Stony Brook's Interlibrary Loan Department, the confirmation of Woodhull's lecture tours in Chapter 4 would have been nothing more than an interesting idea. Pamela Arceneaux at the Historic New Orleans Collection and Marian Matyn at the Clarke Historical Library in Michigan went beyond the call of duty to help me track down hard-to-find local papers. Georgia Barnhill at the American Antiquarian Society and Sara W. Duke at the Prints and Photographs Division of the Library of Congress helped me find obscure illustrations and broadsides. At the eleventh hour, David J. Kelly at the Library of Congress helped me try to track down one last reference. To all these archivists and librarians, named and unnamed, I owe a debt of gratitude for their professionalism and intellectual curiosity, without which research of this type would be impossible.

Scholars in the field assisted me throughout. Lois Beachy Underhill generously shared her time and insights with me near the outset of this project. Mari Jo Buhle and Timothy Messer-Kruse responded with encouragement and good advice to specific questions about Woodhull and her history. Mark Summers clarified the workings of Associated Press dispatches in the 1870s. Elizabeth Lemons generously discussed with me her dissertation work on Woodhull's religious evolution. I've been exceptionally lucky in my editor, Bob Lockhart at the University of Pennsylvania Press, who has expertly guided me through the process of publishing my first book with a combination of enthusiasm and tact.

Portions of this book, in earlier versions, have appeared in print and are reprinted by permission. "Sex in Politics: Victoria Woodhull as an American Public Woman," came out in the *Journal of Women's History* (Spring 2000). "'A Shameless Prostitute and a Negro': Miscegenation Fears in the Election of 1872" appeared in the collection *Fear Itself: Enemies Real and Imagined in American Culture*, edited by Nancy Schultz and published by Purdue University Press in 1998. "Re/covering Victoria Woodhull: A Review Essay" appeared in the *Long Island Historical Journal* (Spring 1996). I thank the editors and anonymous reviewers for their invaluable suggestions. Over these years, I also benefited from the comments at conferences and workshops from Barbara Balliet, Josh Brown, Joan Jacobs Brumberg, Peter Buckley, Faye Dudden, and Nancy Hewitt.

Several people read the manuscript in its various stages of development along the way. In particular, Temma Kaplan brought her warmhearted criticism to bear on both content and form. I am also indebted to Matthew Guterl, Gary Marker, Catherine McKeen, Joel Rosenthal, Naomi Rosenthal, and Diane Samuels for their comments and suggestions, and to the late Roger Wunderlich's fierce editorial eye and intimate knowledge of 1870s radical culture.

Financial support from Stony Brook and Old Westbury made research and professional travel possible on a number of occasions. Graduate Teaching

Assistantships from the Women's Studies Program and the History Department at Stony Brook gave me crucial assistance early in my graduate career. I am particularly indebted to Adrienne Munich and Sally Sternglanz in Women's Studies at Stony Brook for their financial and intellectual encouragement over many years. In addition, support from Stony Brook's History Department's Angress fund and the Graduate Student Organization funded travel to archives and conferences. Since coming to Old Westbury, I received generous support from the Professional Development Fund of the faculty union, United University Professions.

Some debts are longstanding ones. I owe a lot to high school teachers G. Baker and H. Piper for making me love and respect history. I am also grateful to John H. Thompson for introducing me to cultural history, the Canadian perspective on the United States, and Captain Canuck.

Good friends have sustained my faith in this project long after they must have grown tired of hearing about it. I am indebted to Lisa Handler, Annulla Linders, Susanna Taipale, Carolyn Cocca, and Shirley Lim for their willingness to talk not only about the ins and outs of 1870s radical culture, but also about the processes of researching and writing over many long years.

The project could never have been completed without more than a decade of material and emotional assistance from my family. Generous support from my grandparents, Joan and Jack Code and Chalmers Frisken helped make graduate school an option in difficult times. Anni and Sidney Heller's generosity has enabled my professional growth over many years. My parents, Bill and Frances Frisken, and my sisters Sarah and Barbara Frisken showed me by example that the pursuit of knowledge through research was a worthy goal. Oscar, Benny, and Dusa Heller have continually put such work into perspective; I am grateful to them and to Jacob Heller for always reminding me what is important in life.

CPSIA information can be obtained
at www.ICGtesting.com
Printed in the USA
JSHW031915210820
7408JS00001B/20